just peacemaking

TEN PRACTICES FOR ABOLISHING WAR

D1491164

Edited by Glen Stassen

The Pilgrim Press
Cleveland, Ohio

The Pilgrim Press, Cleveland, Ohio 44115
© 1998 by Glen Stassen

Printed in the United States of America on acid-free paper

03   02   01   00   99   98   5   4   3   2   1

Library of Congress Cataloging-in-Publication Data

Just peacemaking : ten practices for abolishing war / edited by Glen Stassen.
    p.   cm.
  Includes bibliographical references and index.
    ISBN 0-8298-1266-0 (cloth : alk. paper). — ISBN 0-8298-1261-X (pbk. : alk.
paper)
    1. Peace—Religious aspects—Christianity.   2. Christianity and justice.
I. Stassen, Glen Harold, 1936–   .
BT736.4.J88   1998
261.8'73—DC21

                                                  97-50286
                                                  CIP

CONTENTS

Contents

COLLABORATORS

Steven Brion-Meisels is co-chair of Peace Action, Washington, D.C.

David Bronkema is a Ph.D. candidate in anthropology, Yale University, New Haven, Connecticut.

John Cartwright is professor of Christian ethics, Boston University, Boston, Massachusetts.

Michael Dyson is professor of African American studies at Columbia University, New York, New York.

Duane K. Friesen is professor of Bible and religion, Bethel College, North Newton, Kansas.

Alan Geyer is professor emeritus of political ethics and ecumenics, Wesley Theological Seminary, Washington, D.C.

Barbara Green is associate for peace, Africa, and Europe issues, the Presbyterian Church (USA), Washington, D.C., Office.

Gary Gunderson is director of the Interfaith Health Program, the Carter Center, Atlanta, Georgia.

Judith Gundry-Volf is associate professor of New Testament, Fuller Theological Seminary, Pasadena, California.

Theodore Koontz is professor of peace studies, Associated Mennonite Biblical Seminary, Elkhart, Indiana.

John Langan, S.J., is Rose F. Kennedy Professor of Christian Ethics, Kennedy Institute of Ethics, Georgetown University, Washington, D.C.

Edward LeRoy Long Jr. is professor emeritus of Christian ethics, Drew University, Madison, New Jersey.

David Lumsdaine is adjunct professor of international relations, Yale University, New Haven, Connecticut.

Patricia McCullough is past co-chair of the Nuclear Weapons Freeze Campaign, Washington, D.C.

Peter Paris is Elmer G. Homrighausen Professor of Social Ethics, Princeton Theological Seminary, Princeton, New Jersey.

Rodger A. Payne is associate professor of political science, University of Louisville, Louisville, Kentucky.

Bruce Russett is professor of international relations, Yale University, New Haven, Connecticut.

Paul W. Schroeder is professor of international history, University of Illinois, Urbana, Illinois.

Michael Joseph Smith is associate professor of government and foreign affairs and associate director of the Program in Political and Social Thought, University of Virginia, Charlottesville, Virginia.

Glen Stassen is Lewis B. Smedes Professor of Christian Ethics, Fuller Theological Seminary, Pasadena, California.

David Steele is project director of religion—conflict resolution, Center for Strategic and International Studies, Washington, D.C.

Ronald Stone is professor of Christian ethics, Pittsburgh Theological Seminary, Pittsburgh, Pennsylvania.

Susan Thistlethwaite is president, Chicago Theological Seminary, Chicago, Illinois.

Introduction JUST PEACEMAKING AS A NEW ETHIC

Duane K. Friesen

John Langan, S.J.

Glen Stassen

During the violence of the early 1980s, many women, especially indigenous women, became widows as their husbands were killed by the military forces of the government. . . . In addition to the deaths of husbands, sons and fathers disappeared or were forced into military service, never to be seen again. Daughters and mothers were violated by soldiers and members of the civil patrol. . . .

Women watched powerlessly as soldiers entered their villages, burned houses and fields, kidnapped husbands and children. They watched as soldiers threw babies into fires or boiling water. They watched as half-dead husbands were buried alive. In front of children members of the military raped mothers and daughters.[1]

This is the experience of women in Guatemala, as told by Michelle Tooley in her book *Voices of the Voiceless*. An analogous first-hand testimony could come from elsewhere in Latin America, or Rwanda, Liberia, Zaire, the Sudan, Burma, Cambodia, Bosnia, Afghanistan, or Iraq. Other kinds of war and terrorism victimize untold thousands in other countries on each continent. Almost infinitely worse would be nuclear war if it were to fall on us.

And even where war is not being waged, large expenditures of scarce money pay for military forces to support unjust governments and grossly unequal concentrations of wealth in countries where the large majority of the people are miserably poor. Suffering and hopelessness result from militarily supported dictatorships and other injustices.

What can we do? Who knows? If no one knows what can be done, who cares? Why waste caring when we don't know how to stop such admittedly tragic, personal suffering?

We, the authors of *Just Peacemaking,* have been working together for five years to develop a road map for actions that actually participate in effective forces that are turning major parts of our world from war to peace. When actions participate in these world-changing forces, they are not mere ideals; they are not isolated and random; rather, they are forces multiplied in strength and effectiveness.

The result of our work is a theory designed to guide our just peacemaking in this new era. It is the unanimous consensus of twenty-three scholars—Christian ethicists, biblical and moral theologians, international relations scholars, peace activists, and conflict resolution practitioners—all of whom have specialized in peacemaking but come from different perspectives. We intend this work to take its place along with, but not to replace, the established paradigms of pacifism and just war theory, to guide our ethics in peace and war. We have worked together for four years in meetings of the Society of Christian Ethics, by research and correspondence between meetings, and in major working conferences at the Abbey of Gethsemani in Trappist, Kentucky, and at the Carter Center in Atlanta. Each chapter describes one of the practices of our consensus ten-point just peacemaking theory.

The ten just peacemaking practices in our consensus model are not merely a wish list. They are empirical practices in our present history that are, in fact, spreading peace. They are engendering positive-feedback loops, so they are growing in strength. They are pushing back the frontiers of war and spreading the zones of peace. We believe that because these emerging empirical practices are changing our world for the better and pushing back the frontiers of war, they are moral as well as empirical guides for all responsible and caring persons. They call all persons of good will to lend their shoulders to the effort. They give realistic guidance for grassroots groups, voluntary associations, and groups in churches, synagogues, meetings, and mosques.

We are saying that something intriguing and history-changing is happening in our time. Peacemaking is spreading in ways most people have not noticed. In Atlanta, during our Quaker-meeting-style worship service, Edward L. Long Jr. said, "this project will take hold, if it does, not because we created it but because it meets the historical moment. It is a *kairos* moment, a moment of meaning and spiritual inbreaking, because people want to know what is happening in our time."[2]

THE HISTORICAL *KAIROS*

Several historical forces have come together as signs of our time to produce the just peacemaking theory.

1. After World War II, the world was stunned by the devastation of the war and the threat of nuclear weapons. The reality of that universally perceived threat persuaded people and institutions to develop new practices and networks to prevent another world war and the use of nuclear weapons. Now over fifty years have passed, and so far we have avoided those two specters. New practices are actually getting results in ways many have not noticed. We believe we live in a moment of kairos when it can serve useful purposes to name these practices, to call attention to them, to support them ethically.

3

2. Now, at the end of the Cold War and the turning of the millennium, people lack a clear vision of what sort of peacemaking is effective and is in fact happening. When the problems were the hostile rivalry between the United States and the Soviet Union and their mutual nuclear escalation, we knew clearly what peacemaking was needed. Now that the Cold War is over, the problem seems more diffuse. The enemy of peace is not so easily identifiable. Hence, people do not know how they can contribute. The results are confusion, cognitive dissonance, apathy, and a dangerous, romantic, inward emigration from effective and responsible involvement—ironically just when the opportunity and need for spreading the zones of peace are most imminent.

Paul Schroeder, the respected diplomatic historian of international relations, writes in his chapter: "This makes just peacemaking into a task for action by ordinary citizens individually and in groups to sustain, criticize, goad, influence, reform, and lead the many kinds of voluntary associations, governmental and private, which can contribute to transcending the contradictions and managing and overcoming the conflicts of an anarchic international society. . . . It is our task to encourage and strengthen the underlying trends that enable cooperation to fly."[3]

3. In our time, there is a growing sense of the inadequacy of the debate between just war theory and pacifism. Debates dominated by those paradigms inevitably focus on whether or not to make war. That crucial question and those two paradigms will not go away if the just peacemaking paradigm succeeds.

But in that debate another question frequently is overlooked: What essential steps should be taken to make peace? Have they been taken, or should they yet be taken? The just peacemaking paradigm fills out the original intention of the other two paradigms. It encourages pacifists to fulfill what their name (derived from the Latin *pacem-facere*) means, "peacemakers." And it calls just war theorists to fill in the contents of their underdeveloped principles of last resort and just intention—to spell out what resorts must be tried before trying the last resort of war, and what intention there is to restore a just and enduring peace. It asks both to act on their stated intentions.

4. Most of the church statements on peace issued by major Christian denominations during the 1980s call for developing a just peacemaking theory or a theology of peace. For example, in their pastoral letter "The Challenge of Peace," the U.S. Catholic Bishops say:

> Recognition of the Church's responsibility to join with others in the work of peace is a major force behind the call today to develop a theology of peace. Much of the history of Catholic theology on war and peace has focused on limiting the resort to force in human affairs; this task is still necessary, . . . but it is not a sufficient response.
>
> A fresh reappraisal which includes a developed theology of peace will require contributions from several sectors of the Church's life: biblical studies, systematic and moral theology, ecclesiology, and the experience and insights of members of the church who have struggled in various ways to make and keep the peace in this often violent age.[4]

Official statements of the Presbyterian Church, United Methodist Church, and United Church of Christ proclaimed similarly that while the two predominant paradigms of limiting the resort to force, just war theory and pacifism, are still necessary, we also need a positive theory of just peacemaking. In addition, several Christian ethicists from different denominations, both just war theorists and pacifists, have authored books calling for the development of a just peacemaking theory. Key authors of all those church statements and books participated in the project to develop a consensus just peacemaking theory.

5. The worldwide peacemaking movement, linking together many groups with different emphases, provides the troops that support and implement just peacemaking theory. It is not merely an academic theory. It can provide overarching comprehension, guidance, and encouragement, showing how diverse actions weave together into a strong supporting web of peacemaking.

A THEOLOGICAL BASIS FOR JUST PEACEMAKING

We believe the practices of just peacemaking are ethically normative because they bring peace, they solve problems, they promote justice and cooperation in a world whose wars are immeasurably destructive. We see historical evidence that when these normative practices are carried out, they can accomplish the goals of peace and justice. Therefore the twenty-three scholars were able to reach consensus on the ten practices of just peacemaking on pragmatic grounds. We purposely fashioned the wording of the ten practices of just peacemaking so they could be adopted by persons of many faiths or no official faith. We wrote chapters explaining each practice so its basis can be seen clearly in what is actually happening in our time to change the world. We appeal to all people of good will to adopt these practices and work for them, grounding themselves in a commitment to change our world (or at least their own little briar patch) to peace rather than war and oppression. Each person can base these practices on his or her own faith. A Muslim or Buddhist or simply a social scientist or human being whose experience has led her or him to care about making peace, not war, can say, "Yes, this is happening in ways I had not fully realized, and it is making a huge difference for good, and I want to support it." We hope many, from diverse perspectives, will make these peacemaking practices their own.

At the same time, many of us arrive at these normative practices of just peacemaking not only on pragmatic grounds, but from deeply held faith perspectives. With the eyes of faith, we attribute the evidence that just peacemaking works to God's reign in history, though we arrive at this historical perspective in different ways. Evangelicals among our group do our ethics with more biblical concreteness;

5

mainline Protestants among us prefer more general theological grounding or middle axioms; some who do not identify themselves as explicitly faith-based shy away from theological reasons; Roman Catholics among us work with general moral norms, natural law, and natural rights; and peace-church members want arguments explicitly theological and faith-based. All of us appeal to persons and groups of various faiths to join with us in seeking to make peace.

In this introduction, we three who have been involved in the process from the beginning (Duane Friesen, a Mennonite; John Langan, S.J., a Roman Catholic; and Glen Stassen, a Baptist) want to share something of the specifically Christian faith perspective that informs us.[5] Our vision is grounded in three theological convictions:

1. *Initiatives:* A biblically informed concept of discipleship and peacemaking initiatives grounded in the life, teachings, death, and resurrection of Jesus Christ.

2. *Justice:* A church committed to seek the peace of the city where its people dwell (Jer. 29:7); to further God's reign, not by withdrawal or quietism or by uncritical support of or reliance on the government, but by engaging the issues of peace and justice—especially justice—actively within the brokenness of the world.

3. *Love and community:* The church community as the eschatological sign of God's love and reign in the world, embodied in a concrete gathering of persons who seek to discern together what just peacemaking means and to model peacemaking practices in our corporate and individual lives.

These three theological convictions form, or correspond to, the three basic imperatives of peacemaking and to the basic divisions of this book: peacemaking initiatives (part 1), justice (part 2), and love-community (part 3). They provide a logical ordering for the ten essential practices of peacemaking.

Discipleship and Peacemaking Initiatives

Discipleship is based on an embodied or incarnational Christology, a view of Christ as representing a specific and concrete alternative way of life meant to be followed. We advocate an embodied Christology which is an alternative to views of Christ that, though they make Godlike claims for the Savior, fail to see Christ's way as the authoritative model for our ethical practice. We advocate Christologies that

6

a) see Christ as divine Sovereign of all of life, not only Sovereign over a "separate" sphere of life (the spiritual); b) define the meaning of Christ in terms that include faithfully following Christ now; c) interpret Jesus' teaching as related to concrete practices that can guide us to live in the real world, not merely as high and abstract ideals; and d) are attentive to Jesus' humanity as one who modeled a way to be followed and saw himself as fulfilling the tradition of the Law and the Prophets, not a Constantinian tradition of alignment with political and economic power. We want to build our peacemaking on a Christology that stays close to the Jewish servant Lord of the Gospels who called his disciples humbly to follow his way of nonviolent love, community-restoring justice, and peacemaking initiatives.

A reexamination of an embodied Christology of Christ's way, an incarnational discipleship, requires a serious reexamination of how the Christian church has related to those of other faiths, most notably its relationship to Jews. Larry Rasmussen states the issue forcefully:

> Developments after the ecumenical councils, including the Reformation, only solidified the massive shift from the God-centered Christology of an alternative servant community within the wider world to the Christ-centered theology of a universalizing empire. . . . This absorption of virtually all of God into the Jesus of imperial Christianity is at the greatest possible remove from the theocentric Jesus and his yeasty, salty, seedy community way. Deadly results for Jews, pagans, indigenous people and cultures would eventually follow. [6]

7

Our perspective should not be understood, however, as a simple claim about the historical Jesus. The Gospels and the other writings of the New Testament portray various images of the Christ of faith. The portrayal of Jesus in these accounts is what the early church believed Jesus to be in a variety of different contexts where they faced a variety of practical issues. The New Testament represents not one unified Christology but various images that suggest different nuances and emphases. But even the high logos Christology of the Gospel of John teaches Jesus' servant role as one who incarnationally and sacrificially embodies God's love for all of humanity, a model of love for all who follow him. Similarly, Paul's theology of justification by faith is integrally connected to his concern for the formation of an ethical community in which divisions between Jew and Gentile are overcome in Christ (as in Gal. 3:24f., where Paul says that in Christ there is neither Jew nor Greek, slave nor free, male nor female).

We can illustrate what an embodied Christology looks like by a brief examination of the *locus classicus* of Christian peacemaking, the Sermon on the Mount (Matt. 5–7). In Matthew's portrayal of Jesus' teachings, we see a way to confront evil—not through violent force but through transforming initiatives as an alternative to either passive withdrawal or violent confrontation. John H. Yoder's *Politics of Jesus*, Walter Wink's *Engaging the Powers*, and Glen Stassen's *Just Peacemaking: Transforming Initiatives for Justice and Peace* spell out this model in much more detail than we can do here.[7]

Most interpretations of the Sermon on the Mount view Jesus as teaching an impossible ideal that cannot be realized in a sinful world. The Sermon on the Mount has usually been interpreted with a dyadic structural analysis, such as (1) "you have heard of old, don't kill"; (2) "but I say don't even be angry" (Matt. 5:21, 22). In this interpretation, the focus is on not being angry, which is easy to dismiss as being impossible. In fact, the Sermon is organized as triads:

1. Traditional piety (e.g., "you shall not kill" [Matt. 5:21]).

2. Mechanisms of bondage (e.g., nursing anger or saying 'you fool'" [Matt. 5:22]).

3. Transforming initiative (e.g., "go, therefore, be reconciled" [Matt. 5:23]).

Matthew 5:21–7:11 consists of fourteen such triads. In each of them, the second member of the triad (the mechanism of bondage or vicious cycle) does not use imperatives, but continuing-action verbs, diagnosing the ongoing process of trouble that we get ourselves into when we serve some other lord than God. When anger rules us, we often fail, in fact, to take the steps necessary to correct a problem. If we recognize the triadic structure of the Sermon on the Mount, we can see that the emphasis is on the concrete commands of Jesus which are practical and doable (in this case, "go be reconciled").

We see that the third element is always an initiative, not merely a prohibition. It is always a practical participation in deliverance from a vicious cycle of bondage, hostility, idolatry, and judgment. Each moves us away from the so-called hard-saying or high-ideal interpretation that has caused resistance, evasion, and a dualistic split between inner intentions of the heart and outer deeds in society. Each moves us instead into participation in God's grace, God's deliverance, God's reign.[8]

In preaching, teaching, and living this good news, Jesus modeled a way to confront evil in order to restore right relationships (righteousness or justice). We have a vivid picture or model in the New Testament, in images, stories, sayings, accounts of Jesus' life, and ethical exhortations, not only in the Gospels but in the ethical injunctions and practices expressed in other writings (the ethical exhortations of Paul, for example, in Rom. 12) of how the followers of Jesus envisioned what it means to follow him in a life of discipleship.

Therefore one basic imperative is peacemaking initiatives. A positive theology of peace is not simply reactive, but proactive. It takes initiatives. It creates peace. It sees peace not as something to be achieved merely by refraining from war, but by taking peacemaking initiatives. Peace, like war, must be waged. It must be waged courageously, persistently, creatively, with imagination, heart, and wisdom. Peacemaking is rooted in the heart of the biblical understanding of God's grace, which does not merely refrain from punishing but takes dramatic initiatives in coming to us, speaking in the burning bush (Exod. 3), pouring love into us in Jesus Christ while we were God's enemies (Rom. 5:1–21). New emphasis on the initiatives of God's grace is transforming our understanding of peacemaking in our time.

Four of our ten practices of just peacemaking embody the imperative of peacemaking initiatives: (1) strategies of nonviolent direct action enacted by millions of people taking inspiration from Gandhi and Martin Luther King; (2) strategies of independent initiatives developed by Charles Osgood and spread by citizens' movements to governments; (3) strategies of conflict resolution now spreading widely; and (4) strategies of acknowledging responsibility, repentance, and forgiveness described by Donald Shriver in *An Ethic for Enemies*.[9]

These four practices embody the same seven essential ingredients of Christian peacemaking: (1) they are not simply passive withdrawal, but proactive ways of grace that empower us to take peacemaking initiatives; (2) they acknowledge the log in our own eye and take our own responsibility for peacemaking rather than simply judging the other; (3) they affirm the dignity and interests of the enemy, even while rejecting sinful or wrong practices; (4) they confront the

9

other with an invitation to making peace and justice; (5) they invite into community in a way that includes, rather than excludes, former enemies and outcasts; (6) they are historically embodied or situated— they are in fact happening in our history; (7) they are empirically validated—they are making a significant difference in international relations and domestic conflict. Thus these practices are not simply unrelated items; they are parallel ways of embodying the historically embodied strategy of transforming initiatives.

We appeal directly to Christians for whom God's grace matters to join us in the sort of initiatives that God wills for us and takes for us in Jesus Christ.

Advance Justice for All

A second basic imperative is justice. Injustice is a major cause of war. To make peace, we must make justice. Two central sets of practices move nations toward justice and away from injustice. They are practices that (1) promote democracy, human rights, and religious liberty and (2) foster just and sustainable economic development.

Just peace is spreading because human rights and democracy are spreading. But to flourish, human rights and democracy require a world economy in which extreme differences in wealth, power, and participation are progressively overcome. The just peacemaking practice of sustainable economic development is an expression of this need, and of Jesus' teachings about wealth, poverty, feeding the hungry, and covenant justice.

Justice is central to the biblical story, from beginning to end. The four basic words for justice in Hebrew and Greek are repeated 1,060 times in the Bible—more frequently than almost any other term. Time and again, the prophets teach that the way to avoid the judgment and destruction of war is to return to God and practice justice. Jesus identifies with the prophetic tradition and repeatedly criticizes those in authority who seek prestige for themselves, neglect justice, faithfulness, and mercy, and cover their sins with the temple sacrifices—just as the prophet Jeremiah had charged (Jer. 7). Jesus' peacemaking teachings in the Sermon on the Mount and elsewhere focus much attention on giving alms to the poor and seeking justice (righteousness) and God's reign.

Jesus taught and practiced a total devotion to God's reign that called into question the human devotion to acquisitive ends. Although Jesus does not deny the importance of material goods that sustain bodily well-being, the gospels severely condemn those devoted to the accumulation of wealth and the goods of this world. Walter Wink summarizes Jesus' teachings:

> Jesus . . . pours scorn on those who are clothed in soft raiment and dwell in king's houses (Matt. 11:8; Luke 7:25). He challenges creditors, not only to forgo interest, but to ask no repayment whatever. To those who wish to follow him, he counsels selling everything, and warns the rich that they have no access whatever to the new society coming. Those who hoard luxuries and neglect the poor at their doors are presented with the prospect of their own death and divine judgment (Luke 12:13–21; 16:19–31). To the religionist's dream of being able to be "spiritual" and still amass wealth within an unjust system, Jesus pronounces an unconditional no. "You cannot serve God and wealth" (Matt. 6:24; Luke 16:13).[10]

11

Compassionate presence is at the heart of the Christian faith. The New Testament portrayal of Jesus reveals a God who is not a detached sovereign ruling over the universe from a distance. The Greek word for compassion in the New Testament, *splagchnisomai*— a word that perhaps best characterizes Jesus—means to "let one's innards embrace the feeling or situation of another." Jesus as a compassionate presence with those who suffer is evident in many of the stories of the Gospels.

Jesus stands in solidarity with the marginalized. Those who are treated as outcasts within the social context of Jesus' time are just the ones upon whom he has compassion: the poor, widows, the sick, Samaritans, those labeled sinners. Jesus' attitude and behavior toward women and children is revolutionary, particularly when viewed in the cultural context of first-century Palestine.

The church is engaged in mission beyond its own borders. It does not exist simply for itself, but to participate in the liberating power of God's reign in the world. The Gospels portray Jesus as an agent of deliverance, God's anointed one (Messiah), who is commissioned to bring God's dominion or reign into the world. The vision of the dominion of God is not a sectarian model simply for the church, but a call to transform the world.

Though God's reign is a reality which is still future in terms of its full manifestation, it is present already where God's authority is breaking into history. It becomes present through Jesus when he gives sight to the blind, feeds the hungry, liberates people from demonic possession, and forgives sin so that people can live a life of wholeness.

Luke 4:18–19 (quoting Isa. 61:1–2) expresses the purpose of Jesus' messiahship:

> *The Spirit of the Lord is upon me,*
> > *because he has anointed me to bring good news*
> > *to the poor.*
> *He has sent me to proclaim release to the captives*
> > *and recovery of sight to the blind,*
> > *to let the oppressed go free,*
> *to proclaim the year of the Lord's favor.*

Christ's call to discipleship means the church will find itself frequently at odds with the dominant culture in which it exists. In some sense, like the Hebrews in Babylon at the time of Jeremiah, the church is an exile community. But exile does not mean withdrawal into a special enclave separate from the world. Rather, like the Hebrews of Jeremiah's time, the church is called to "seek the shalom of the city where it dwells" (Jer. 29:7). The church exists not for itself, but for the world, to be God's body in the world. The advice of Jeremiah to pray to God on behalf of the city in which we live is not a call for passivity—to let God act while the church watches and waits. To pray genuinely to God for the welfare of the city is to yearn with all one's heart for its well-being. So, as David Hollenbach, S.J., writes:

> The 1971 Synod of Bishops of the Roman Catholic church introduced its reflections on the meaning of justice in world society with a statement that has become the platform and legitimation for a whole series of new initiatives in sociopolitical life by Roman Catholics. The bishops stated: "Action on behalf of justice and participation in the transformation of the world fully appear to us as a constitutive dimension of the preaching of the Gospel, or, in other words, of the Church's mission for the redemption of the human race and its liberation from every oppressive situation."[11]

The worldwide push and pull for human rights for minorities and oppressed peoples since World War II, since the U.N. Declaration of Human Rights and the active work of many church groups as well as secular groups, has been a major factor in advancing justice and democracy and is a crucial practice for peacemaking. The push for human rights in the second half of the twentieth century has contributed mightily to the spread of democracy and thus to the receding of the fires of war from half of the world's regions.[12]

Some, however, oppose Christian support of justice and human rights. They may be influenced by philosophical criticism of the possessive individualism of the eighteenth-century Lockean tradition. They may also be influenced (perhaps unknowingly) by authoritarian traditions that opposed historical struggles for civil rights, struggles for the rights of Jews against Nazi racism, or for the rights of oppressed groups in the southern hemisphere; traditions that have claimed that struggles for human rights are selfish.

We want to point out clearly that there are two quite different narratives of human rights. One is the eighteenth-century individualistic narrative shaped by John Locke. It emphasizes liberty as autonomy, rejecting monarchy and authoritarianism; and it emphasizes the pursuit of property, reducing the earth's resources to individual possessions once they are mined, used, or exploited. The other emphasizes community, responsibility, and basic human needs. It preceded Locke historically, being rooted in older Hebraic traditions of covenant justice, Catholic traditions of social responsibility, and early free-church Puritan traditions of religious liberty and covenant responsibility.

This more socially responsible tradition connects with the twentieth-century narrative of the oppressed and discriminated, seen in the revulsion against the discrimination of Adolf Hitler's Third Reich; in the drive of former colonies for independence; of those suffering from racial hatred; of Latin American people's movements; of movements for justice in the former Soviet Bloc, the Philippines, South Africa, and elsewhere; in all struggles for justice. This is a narrative of rights to liberty (rejecting oppression and affirming participation), to life (including basic human needs), and to community (including membership and responsibility). It is this narrative toward which Michelle Tooley and we are pointing. It is expressed in the U.N. Universal Declaration of Human Rights; and it, not the possessive

13

individualism of the Lockean narrative, is represented by the commitment of many churches and Christian movements to champion human rights.[12]

Thus John Langan, S.J., writes that a human right is, first,

> a right that a human person has simply by virtue of being a human person, irrespective of his or her social status, cultural accomplishments, moral merits, religious beliefs, class memberships, or contractual relationships. . . . Rights include economic and social rights such as rights to social security, to work, to education, and to a "standard of living adequate for the well-being of [one]self and [one's] family, including food, clothing, housing and medical care, and necessary social services." Economic and social rights were unknown to Locke and the eighteenth century natural rights theorists, . . . [and] this is a fundamental error.[13]

Langan clarifies that, within Catholic teaching, rights claims are situated in a social context where "rights are to be balanced with duties, and individual claims are to be integrated into the pursuit of the common good. . . . The duty [of] meeting basic human needs . . . falls on all human persons to the extent of their ability. . . . A fundamental commitment to human rights requires that one be critical of abuses of power and neglect of the needs of the disadvantaged, whether these occur under oligopolistic capitalism or state socialism or the national security state."[14]

Langan concludes with the emphasis on *community* that is found in the covenant community tradition of the Old Testament, the early Puritan human-rights tradition prior to Locke, the Roman Catholic tradition, and the twentieth-century narrative to which we are pointing.

> Recognition of the social and economic rights of others constrains the free pursuit of interest and of one's own plans on the part of some. . . . [This] creates the basis of a comprehensive and nonexclusive form of community. For to acknowledge the rights of others is to enter into a form of community with them, a community which is both presupposed and realized by the common task of satisfying those claims that we recognize as universal moral rights. Our common humanity leads us to acknowledge and

respect each other's human rights; satisfying these rights requires us to live as a community in deed and not merely in word. Acknowledging the needs, the liberty, and the worth of other individuals in this view is not a retreat into selfishness but a step to a just ordering of the world.[15]

To try to force this tradition into the Lockean narrative is to engage in ideological distortion.

Love and Community: Strengthen Cooperative Forces

The individualism of our culture and of our traditions has caused us to slight the gospel's emphasis on community. We need to recover the Hebraic emphasis on covenant community. We need to recover Jesus' emphasis that love includes enemies, outcasts, and the neglected in community. Otherwise, our peacemaking ignores structural forces beyond interpersonal peacemaking. Essential to peacemaking is attention to those structural forces of cooperation that work steadily to build regular relationships and include enemies, outcasts, and the neglected in community with us. These forces bind nations together in ways that go beyond what any individual may do. Like the Energizer bunny, they just keep on working—beyond what individuals may do. They are bigger than any one of us. Yet they need our support, so that governments and people will strengthen them rather than weaken them.

We put these cooperative forces last in our book. This is a sign of the way individualism in our culture narrows our understanding. Students who read the first draft told us that we should first point to forces such as conflict resolution and nonviolent direct action, because people readily grasp them. Structural forces of cooperation seem like a foreign language to many—foreign to the individualistic language of our culture. But these forces are changing the world dramatically in ways many have not noticed. They are hugely important for peacemaking. They need to be understood. And they need our support.

Cooperative forces may be seen as a dimension of love, if love is understood realistically rather than sentimentally. Love as a feeling for certain persons is not enough; love must mean building reliable community with others, and it must include enemies. This community-building love is central to the gospel.

So Judy Gundry-Volf shows how the Gospel stories of Jesus' encounters with the Samaritan woman and the Syrophoenician woman (John 4:1–30; Mark 7:24–30) are stories "about the inclusion of the 'other,' about crossing the boundaries caused by ethnic, religious, social and gender otherness and bringing about a new, inclusive community of salvation."[16] She tells of the history of hostility and avoidance, war and temple desecration, between Samaritans and Jews, as well as the male avoidance of mutual discussion with women. But in Jesus, the Samaritan woman found "a Jew who did not impose on her the Jewish stereotype of a Samaritan. . . . a man who did not impose on her the stereotype of a woman. . . . The living water also overflows the boundaries dividing the figures in this story and envelops them in a new, inclusive [communion]." The woman had been alienated from her own Samaritan community, but through Jesus she "regains a voice in her community, her witness is heard and believed, and her key role in the salvation of the Samaritans is recognized." Because of her witness, the Samaritans press Jesus to stay with them, and "he accepts their offer and stays two days with the Samaritans."[17] Similarly, Jews were oppressed politically and economically by Tyre and Sidon, "notoriously our bitterest enemies."[18] The woman from Tyre and Sidon was excluded from Jesus' Jewish mission. But her clever appeal to the practice and experience of mercy over "both exclusivism and sequential priority in salvation based on ethnic identity" persuades him that his mission extends to Gentiles as well. He immediately goes to the Sea of Galilee, attracts great crowds of Gentiles, expresses compassion for them, and feeds four thousand of them. They are part of the community of compassion. God's mercy has triumphed over "the prejudice-based distance between nations and cultures."[19]

So also Duane Friesen writes that Jesus gives the concept of trust in God a

> nonviolent interpretation by extending the meaning of who are God's people universally to include even God's enemies. Love is to be shown to enemies, for they are objects of God's saving activity, potentially members of the covenant community. . . . This universalization of the meaning of peoplehood had already taken place in the Hebrew prophets. . . .

The cross is both the negative consequence of Jesus' nonconformity to institutions threatened by his life and message, and also a positive demonstration of his radical love. The cross, above all, demonstrates his willingness to lay down his life for us. In demonstrating an alternative to revolutionary violence, Jesus introduces into the historical process the possibility of genuine reconciliation. Genuine reconciliation is possible because love overcomes all barriers, even the barrier between enemies. . . . The ethic of the kingdom extends beyond the narrow loyalties of nation, class, and race to the whole of humankind, even to one's enemies.[20]

And Lisa Sowle Cahill writes, "The New Testament makes it abundantly clear that to love and forgive one's enemies is not only intrinsic to the kingdom, but that a life of love and forgiveness is a concrete alternative now."[21]

American culture-conforming Protestant individualism needs correction by an understanding of the church as a discerning community. Discipleship is not primarily realized in the practice of heroic individuals, but is potent where it is embodied in the practices of a concrete community, in a social group which, by its very existence as an alternative community in the world, becomes a sign of God's reign, albeit in earthen vessels.

> To organized opposition, Jesus responds with the formal founding of a new social reality. New teachings are no threat, as long as the teacher stands alone; a movement, extending his personality in both time and space, presenting an alternative to the structures that were there before, challenges the system as no mere words could.[22]

First, the church functions as a community of memory and hope to nurture the paradigmatic story that orients the community in time and sustains a vision of God's reign. Deliberate attention to the nurture of the church, which keeps alive the memory of its paradigmatic stories (such as the Exodus or the parable of the good Samaritan [Luke 10:30–37]), is essential to the moral formation of people of character. Wuthnow notes that there is widespread knowledge in American society of the good Samaritan story, which many cite when they explain their concept of compassion. Those who participate little or

17

not at all in a religious community, however, tend to have a vague understanding of the story, about someone who helped another person beside a road. We need a community that retells and embodies this story, and other gospel stories; it speaks vitally to the social conditions we experience.

> It provides a framework that helps us define—and therefore see—the possibilities for compassion in our own world. . . . For us the story of the Good Samaritan is fundamentally about the possibility of human kindness existing in a society of strangers. . . . The story of the Good Samaritan tells us that some basic element of our humanity can bridge the gap and create community even among strangers. . . . It is also a story that reveals our diversity as a society—the divisions that ordinarily separate rich and poor, black and white, male and female, citizen and alien—and yet it shows that these divisions can be overcome. . . . People who know the story understand that the Samaritan is a social outcast and yet he is the one who shows compassion. . . . We hear this message of reconciliation when we recognize who the outcasts are today who play the role of the Good Samaritan.[23]

Second, the church structures a process of practical moral reasoning where the members of the community can listen to one another as they discern together what discipleship means. To be a member of a church means to commit oneself to a process of conversation. If a church is the community that follows its God, it embodies a conflict resolution process that assumes active participation by the entire membership (based on New Testament models outlined in 1 Cor. and Matt. 18:15–18). Commitment is not primarily to a fixed system of ethics. The church is a gathering of persons committed to speaking and listening to one another to discern what faithfulness means in the light of the vision of life revealed in Jesus Christ. This participatory model, when it functions well, can be a school of learning for the participatory democracy that is a key practice of peacemaking. It has been such historically, and it can be so in our contemporary setting.

It should be clear why we strongly emphasize the tenth practice of just peacemaking, "encourage grassroots peacemaking groups," which we principally interpret as those churches, church groups, and peacemaking groups that embody the peacemaking the Jesus Christ of the New Testament teaches and for which he dies.

Our emphasis on the church as community (as opposed to individualism) also influences us to see the importance of the eighth and ninth practices. These are cooperative forces in the international system, including the United Nations and regional organizations that function not only as deliberative bodies but encourage mutual admonition, mutual understanding, communication, and common memories and narratives rather than simply national narcissism. Like churches, these secular organizations have their own power struggles, antagonisms, self-interest, inefficiencies, and internal conflict. Yet they do nudge nations, groups, and economic institutions into cooperative communities, even across lines of enmity.

We have learned from John Howard Yoder to notice that New Testament practices such as building inclusive community that includes even enemies are processes that a secular social scientist could observe among the early Christian community and that resemble analogous secular processes in the world. In fact, some of those secular processes historically were set in motion or strongly supported by Jewish and Christian community. Our correction of our own individualism by our appreciation of the importance of the church as community opens our eyes to see the importance of processes of community that are transforming our anarchic world into a society. We see secular organizations such as the United Nations, international communication and trade, and a hundred kinds of community-building processes as secular analogies to community-building love which encourages nations, economic organizations, and people to build increasingly strong community with one another, often including those who are enemies or potential enemies. These, in fact, are transforming international relations in ways many have not noticed. "Today the world is knitted together not just by the printed word, but by wires, cables and satellite links buzzing with everything from breaking news to e-mailed Valentine's Day messages. What will such connectedness mean to the leaders of tomorrow?"[24] Thambo Mbeki, heir-apparent to Nelson Mandela in South Africa, says that multiple international connections will make people much better informed and less dependent on political rulers for their information. Asked if there could have been apartheid in a South Africa connected to e-mail, international television news, and the like, he replied flatly, "There could not have been."[25] Empirical research shows that nations with many international ties and relationships are significantly less likely to make war with each other. Extensive and even surprising evidence of this will be presented in chapters 7, 8, and 10.

HOPE WITH EMPIRICAL REALISM

Reinhold Niebuhr, the Christian realist, influenced us to be suspicious of cries of "peace, peace" as an ideal when there is no peace in practice. Niebuhr the realist repeatedly asked what are the empirical power realities and interests, and what real steps of peacemaking are actually being taken now.

We are not simply talking about peace as a utopian ideal. We are not predicting that there will be fewer and fewer wars. We are, in fact, saying that conflicts of interest are strong and the instruments of destruction are now so devastating that the judgment of war can become a worldwide experience in ways too horrible to imagine. With all our beings we warn against the false optimism that has caused many to relax their peacemaking after the Cold War, precisely when our peacemaking is terribly needed and when it has the global opportunity to spread peace widely and greatly reduce the likelihood of local wars and global holocaust. We are not saying we can abolish war tomorrow. We are saying that these ten practices have in fact abolished wars in specific places and that they need our support to spread.

Some of us were students of Niebuhr, the realist. He taught us to be skeptical of major change in history. But we now see the empirical evidence that these practices are incrementally changing the way nations relate. The combination of these various kinds of incremental change is adding up to a system change that is still insufficiently recognized. Niebuhr himself said that utopian hopes are not helpful, but day-by-day practices can build changed relationships and structures that change reality and make peace.

We are pointing to such day-by-day practices. We are showing in our ten chapters that they are actually happening, spreading, and stamping out the likelihood of war in major regions of the world. In places, however, such as Bosnia, Croatia, Serbia, Rwanda, Somalia, Sudan, Burma (Myanmar), and North Korea, these practices are absent or are only beginning to occur, and they are much needed. In other places such as Russia, they have begun but need much more support and strength.

In our unprogrammed meeting/worship service on the last day of our working conference at the Carter Center, Susan Thistlethwaite read from Adrienne Rich's poem "Spider's Web." In weaving a web, a spider weaves over and over and over again, building a strong web in spite of the fragility of each strand. She called us to a similar modest hope, weaving our practices over and over and over again. Ted Koontz said he had moved from "this world is a mess and I need to fix it" to "God is moving in history to do something, and I can join in." We are trying to describe what we see God doing in our history so that people can join in.

Some Christians resist, expressing fatalism. They cite the book of Revelation to support their belief that we cannot spread peacemaking. We should not hope to reduce or eliminate war, they say, because the Bible says there will be wars and rumors of war. We believe this misreads the message of the book of Revelation. Throughout the biblical drama, we are taught that though the powers and authorities seem in control, God is sovereign; and we are to be faithful to God's teachings. This is also the message of the book of Revelation: God is the real ruler; God is judging the powers who seem to be ruling for now and who are causing wars. God will redeem the followers of the Lamb; therefore, do not lose hope; follow the teachings of the Lamb. The followers of the Lamb do the deeds Jesus teaches. The same point is repeated again and again in varieties of phrasing, so often that one wonders how people could miss it: The followers of the Lamb are those who do the deeds Jesus teaches, who do God's will, keep God's Word, keep God's commandments, hold faithful to the testimony of Jesus, do the teachings of Jesus, follow God's teachings as given through Jesus, obey God's commands (Rev. 2:2; 2:23; 2:19; 2:26; 3:8, 10; 9:20–21; 12:17; 14:4; 14:12; 16:11; 19:10; 20:12–13; 22:11).

The book of Revelation does not teach that we should avoid taking peacemaking initiatives because God will do everything; it teaches that we should take the peacemaking initiatives that Jesus teaches: Do the deeds of Jesus. It does not teach that we cannot do anything about the future and so should fall back into fatalistic inaction; it teaches that when we do peacemaking deeds as Jesus commands, we are participating in the great drama of God's redemption of the world through the Lamb: Do the deeds of Jesus. The point is not that because things will get worse before they can get better, there is nothing we can do. The point is that things will not get better by trusting in the power of the violent beasts; we can expect violent trauma as judgment on their violence. Things will get better through God's delivering action, so we are to do the deeds of Jesus. God is working in our history to overcome the violence and injustice and to bring forth the New Jerusalem of Shalom. This will happen not by a simple belief in progress, nor by our own power, nor without suffering and trauma. It will happen by God's grace; we are called to believe in God's grace and to be faithful participants in it: Do the deeds of Jesus. The central question in the book of Revelation is whether we are followers of the Lamb or followers of the beasts who kill and destroy; whether we do the deeds of Jesus or the deeds of the evil rulers; our answer decides whether we are participants in God's present and eternal purpose and rule: Do the deeds of Jesus.[26] The deeds that Jesus teaches include deeds of peacemaking.

The church can serve a special role in nurturing a spirituality that sustains courage when just peacemaking is unpopular, hope when despair or cynicism is tempting, and a sense of grace and the possibility of forgiveness when just peacemaking fails. A church nurtured by an eschatological vision of God's reign, grounded in a vision that the slain Lamb is the Sovereign of history, is particularly needed when popular culture fosters a mass spirit of hatred toward enemies and fans the flames of war. Peacemakers need to be sustained by a willingness to suffer if necessary, to overcome hatred of the enemy and the ability to endure abuse without retaliation, and to keep hope and patience alive during a long period of struggle. The church can sustain trust in the possibility of the miracle of transformation when the evidence for change appears bleak, and joy even in the midst of suffering and pain. Just peacemaking will not long endure if its theological roots are based upon the assurance of success, though we live at a moment when historical evidence of the promise of just peacemaking surrounds us. We still need a realism about the depth of evil that guards people from disillusionment. Aware of the limits of our own ability to predict and control the future, we can still, through the gracious power of God, embrace our common humanity through simple deeds of kindness and charity. In the context of hatred and violence, such acts may disarm an opponent and become the occasion for a transforming initiative for justice and peace.

PRACTICES VERSUS THE FACT-VALUE SPLIT

At our first working conference at the Abbey of Gethsemani, a form of the fact-value split arose. The question was raised whether we should emphasize moral principles or political strategies. That led us toward abstract, historically disembodied principles or ideals rather than historically situated practices. It led us away from concreteness and historical actuality. It was ironic—or providential—that this struggle between empirical description and moral imperative took place at the Abbey of Gethsemani, where right before our eyes the monks were actually, empirically, engaging in the normative practice of prayer, beginning at 3:20 each morning. A few of us participated in those early-morning prayers, and the monks' normative practice may have been what led us forward into integrated embodiment.

We found our reintegration by explicitly turning to the ethics of normative practices. Several ethicists of different schools have written recently of practices as normative for ethics: first, John Howard Yoder and Michael Walzer; followed by Sharon Welch, Theophus Smith, Larry Rasmussen, Stanley Hauerwas, James William McClendon, and others.[27]

A practice is neither an ideal nor a rule, but a human activity that regularly takes place and that a sociologist could observe. Such activities include monks praying; churches worshipping by sharing bread and wine in Jesus' name and feeding, clothing, and housing the poor and hungry; Gentiles and Jews becoming one in the early Christian community; Jimmy Carter practicing conflict resolution; East Germany practicing nonviolent direct action while studying Martin Luther King; and Guatemalan women meeting together to struggle for human rights.

We have judged some practices to be ethically normative because they embody love, justice, and peacemaking initiatives and because they do, in fact, spread peace. But we have not simply derived our ten practices of peacemaking deductively from love, justice, and peacemaking initiatives; we have observed them inductively as actually happening in our history and then have judged them to be ethically normative. Some, of course, like nonviolent direct action and feeding the hungry, have arisen out of practices of faith; the relation between empirical observation and ethical assessment is a mutual interweaving.

Casting our just peacemaking theory in the form of normative practices brought together the empirical research of the international relations experts among us and the ethical arguments of the Christian ethicists and moral theologians. It brought together the realists and the advocates of a liberal-democratic peace, the pacifists, and the empiricists and historians among us. Realism says the world is characterized by power struggles and conflicts of interest, and history does not take leaps; therefore, we have to learn to deal with the world as it is. Idealists say we should focus on ideals and imagine how we can move the world toward them. The practices of peacemaking that we are pointing to happen empirically in the real world, in the context of real threat, power struggle, and drive for security. They make power's expression in war less likely and peace more likely.

Casting our theory in the form of practices remedied the tension we experienced about the role of justice in peacemaking. When justice means historically actual practices that restore community, and we acknowledge our own complicity in injustice, then we can participate in modest and realistic ways that do lead to peace. When, on the other hand, justice is thought of as an absolute ideal or a truth that we already know, the result often is self-righteous crusading or postponing peace until the reign of God arrives in its fullness.

Focusing on practices grounded our normative recommendations in peacemaking processes that are, in fact, taking place in our historical period and growing via positive feedback loops. When we notice that these ten practices are already happening, resolving conflicts, proving useful, and therefore spreading and making reliance on war unlikely in many regions, then we sense that ours is a historic moment in which we may be able to encourage a transition from war as normal to war as abnormal. We are not just expressing a wish, but calling all to notice what new processes of deliverance are happening among us and spreading globally. We are urging not disembodied ideals or ahistorical "oughts" to impose on an alien history they do not fit, but support for what is serving functional needs in the midst of power realities.

These practices can be perceived by all. They are seen from the perspective of peace and justice, and some faith and hope. The empirical practices that we present are not merely a dispassionate statistical summary. By no means are all practices in our time ethically normative. There are powerful economic interests and natural drives for national security that can work good or evil. There are interests that do not want to make peace, and interests that think they want to make peace but perceive things in such a way, and with such loyalties, that their actions work at cross-purposes to peace. Some think that the way to peace is to wipe out the enemy. There are enormous forces of evil: nuclear weapons and their delivery systems; chemical and biological weapons; devastating poverty and its off-spring, population explosion; ecological devastation and nonrenew-able energy consumption; ethnic and religious wars within nations such as Cambodia, Bosnia, and Zaire. "Some 2 million children have died in dozens of wars during the past decade. . . . This is more than three times the number of battlefield deaths of American soldiers in all their wars since 1776. . . . Today, civilians account for more than 90 percent of war casualties."[28] Whenever the peacemaking practices we point to work their way into areas where they are still foreign, each practice recognizes and seeks to resolve, lessen, discipline, or check and balance one or more of these evil forces.

25

Our focus on practices, and on churches and groups that encourage and foster those practices, means that we recommend to every individual and every church that they form groups to nurture such practices. Most church groups and denominations have a church peacemaking program. We urge each church to link up actively with its group's peacemaking program. We also urge linking up with networks that provide action alerts so we can know when to join with others in putting our shoulders to the wheel of peacemaking, so that in our numbers there is strength and in our timing there is effectiveness. Some will join Peace Action and/or Bread for the World, Amnesty International, World Peacemakers, Greenpeace and Greencross, or the Sierra Club.[29]

In isolation is passivity; in working together is empowerment. The acting unit, for us, is not the isolated individual but the individual in a local group that is connected with a national network of peacemakers. Churches should have a peacemaker group, a Peace and World Hunger committee, or a Peace and Justice leadership group that will lead the church in peacemaking action. Denominational peacemaking programs and World Peacemakers have suggestions for how to organize church peacemaking groups. Alone, as individuals, we lack the information, the group support, the sense of empowerment, and the ability to act in concert with other peace-makers to become a strong force for peace. Together, in groups, we can experience the fun of mutual support and friendship as well as the spiritual growth of the arcane discipline of prayer and action.[30]

CONSENSUS WITHOUT UNANIMITY

Churches and peacemaking groups, and governments and citizens, have an obligation to support these peacemaking practices in long-term work to build conditions that make peace more likely as well as in crises, where peacemaking initiatives can make war less likely. Whether a government employs these practices is a test of the sincerity of its claim to be trying to make peace. Whether a church supports these practices tests its sincerity in claiming to follow Jesus.

We recognize that our work is incomplete. We hope to offer our best thinking, and we ask: Does it make new sense of our historical context, and point to faith-based, meaningful action and prayer in that context? Can these ten practices of just peacemaking help people participate in the peacemaking practices and forces that are changing our world? Do they grapple with realistic evils that cause war and destroy peace? What improvements can you offer? How would you relate them to your faith or core beliefs and values? We are addressing all persons of various faiths or no claimed faith who are concerned about peacemaking, or who could become concerned if they had a map that would make sense of events and of peacemaking trends for them and that would indicate directions their participation can take.

Coming from diverse perspectives, we reached consensus. We celebrated; we were energized by our agreement. But we also recognized differences and omissions. John Cartwright observed that we had ideological differences in the essays, and he thought that was good; heads nodded in agreement. We need more on the nuclearized world; we believe many have relaxed too soon. We lack enough attention to racial-ethnic-religious conflict, but we have made efforts to emphasize this concern. We do not all agree with Michael Smith's affirmation of humanitarian intervention, but we think it should be included. We have definite disagreements over the international economy in its complexities, power realities, and injustices. We should say more about structural adjustment policies of the International Monetary Fund. Empirically, international trade decreases war, but the globalized economy is setting millions of the poor back further. The question of how we can make global corporations ethically and legally responsible in each country where they operate, despite their enormous power and their ability to leave any country, is one of the most crucial ethical questions for the next decades. We have not tried to answer it; we have only pointed to some effects on peacemaking. Being based in members of the Society of Christian Ethics who have authored calls for a just peacemaking, we lack Third World voices. Although we listen to voices from the developing nations, read Third World books, visit Third World countries, and seek to incorporate insights from those sources in what we have written, this book would be different if it had been written in Nicaragua or Uganda, El Salvador or the Sudan. From the perspective of our First World location, our practice should be confession and repentance for the injustice of the system, of international power, of economic practices. But one participant pointed out that our focus is not so much on condemning wickedness as on naming practices that can make it better, such as the practice of sustainable economic development.

27

Peace activists are located in the struggle for change, and this gives them a strongly critical tone toward present government policies, institutions, leaders, and other status-quo forces. Many members of established faith communities tend to be more a part of established institutions, more oriented toward gradual, incremental change, and often defensive in the face of more-radical criticism of the status quo. Academics tend to be part of a would-be scientific and detached community, and so speak in distanced language. The distinctions are not airtight; many peace activists are deeply involved in faith communities; many academics are engaged in congregations, and many are more radically critical of the status quo. Most of us who have produced this just peacemaking paradigm are academics; many have been engaged in peace activism on the national, local, and church levels. Many of us are a synthesis: academic church peace activists.

The result is that, for some peace activists, we may not be critical enough of U.S. policies; for some church people, we may be too critical; for some academics, we may say too little about systemic theory. All we can say is that, yes, there are logs in our own eyes. We have those tensions in our group as well. But the more we have worked together, the more we have learned to appreciate one another's diverse perspectives, and the more we have become committed to the importance of these practices. We believe these practices are so important that we are genuinely eager for them to reach a wide audience. It has been fun to watch our enthusiasm grow out of initial skepticism as we have experienced the result taking shape. We ask you to focus on the sense the practices make; on how they can help you notice what is happening in our world, in our time; and on how you can be a part of them on the level of your personal practice, your group and congregational involvements, and your encouragement and criticism of governments. In Michelle Tooley's study of women working for human rights in Guatemala, she found that what empowered them was working together in groups with specific, shared practices of peacemaking.[31] We can do likewise.

peacemaking initiatives

SUPPORT NONVIOLENT DIRECT ACTION

John Cartwright
Susan Thistlethwaite

Nonviolent Direct Action came to the attention of most of us in the United States as the method used effectively by Martin Luther King Jr. and the civil rights movement; that application borrowed from the *satyagraha* campaign led by Mahatma Mohandas Gandhi for independence in India. And nonviolent direct action has been further refined through the nonviolent movement that ended dictatorship in the Philippines; the nonviolent campaign that ended rule by the shah in Iran; the recent revolutions in Poland, East Germany, and Central Europe; human-rights movements in Guatemala, Argentina, and elsewhere in Latin America; the nonviolent parts of the *intifadah* campaign in Palestine; and the freedom campaign in South Africa.

Nonviolent direct action is a strategy that lances the festering boil of violence and produces healing without resort to war. Citizens and governments must support and work with such campaigns in situations of actual or potential conflict before the condition of "last resort" can be employed to justify violence. Hence the practice of nonviolent direct action is an obligatory norm where nonviolently it can transform festering injustice into constructive change.

Nonviolent direct action is designed to deal with injustice that is already happening. It becomes an action that transforms a situation from greater to lesser violence, from greater to lesser injustice, when it is employed out of an analysis of the violence and injustice that is currently underway. That is to say that none of the nonviolent direct actions described below, taken out of this context, guarantees that greater justice and peace will automatically result. Any of these nonviolent direct actions can be and has been employed to increase violent confrontation for unjust ends.

As a general guideline, grassroots movements for peace and justice, nongovernmental organizations, or even government agencies and the military, when they are considering any of these practice norms, must engage in rigorous contextual analysis of the forces in the situation that are increasing violence and injustice and the current or proposed options for increased peace and justice. This analysis must be concrete and must be done in consultation with the many groups, agencies or instrumentalities involved. Peacemaking is never simple. It always requires the broadest kind of consultation with *all* the parties involved. Then a decision as to which practice norm, several norms, or none at all, best serves the interests of justice and peace in any given situation.

As Daniel L. Buttry says:

> The 1980s and early 1990s witnessed a transformation of the way people engage in struggles for freedom, justice, peace, and human rights. Wars, insurgencies, ethnic violence, and acts of terrorism still occur with horrifying frequency and tragic consequences, but for the first time in human history a global phenomenon of nonviolent movements shook up political powers, redrew national boundaries, and brought hope to millions of people ground down by oppression and poverty. . . . Through nonviolent action, ordinary people who had often been locked out of political decision-making processes became agents shaping their own destinies.[1]

As part of this global movement, the teachings and works of Gandhi and Martin Luther King Jr. spread around the world. Chinese students in Tiananmen Square quoted King. The movie *Gandhi* played in Lithuania in 1987 just as the Sajudis independence movement was beginning. The International Fellowship of Reconciliation provided nonviolence training in Brazil, the Philippines, South Africa, Burma, Korea, and a host of other countries. Hildegard and Jean Goss-Mayr of the International Fellowship of Reconciliation were nominated for the Nobel Peace Prize for their efforts to disseminate nonviolence through their workshops. Adolfo Pérez Esquivel from Argentina received the Nobel Prize in 1980 for his work in linking together nonviolent movements as diverse as the Mothers of the Plaza in Argentina protesting the disappearance of their relatives, cement workers in Brazil striking for better working conditions, and Indians in Ecuador struggling for land reform. The theory and history of nonviolence has received more scholarly attention by people such as Gene Sharp, whose three-volume work *The Politics of Nonviolent Action* has become a classic in the field. These connections have helped to break down the walls of isolation that have aided repression, and have provided new insights, creative examples, and moral solidarity for people in a wide range of contexts as they struggle to better their lives and shape their destiny.

The practice of nonviolent direct action actually includes a set of practices, outlined in the sections that follow.

BOYCOTTS

A *boycott* is a concerted action designed to isolate an individual, group, or nation in order to express disapproval and to coerce change. The term "boycott" is taken from Charles Boycott, an English estate manager whose rent collection tactics in the 1880s so enraged Irish tenants that they refused to harvest crops for him. The withholding of labor was first used, therefore, on Boycott himself, and its success was demonstrated by his need for fifty volunteers from Ulster, working under an armed escort of nine hundred soldiers, to harvest his crops.

After 1880 the term soon came into common use, broadening to describe and include all forms of nonviolent intimidation. The nineteenth-century Abolitionist movement, for example, was the first organized effort to change national policy in the United States through nonviolent means. Boycotting slave-made products was a common tactic in that endeavor. Indeed, product boycotts were common in the late nineteenth century when the nascent labor-union movement attempted to discourage the public from buying goods made by nonunion companies with unfair labor practices.

Numerous and varied examples of the use of the boycott pervade the twentieth century. In the 1930s, Gandhi encouraged Indians to boycott British textiles and to substitute their own homespun cloth, a significant factor in the success of the movement for Indian self-determination. The Montgomery bus boycott of 1955–1956 launched the Martin Luther King-led civil rights movement, and boycotts of stores and business districts that supported segregation were integral to the movement's success in many cities. César Chávez, who founded the National Farm Workers Association in 1962, organized national consumer boycotts of lettuce, grapes, and wines in order to protest the plight of migrant farm workers. In the 1970s and 1980s, organizations concerned about the abuse of infant-formula marketing practices organized a successful global boycott focused on Nestlé, which resulted in new standards of marketing.

Although the boycott is most frequently used in labor disputes, it has had a much wider range of application and use. In recent history, perhaps the most impressive example of a global boycott which contributed to nonviolent political change was the action against South Africa. Boycotts of companies that invested in South Africa and economic sanctions against that state were a major force in persuading the government to drop apartheid and to enter into democratic elections and peaceful integration, when most observers had expected apartheid would end, if at all, only after very bloody violence.

That action demonstrated the increased ability of nonviolent activists to penetrate the complex corporate patterns of ownership and control. Activists were able to coordinate their research, confrontation, and publicity globally—a sophisticated model of boycott that has become easier with the increased availability of communication tools to activists around the world. This boycott was crucial in persuading the moderate (or, perhaps more accurately, amoral or morally ambivalent) parts of the South African business community of the eventual higher cost of resistance to change.

In the final analysis, all boycotts depend for their effectiveness on broad concerted action that is focused on a limited issue or problem. Since the purpose of a boycott is to change rather than annihilate the offending party, careful management of the boycott process is required. Furthermore, serious economic, political, and moral questions may arise from a miscalculation or disregard of the effects of a boycott on secondary parties or the community as a whole. This suggests a certain degree of control, foresight, and attention to both the manifest and the latent consequences of this type of concerted action.

In a thoughtful book, Mark W. Charlton concludes that international economic sanctions can produce corrections of systemic injustice without the violence of war, or they can violate basic human rights and even contribute directly to extensive loss of life. They must be evaluated not by abstract general principles but by an ethical framework of violence-reduction criteria that evaluate them in the context of specific policy situations:

1. The target country must have committed a grave injustice.
2. Less-coercive measures must have been tried first.
3. A significant portion of the population must not already be living at a subsistence level and pushed over the brink by the sanctions; and neutral authorities—not the enforcers—must monitor the effects.
4. Humanitarian provisions must be included so that fundamental rights to food, medicine, and shelter are not violated.
5. Preference should be given to targeting the interests of those responsible for the wrongdoing, and to avoid enriching them at the expense of the victims.
6. If domestic reform is the main objective, there must be widespread support for the sanctions within the targeted population.
7. Sanctions should be applied in a manner likely to lead to a long-term, just resolution: by upholding international law and widely accepted moral values; by being part of a broader political strategy to find a peaceful and just solution; by having clearly announced objectives that indicate what behaviors will result in lifting the sanctions; and by refraining from adding new conditions or objectives.[2]

STRIKES

A *strike* is a collective refusal by employees to work under the conditions required by employers. It can take the form of an outright walkout, a sitdown strike, a work slowdown, or a hunger strike. It is a practice norm in peacemaking when it is directed at noncooperation with unjust economic practice, or is combined with larger movements of noncooperation with unjust political and/or social orders. One could say that worker noncooperation with oppressive conditions is as old as history itself. Pharaoh experienced both a work slowdown on the part of the midwives and a complete walkout on the part of the Hebrews (Exod. 1:13).

Strikes as an organized effort of the labor movement date from the nineteenth-century Industrial Revolution in Europe and the early twentieth century in the United States. They were used as a tactic of labor organizing, particularly in Great Britain. Unions did not become legal in England until 1871, and not until 1935 did the National Labor Relations Act make labor organizing and collective bargaining legal in the United States. The Solidarity union in Poland achieved considerable social change through strikes in the 1980s. Local and national strikes as well as work stoppages and slowdowns formed a cornerstone of the struggle against apartheid in South Africa.

Strikes have often met with considerable violence on the part of both business owners and government. In Colorado in the early twentieth century, strikebreakers burned striking gold miners alive while they were gathered in a meeting hall. The leaders of striking Bolivian tin miners in 1977 were imprisoned, beaten, or exiled. Officials have called on police and even the National Guard, as Calvin Coolidge did in breaking the strike of the Boston police force in 1919. Owners have used scabs or nonunion workers to replace striking workers. Several states in the United States now have right-to-work laws which weaken unions by making closed shops—that is, only union shops—illegal.

Strikes and work slowdowns were used effectively in combination with consumer boycotts by a Mexican-American, César Chávez. Chávez organized migrant farm workers in California, founding the National Farm Workers Association in 1962. Agricultural workers are among the most exploited segment of the U.S. labor force, being exempt from Occupational Health and Safety Standards and minimum-wage laws. Child labor still exists in farm work. Chávez gave these workers a sense of control over their own lives through this type of action.

Hunger strikes are sometimes a part of the strike effort. Certainly Gandhi elevated the hunger strike to a new level of spirituality. As he said in the Fast unto Death in January 1948, "My fast should not be considered a political move in any sense of the term. It is obedience to the peremptory call of conscience and duty. It comes out of felt agony."[3] Women leaders in the suffrage movement in England, such as Emmeline Pankhurst, effectively used hunger strikes as part of their struggle to secure women's right to vote. Arrested for her increased militancy in the struggle for women's suffrage, Pankhurst went on a hunger strike in prison in 1913. Hunger-striking prisoners had been force-fed in British prisons, and some had choked to death. The resultant public outcry had caused the government to release hunger strikers until they regained their health, after which they would be reincarcerated. Pankhurst was released and rearrested under this law twelve times in one year.

César Chávez used a thirty-six-day hunger strike to protest hazardous pesticide use. After the Bolivian tin miners' union leaders were killed, imprisoned, or exiled, four wives of imprisoned miners—Nellie Paniagua, Angelica Flores, Aurora Lora, and Luzmila Penmentel—began a hunger strike on Christmas Day 1977. This story deserves to be related in detail.

Archbishop Jorge Manrique allowed the women to hold the hunger strike in his own residence. On December 28, the Feast of Holy Innocents, which commemorates the children slaughtered by Herod, the women's children joined the hunger strike. When people protested, the mothers said they would release the children as soon as adults came to take their places. Soon almost fourteen hundred people had joined this hunger strike. As the tension mounted, international human-rights organizations, church representatives, and other nongovernmental agencies tried to mediate. Negotiations broke down at one point, and some strikers and human-rights observers were arrested. The four women then began to refuse water as well as food.

The government acceded to the striking women's demands in full, providing amnesty for nineteen thousand political prisoners and exiles, reinstating jobs for union activists, and granting freedom to all arrested during the strike as well as the right to organize unions in the future.

The application of strikes as a practice norm is broad. Because unjust economic practice frequently is a form of institutionalized violence, strikes point directly to that often-hidden form of violence. Strikes are particularly effective when combined with other practices such as public disclosure, since the reason for the strike will be obscured or distorted by the business or government leaders who oppose it.

Noncooperation is a historically effective nonviolent method of achieving social change. In the form of strikes, whether to organize a union or to call attention to widespread political and social injustice, noncooperation involves many people making a commitment not to participate, even for a short time, in the structures they wish to change.

Hunger strikes can be used separately from broader strike activity but are often used in conjunction with economic noncooperation to draw attention to the spiritual dimension of the effort.

MARCHES

A *march* is a mass public demonstration by a group or groups seeking to dramatize an issue, a concern, a point of view, or an injustice. Externally, its purposes may include one or more of the following: education, fund raising, a show of force (in terms of numbers), recruitment of new or marginal adherents, or engendering of so-called creative tension and crisis. Internally, the march serves to build group morale, to identify the sympathetic, and to foster cohesion among the participants with regard to the group's aims and goals. A march usually involves both a *parade* and a *rally*, the latter characterized by speeches and celebration.

38   Marches in the context of conflict resolution and peacemaking appear to be quite modern. In the United States, marches most often have been associated with dramatizing a particular issue or cause such as temperance, suffrage, labor-management conflict, civil rights, opposition to war, or gay rights. Recently, the celebrated March on Washington in 1963 and the Million Man March of 1995 have become particularly potent examples of the attention-getting effect of a well-executed mass demonstration.

King orchestrated the march to an art form. He saw that the non-violent march should intentionally seek to create such a crisis and foster such a tension that a community which previously had refused to hear must now confront the issue in the form of living persons; such a live dramatization of an issue can no longer be ignored. As King stated in his classic "Letter from Birmingham Jail," conflict must be brought into the open in order to be healed:

> Actually we who engage in nonviolent direct action are not the creators of tension. We merely bring to the surface the hidden tension that is already alive. We bring it out in the open, where it can be seen and dealt with. Like a boil that can never be cured so long as it is covered up but must be opened with all its ugliness to the natural medicines of

air and light, injustice must be exposed, with all the tension its exposure creates, to the light of human conscience and the air of national opinion before it can be cured.[4]

The march, therefore, is predicated on the faith that the exposure to truth creates its own dynamic and makes for resolution around the true issues rather than false or superficial ones.

In the United States, East Germany, South Africa, Argentina, and elsewhere, marches have brought dramatic nonviolent change that had been thought impossible without massive violence.

CIVIL DISOBEDIENCE

Civil disobedience is the act of disobeying or refusing to obey civil laws or decrees on grounds of moral, political, or religious principle. Persons who practice civil disobedience break the law because they consider the law unjust, want to call attention to its injustice, and hope to bring about its repeal or amendment. Although it adopts the tactics of nonviolence, civil disobedience is usually more than mere passive resistance. It often takes such active forms as illegal demonstrations or peaceful occupation of premises. As distinguished from other forms of rebellion, civil disobedience tends to invite a confrontation with civil authorities (most often leading to arrest) and willingly accepts the penalty for breaking the law.

Civil disobedience can be traced back at least to the Exodus of the Jews from Pharaoh's authority in Egypt and to the earliest Christians, who engaged in limited forms of civil disobedience on religious grounds. Religion often has been a basis for refusing to obey laws perceived as contrary to belief, as when the Doukhobors in Canada refused to send their children to state-operated schools. The Doukhobors then paraded nude in public to protest their prosecution for passive resistance to the school laws.

The classic exposition of civil disobedience is Henry David Thoreau's essay "Resistance to Civil Government" (1849), later retitled "On the Duty of Civil Disobedience." Thoreau said that when one's conscience and the laws clash, one must follow one's conscience. This stress on personal conscience and on the need to act now rather than wait for legal change have become recurring elements in civil disobedience movements.[5]

Perhaps the most ambitious and most successful examples of mass civil disobedience were those of Mohandas Gandhi and Martin

39

Luther King Jr. Gandhi called civil disobedience *satyagraha* (a term meaning "truth force") and taught it as an austere practice requiring great self-discipline and moral purity. With a versatile use of civil disobedience, Gandhi led the campaign for Indian independence in the 1930s and 1940s.

Also in the 1940s, Blacks along with white sympathizers began to use forms of civil disobedience in order to challenge discrimination in public transportation and restaurants. The major movement, however, began in 1955 with the Montgomery bus boycott and the ensuing illegal sit-ins in support of boycotts of segregated public facilities. King was a disciple of Gandhi and became the chief advocate of nonviolent civil disobedience in the civil rights movement of the 1960s.

Civil disobedience has been practiced by pacifists and by individuals devoted to such causes as prohibition and women's suffrage. It also has been widely employed worldwide by oppressed groups that want to emulate the success of Gandhi and King. The tactic is often effective in changing laws and protecting liberties. Resistance to war and military preparations is a frequent reason for civil disobedience. It can take the form of refusal to serve in the armed forces (conscientious objection) or unlawful demonstrations such as those aimed at nuclear armament and the Vietnam War.

Civil disobedience has been shown to be a powerful political force when people have sought to liberate themselves from foreign domination within their own countries. In such cases, civil disobedience, when combined with mass withdrawal of cooperation in the form of strikes, boycotts, mass demonstrations, and the like, holds great promise of effectiveness.

PUBLIC DISCLOSURE

Public disclosure is publicizing the complete facts or events relevant to a conflict but which are being kept hidden or falsified due to deliberate strategies of disinformation. Violence loves the lie. Its operations are best done in secret and, where unavoidably visible, cloaked in justification and even glorification. Exposing the lie is as old as the first codes of moral conduct: "Thou shalt not bear false witness against thy neighbor" (Exod. 20:16). Yet the practice of public disclosure as a regular strategy of peacemaking is far more recent.

In a sense, public disclosure as a practice norm is a child of the information age. The forces of disinformation make excellent use of the modern ability to disseminate information quickly to large numbers of people, and their responsibility for distortions must be made public in order to check this misuse. Historian Margaret Miles has argued that the first use of the printed page was to stir up hostility and violence against witches.[6] The rise of anti-Semitism in Europe prior to the World War II was led by a hysterical press. Lies about Jewish bankers ruining economies, controlling the media, and corrupting so-called pure societies flooded first the population of Germany and then, as the Germans swept across Europe, other populations. These lies were extremely effective.

Public disclosure as a deliberate practice norm for peace may be traced most directly to the thought and practice of Mohandas K. Gandhi. "I claim to be a passionate seeker after truth, which is but another name for God," wrote Gandhi in *Nonviolence in Peace and War.*[7] *Satyagraha*, the name Gandhi gave to nonviolent action, can also be translated as "passionate seeking of truth." Change in India resulted not only from the work of the *satyagrahas* in nonviolently resisting the British troops but also from the public disclosure of their resistance. And when Martin Luther King Jr. led marches in Birmingham and Selma and was met with firehose-wielding police, the lie that race relations were just fine was met with the force of public disclosure. It was surely the pictures of the body bags coming off the airplanes that accelerated resistance to the Vietnam War; and that was certainly the reason why, in the Gulf War, the phrase "body bag" was replaced by "human remains containers" and no photographs were allowed.

As with other nonviolent practice norms, the spiral of violence of which Dom Helder Camara has written will be revealed.[8] Public disclosure of overt or covert violence usually leads the perpetrators of violence to produce yet more disinformation and increased violence. This becomes so obvious that they lose credibility, to the point where the violent will no longer be able to maintain the fiction that their course is honorable and justified.

Positively, public disclosure as a practice norm is rooted in the fact that an unacknowledged conflict cannot be mediated. Open communication regarding the existence of conflict and its contents is the first step in mediation.

Public disclosure has been effective where there are disinformation and denial that a conflict exists. Recent examples of the effectiveness of public disclosure include Karen Silkwood's disclosure of the dangers of nuclear power, the use of the Internet by Chinese students to get word to the international community about the massacre in Tiananmen Square, the witness of the COMADRES (Committee of the Mothers and Relatives of the Disappeared, Political Prisoners, and Assassinated of El Salvador), the demonstrations of the Mothers of the Plaza de Mayo in Argentina about their "disappeared," the coverage by CNN and Peter Arnet of the bombing of Baghdad during the Gulf War when the true extent of the violence was being hidden, and the witness of the Women of Greenham Common to the dangers of the impending installation of ground-launched cruise missiles.

ACCOMPANIMENT

Accompaniment is the practice of independent monitors accompanying those most exposed to potential violence. This practice is closely related to public disclosure. For example, during the civil rights movement, prominent citizens, members of the clergy, and many others participated in demonstrations and sit-ins in order to add their public witness and increase public attention to the injustices.

There are two major models of accompaniment. In the first model, human-rights monitors make third-party witnesses present and visible so that the potential calculus of violence must take into account public knowledge of the actions. The monitors remove the veil of secrecy. Even if the world is not particularly interested in the conflict at the moment, the monitors ensure that eventually the truth will be told. The genocide in Burundi and Rwanda seeks not resolution of a competing claim but elimination of the competitor. The presence of monitors makes this unjustifiable violence potentially more costly to its perpetrators. Monitors do not intervene and often are resented when they stand by taking notes in relative safety.

In the second model, a more-interventionist accompaniment is pursued. During the war for Nicaragua, thousands of unarmed volunteers placed themselves in harm's way, acting not just as witnesses but as a shield, calling themselves Witness for Peace. This interventionist form of accompaniment is especially effective in decreasing the likelihood of violence if potential perpetrators view those doing the accompanying as unacceptable casualties. In Nicaragua, the likely perpetrators were supported by the U.S. government, which made the deaths of U.S.-citizen witnesses highly disadvantageous to their cause. In contrast, say, Belgian citizens would have had no such deterrent effect on those perpetrating violence in, for example, Rwanda.

The practice of accompaniment is a step of nonviolent defense that lessens the need for those facing attack to engage in defensive violence. It may be sought by a party for its defense or initiated by third-party peacemakers. It exposes peacemakers to serious risks and possible consequences by placing them in harm's way. It also challenges those who offer moral criticism of defensive violence by threatened groups to answer the question: "Do you so oppose violence that you are willing to accompany me and stand vulnerable with me before those I fear?" Hence it forces peacemakers to take a less-abstract view of the relative risks faced by the parties involved.

The accompaniment option can be taken by neutral armed forces. But more often, it is practiced by unarmed, and often unofficial, peacemakers. It need not be agreed to by both defender and attacker; it can be chosen by defenders to decrease violence.

43

SAFE SPACES

Safe space is used either to prevent conflict or during a conflict, when the physical and psychological safety of some—especially traditional noncombatants—is secured. Safe space finds its historical roots in the concept of *sanctuary*, which means "sacred space," set apart from the ordinary, profane world. Originally defined as natural locations, such as mountains or forest groves, sanctuary was extended to mean structures devoted to worship such as a tabernacle, tent, lodge, or church. Because such places were deemed sacred, and therefore the shedding of blood would profane them, they came to be regarded as asylums for those being threatened with violence, often criminals but also refugees.

In Christian law after the fourth century, the space of sanctuary free from violence was extended beyond the walls of the church structure to the surrounding area. Henry VIII abolished many church sanctuaries but established certain "cities of refuge." The practice of sanctuary survived in continental Europe until the French Revolution.

Sanctuary or safe space has been revived in several ways. During American slavery, abolitionists established the underground railroad, a network of safe houses linking transportation routes from the slave states of the South to the North. These safe houses, unlike earlier sanctuaries, were not respected by civil authorities.

In the twentieth century, when refugees from the wars in El Salvador and Guatemala began to cross into the United States, the Immigration and Naturalization Service (INS) began to deport them to almost certain death at home. This was being done despite the U.S. Refugee Act of 1980 and the United Nations Protocol Accords of 1967, which say that no persons can be deported who have a grave fear of persecution if returned to their homeland. A movement within the religious community to provide shelter for these refugees began along the U.S.-Mexico border and spread throughout the country. The U.S. government harassed churches, sanctuary workers, and peace advocates. Eventually eleven sanctuary workers, including two Catholic priests, a Presbyterian minister, and a Catholic nun, were arrested and tried in Tucson, Arizona. The judge refused to allow any evidence about conditions the refugees were fleeing to be entered into the trial. The sanctuary movement continued as long as the refugees were coming. It had a significant impact on U.S. public opinion, which eventually demanded and secured an end to U.S. government funding of the war by the Contras against the legally elected government in Nicaragua.

Another major locus of safe spaces is the battered women's movement, which began out of the women's consciousness raising that took place in the 1970s. Prior to the this movement, only a few safe spaces for women who were victims of domestic violence existed, such as Haven House opened by Al-anon in California in 1964. In the 1970s, the extent of violence against women in the home was revealed. The tired question "Why doesn't she just leave?" was answered: Many of these women would leave in a minute if they had a place to go and the help they needed to get on their feet and live in peace. The earliest safe spaces for battered women were shelters opened in England and the United States during the late 1970s to respond to the degree of domestic violence. This movement is now worldwide. In Costa Rica, the degree of domestic violence is so high that now not only are there state-supported shelters but also women-run police stations. These stations were established because when battered women went to traditional police stations to report domestic violence, often they were sexually harassed by the police.

Safe space as a practice norm has been applied both at the domestic level in battered women's shelters, and at the military level

44

as a no-fly zone or safe zone. Between these two poles, several other applications are possible. In protecting civilian life in conflict, hospital areas have been recognized through the Geneva Convention and other treaties as safe spaces.

Domestically, much work needs to be done in our cities and towns to make schools safe spaces, free from weapons and from drug and gang violence. It might even be possible to extend the concept of "safe school zones" to parks and recreational areas used by children. Internationally, demilitarized zones have been used to separate warring parties and to reduce the chance of incidents that could escalate the conflict. In the war in Bosnia, safe spaces were used in an attempt to reduce the civilian casualties in a war where civilians had been the target of military attack and genocide.

A MENU OF INTERVENTIONS AND DEFENSIVE STRATEGIES

Nonviolent direct action represents an evolving menu of interventions and creative defensive strategies that forces those who easily drift toward violence to justify themselves. The technologies of violence are becoming more lethal and, in terms of just war theory, more unjust, due to the inevitable disproportionate scale of violence and the greatly increased tendency of such powerful and plentiful weapons to wound, maim, and kill innocents.

The technologies and techniques of nonviolent direct action are also evolving in ways that are more powerful and effective. Increasing access to communication tools makes it easier for organizers to coordinate participants, track the companies and governments opposing justice, and reach broad constituencies with the content and meaning of the action. The tools have evolved to the point where nonviolent direct action can be considered a norm that must be pursued before violence can be considered as a just last resort. Governments must make room for, must respect, such movements. And groups of citizens—including church groups, members of synagogues, mosques, and friends' meetings, and other groups united by religious faith, are challenged to engage in nonviolent direct action and thus to lance the boil of injustice before it festers and becomes increasingly violent.

2

TAKE INDEPENDENT INITIATIVES TO REDUCE THREAT

Glen Stassen

The strategy of independent initiatives is a recent innovation in international relations. It was implemented successfully to achieve the Austrian State Treaty in 1955, by which the Soviet Union set Austria free and NATO agreed to Austrian neutrality and nonoffensive military force; by presidents Eisenhower and Kennedy to halt atmospheric testing unilaterally and eventually to achieve the Partial Test Ban Treaty of 1963; in the series of initiatives taken first by Soviet president Gorbachev and the U.S. Congress and then by U.S. president Bush to achieve dramatic reductions in nuclear weapons; and in small initiatives taken by Israel and its Arab neighbors and by adversaries in Northern Ireland to create the climate for recent peacemaking breakthroughs. The strategy was named and affirmed in Catholic, Methodist, Presbyterian, and UCC statements in the 1980s but is not widely enough known. It needs to be understood more widely so that it will be noticed when it causes breakthroughs for peace and so that citizens can press governments to take independent initiatives.

In 1962, the social psychologist Charles Osgood proposed the peacemaking method he called "independent initiatives."[1] Over the next two decades, it was widely adopted by church statements and peace movements in Europe and the United States. Eventually, they persuaded governments to adopt it, with striking success. Osgood argued that in a relationship of distrust and heightened threat perception, nations are blocked from initiating peacemaking steps and misperceive peace initiatives from the other side as insincere manipulation.

The old strategy of building up military threats in times of tension increases threat perception and decreases flexibility. The opposite strategy of unilateral disarmament is politically unlikely. A new strategy is needed—independent initiatives. The strategy is to take initiatives to decrease the other side's distrust or threat perception, in order to induce them to take similar initiatives or to negotiate seriously to remove threats.

Effective initiatives have the following characteristics:

1. They are designed to decrease threat perception and distrust by the other side, such as Gorbachev's removal of tanks and river-crossing equipment from Central Europe, so that NATO would be less fearful of a sudden tank attack. Once NATO no longer feared a tank attack, it became more willing to negotiate reductions in medium-range nuclear missiles (see chapter 9, "Reduce Offensive Weapons and Weapons Trade").

2. They are visible and verifiable actions, so that the other side can see that they are, in fact, being taken. Mere words or invisible actions are insufficient to break through the context of distrust; they will be interpreted with disbelief.

3. They are independent of the slow process of negotiation. One side does not first negotiate what the other side will do if and when it takes this initiative, because that process takes too long; the point is to take surprising, transforming initiatives that create a climate where negotiation can succeed and make a difference, including ratifying and regularizing the initiatives that already have been taken.

4. They are designed to decrease the threat to the other side, but they should not leave the initiator weak. A feeling of weakness often increases distrust and threat perception.

5. Initiatives should be undertaken in a series; one initiative is not likely to decrease threat perception significantly enough.

6. If the other side reciprocates with some independent initiatives of their own, then the series of initiatives can continue in a major way. If the other side holds off from reciprocating, then rela-

tively small initiatives should continue the series in order to keep inviting reciprocation.

7. The timing of each initiative should be announced in advance and carried out regardless of the other side's bluster: To postpone confirms distrust.

8. There should be clear explanation of the purpose: to shift the context toward deescalation and to invite reciprocation.

One of President Eisenhower's initiatives constitutes a historical example. In response to the worldwide movement against testing nuclear bombs by exploding them in the open air, he announced in 1958 that the United States would halt above-ground testing for one year. If the Soviet Union reciprocated, he continued, then the United States would halt for an additional year and perhaps more. The Soviet Union also halted such tests, and the halt lasted almost three years. Both sides already had a nuclear deterrent, and halting tests did not weaken them. After testing had resumed, a similar halt was again initiated by President Kennedy. This led to the 1963 Atmospheric Test Ban Treaty and the beginning of the thaw of the Cold War.

More recently, independent initiatives were a major factor in the peaceful end of the Cold War and the dramatic reductions of nuclear weapons. *Schritte zur Abrüstung*, the group of German political scientists and ethicists who advocated the strategy of independent initiatives, expressed surprise that the Soviet Union under Andropov and Gorbachev adopted the strategy more quickly than the Western governments did. They listed a dozen Soviet independent initiatives, including halting underground nuclear testing and inviting U.S. reciprocation; withdrawing from Afghanistan; destroying all SS-4 and SS-5 medium-range missiles; withdrawing half their tanks, all river-crossing equipment, and a large number of troops from central Europe; and accepting NATO's "zero-option" proposal, which eventually became the turning point in ending the Cold War. These initiatives did succeed, bit by bit, in changing Western perceptions of the Soviet Union, just as Congressional initiatives had given the Soviet Union hope of likely U.S. responsiveness to initiatives the Soviet Union might take.

In the 1980s, the U.S. Congress was persuaded to adopt the strategy bit by bit. The House voted to halt money for:

1. Any MX missiles beyond the fifty in the pipeline.
2. Any missile deployments exceeding SALT II Treaty limits.
3. One-third of the "Star Wars" program (officially named Strategic Defense Initiative or SDI).
4. Star Wars tests violating the Anti-Ballistic Missile Treaty.
5. Half of the chemical weapons program.
6. Contra aid for the war in Nicaragua.
7. Any increase in the military budget.
8. Flight testing of antisatellite missiles.
9. Underground nuclear testing.

The U.S. Senate agreed to all but halting underground testing (they finally approved a total halt in 1992).

Congress's initiatives interacted reciprocally with the Soviet Union's, encouraging yet further initiatives. The result was rapid removal of large quantities of threatening nuclear weapons. Citizen pressure stimulated by peace movements was crucial throughout the process for achieving the congressional initiatives.[2] It is crucial now for citizens' groups to learn the practice of independent initiatives, employ it in their own conflicts, and urge it on governments.

On September 27, 1991, President Bush took up the theme, stating that negotiations take too long (the START talks took ten years) and that the United States needed a sweeping initiative. He announced he would go along with Congress's canceling the mobile MX missile and the short-range attack missile and with the European governments' requests that the short-range missiles be removed. He would also remove shorter-range nuclear missiles from ships and attack submarines and relax the alert readiness of bombers. Gorbachev matched these and stopped nuclear testing. The outcome has been rapid reductions (see chapter 9). The strategy of independent initiatives has made an enormous contribution to our safety. We should push for its employment in other cases of hostility and threat.

During the buildup toward the Gulf War, Harold Saunders, the highly respected advisor on Middle East policy for several administrations, advocated that we try "a scenario of political steps that could lead to changes in the situation," spelling out independent initiatives designed to persuade Iraq to back out of Kuwait without war.[3] His initiatives were not tried.

After the war, the United States persuaded Israel and some Arab states to take small independent initiatives toward one another, opening up some trade, telephone lines, and the like, which helped create willingness to enter into the negotiations that led to Palestinian recognition of Israel and Israeli recognition of self-government for Palestine, and a peace treaty with Jordan. As Israeli-Palestinian relations deteriorated during 1997, the U.S. government urged Prime Minister Netanyahu to take independent initiatives: a withdrawal of Israeli troops from 15 percent of the West Bank and a moratorium on new settlements in Palestinian areas.

The strategy of independent initiatives is advocated especially clearly by the statements of the United Church of Christ, the Methodist bishops, and the Catholic bishops.[4] In East and West Germany, it was a central feature of the strategy advocated by church and peace groups, and was combined with the concept of security partnership: Our security depends on our adversary's perception of its own security.[5]

The U.S. Catholic bishops called for independent initiatives as obligatory, required, of governments:

> We believe the urgent need for control of the arms race requires a willingness for each side to take some first steps. . . . By independent initiatives we mean carefully chosen limited steps which the United States could take for a defined period of time, seeking to elicit a comparable step from the Soviet Union.
>
> In 1963 President Kennedy announced that the United States would unilaterally forgo further nuclear testing; the next month Soviet Premier Nikita Khrushchev proposed a limited test ban which eventually became the basis of the U.S.-Soviet partial test ban treaty. Subsequently, both superpowers removed about 10,000 troops from Central Europe and each announced a cut in production of nuclear material for weapons.[6]

Transforming initiatives are also urged by the United Church of Christ in *A Just Peace Church:*

Unexpected initiatives of friendship and reconciliation can transform interpersonal and international relationships and are essential to restoring community. . . . Each local church [should] become a community . . . willing to take surprising initiatives to transform situations of enmity. . . . We reject any use or threat to use weapons and forces of mass destruction and any doctrine of deterrence based primarily on using such weapons. We also reject unilateral full-scale disarmament. . . . We affirm the development of new policies of common security, using a combination of negotiated agreements, new international institutions and institutional power, nonviolent strategies, unilateral initiatives to lessen tensions, and new policies which will make the global economy more just. . . . We call upon the United States and the Soviet Union and other nations to take unilateral initiatives toward implementing [a mutual nuclear weapons] freeze, contingent upon the other side responding, until such a time as a comprehensive freeze can be negotiated. . . . All nations should . . . make unilateral initiatives toward dismantling their military arsenals, calling upon other nations to reciprocate.[7]

The strategy of transforming initiatives has been studied extensively in experimental psychological research by Svenn Lindskold.[8] And Deborah Welch Larson has studied its effectiveness in achieving the Austrian State Treaty, peacefully freeing Austria from an East-West partitioning of the sort that Germany had to endure for forty-five years. Larson concludes that the parties did act as the independent-initiatives strategy predicts rather than as tit-for-tat strategy predicts—that the strategy did work to elicit reciprocating initiatives, to relax tensions, to defuse a potentially explosive area, to establish a buffer zone, and to produce "the most successful neutralization agreement negotiated during the postwar period. It prevented a dangerous confrontation between Western and Soviet troops over control of this strategic territory in the heart of Europe."[9]

A likely objection is that in order to deter an adversary from aggressive action, it is important sometimes to communicate firm determination to resist; thus, independent initiatives could weaken the perception of determination. Robert Jervis's book *Perception and*

Misperception in International Politics is the preeminent study on the subject.[10] He describes this problem along with the opposite danger that the deterree will perceive signs of firm determination to resist as threats to attack and as intention to reject or take advantage of any moves toward deescalation and away from aggression. It is important to communicate firmness in resisting aggression as well as receptiveness to deescalation. Deterrence is persuasion, and it depends on perception—including the perception that if the adversary does back off, a better and more secure outcome is possible. For this, both firmness against aggression and independent initiatives pointing the way of deescalation are needed.

For example, during the Cuban Missile Crisis, President Kennedy not only communicated firmness, he also took initiatives to avoid confronting the first Soviet (non-missile-bearing) ship and to avoid retaliating when a U.S. spy plane was shot down. He agreed further to remove U.S. Thor and Jupiter missiles from Greece and Turkey.

We conclude that one essential step of just peacemaking is to take independent initiatives that point the way to deescalation, especially when distrust and threat perception are high. Governments that have not taken independent initiatives have not tried one essential resort to make peace. We call on persons of good will to explain the strategy of independent initiatives to others, to notice and point them out when they occur, and to urge governments as well as smaller groups and individuals to take independent initiatives where distrust and threat need a breakthrough.

3

USE COOPERATIVE
CONFLICT RESOLUTION

David Steele
Steven Brion-Meisels
Gary Gunderson
Edward LeRoy Long Jr.

Cooperative conflict resolution (CCR) is an essential practice of just peacemaking. It emphasizes the active coworking of parties in conflict; they attempt to develop creative solutions that each can affirm and support. They take on the process of conflict resolution as a shared enterprise, an active partnership in problem solving, in order to devise mutually beneficial outcomes.[1] The goal is to transform one's view of possible solutions to any given conflict from inevitable deadlock to multiple possibilities and to transform one's view of the other party from adversary to partner. Theologian Jürgen Moltmann states the aim well when he calls for a provisional peace in which fighting enemies can become "quarreling partners" and deadly conflict can become "non-lethal controversy."[2] As a result of such a process, the resolution of current conflicts and prevention of future ones can proceed with maximum success with respect to both peace and justice.

The cooperative conflict resolution process is transparent as well as transformative. It involves self-critical honesty, yet it is nonjudgmental toward others. Therefore it requires risk-taking and spiritual awareness. Its historical roots, in fact, draw deeply from many religious traditions that teach followers to respect and value all persons, even enemies, and that teach healing and forgiveness as crucial to the quest for fullness of life.[3] In their totality, they highlight the importance of often neglected aspects of conflict—the historical, spiritual, cultural, emotional, individual, and social elements of our experience.

First, it is important to set out a list of ten criteria or principles for achieving effective CCR.

1. Those involved in cooperative conflict resolution (CCR) must seek to understand the perspectives and needs of adversaries, even when they may personally disagree. They work to understand the problem from the other's point of view. They see cultural differences as resources rather than deficits. They recognize that creative approaches may challenge their own cultural practices and ways of seeing. They use personal and group histories, stories, and emotions to discover basic needs hidden behind surface positions and strategic interests.

2. Participants in CCR listen carefully before judging or offering solutions. They make space for the voices of all involved, both victims and perpetrators. They listen for content, feeling, and meaning. They withhold judgment even as they are clear about their own principles, positions, and stances.

3. Participants in CCR distinguish judgments about behavior and actions from judgments about persons or cultures. They may need to oppose or condemn particular actions, but their strategies for resolving conflict do not dehumanize or demonize the "other." Rather, all participants hold out the possibility of mutual solutions and mutual survival.

4. Participants in CCR acknowledge their own involvement in the creation or escalation of conflict and work to facilitate personal and social transformation. They are willing to examine basic attitudes and values self-critically. A religious way of saying this is that participants confess their sin, both personal and corporate. A more-secular formulation is to say that all participants must admit their own responsibility, both general and particular, in the history of the conflict. Therefore, facilitators must help adversaries to examine their accountability (confess their sin) and seek forgiveness as well as repentance—knowing that with acknowledgment and transformation come a basic honesty that encourages all parties to avoid arrogance, hubris, and domination.

5. Cooperative conflict resolution is transparent and honest in all aspects of its practice. Goals are clearly stated yet open to negotiation. Strategies are democratic, with negotiators respecting the right of all

parties to know and participate in the process. They recognize and help others to affirm that giving up some individual power increases the likelihood of a potentially transformative collective power.

6. Participants in CCR generate and support a partnership approach to problem solving. They seek to use power *with* rather than power *over*—cooperation rather than domination—in order to confront a mutual problem. They attempt to reconcile basic interests or needs, rather than positions, in order to remove parties from rigid stances. They encourage the brainstorming of multiple options before attempting to select the best solution. They advocate criteria for decision making that are both fair and transformative, representing the full vision of shalom.

7. If force is necessary, it is used to separate, restrain, and create space so that an alternative to violence and injustice can be found through reflection, negotiation, healing, and a partnership approach to problem solving.

8. Those who seek to resolve conflict cooperatively take risks in order to find common ground. They are willing to make themselves vulnerable, in order to create safe spaces for resolution and in order to encourage others to do the same.[4]

9. Participants in CCR seek long-term solutions that help prevent future conflict. They look for prevention strategies, even as they work to heal and resolve conflict through a just peacemaking intervention.

10. They perceive both peace and justice as equal core components. They understand that the pursuit of peace without justice leads to appeasement, while the pursuit of justice without peace leads to a crusade mentality. Neither of these results is consistent with the aims or methods of CCR.

HISTORICAL DEVELOPMENT AND CONTEMPORARY CASES

The principles of cooperative conflict resolution have been at the center of many movements for social change in the twentieth century. For example, Gandhi's principled strategies as well as those of civil rights workers like Martin Luther King Jr. were all built on the ten principles identified above. More recently, in the 1970s, President Jimmy Carter encouraged the creation of the first Neighborhood Justice Centers (soon to be called "community mediation programs"), alternatives to courts in dispute-settlement processes. These programs were democratic and often volunteer-driven. The practitioners who worked in these programs sought resolution instead of judgment or punishment, shared a set of problem-solving skills, and saw themselves as facilitators for community members.

A decade later, a number of community mediation programs sought to extend their work into schools. They saw conflict as a normal part of school life and resolution skills as essential for young people's long-term success. Most importantly, they believed that, with teaching and guidance, most students could learn to resolve their own conflicts—acting as peers, within a democratic and voluntary partnership process.[5]

Successful peer mediation programs address many of the issues which a just peacemaking framework seeks to resolve—including situations that cross lines of race, gender, culture, class, age, and even inequitable power. These practices have been used successfully to squash violence resulting from rumor or other kinds of incomplete or manipulative communication; to deal with issues related to in/out, power relationships—where one group seeks to exclude another; to address issues of racial or cultural intolerance; and to quell threats and intimidation over property, turf, or zones of control in urban gang warfare or neighborhood mediation.

One of the most remarkable organizational developments of the last fifty years has been the dramatic increase in the number and strength of nongovernmental organizations. In many cases, these organizations are committed to a change strategy or humanitarian agenda more than to any nationality or ethnic identity. Their humanitarian agenda often puts them at the center of crises, giving them knowledge and presence relevant to the conflict. This sometimes permits their representatives to play a trusted bipartisan role, accepted by both sides. For instance, during the bitter conflicts in Rwanda, Burundi, and Zaire, MAP International—a U.S.-based nonprofit organization—provided about thirty million dollars in donated medical supplies (their core ministry). Their staff also became citizen-diplomats—playing an important, if quiet, part in the early stages of grassroots conflict resolution because they were known and trusted by parties on different sides.

The value of nongovernmental humanitarian groups and their "citizen-diplomat" staffs is likely to grow as the distinct authority of nations and traditional polities loses its hard edge. Most of the three dozen or so major conflicts that are simmering at any one time are not between recognized nations or even recognized legal entities. Frequently, one of the partners in conflict is a governmental unit while the other is not, and a nongovernmental entity is more likely to be mutually trusted.

One of the most prominent transnational citizen-diplomats is former U.S. President Jimmy Carter. Certainly, Carter's name recognition provides him an entry ability that few people can match. At the same time, Carter's credibility stems from the humanitarian efforts of the Carter Center, from the respect generated by his spiritual commitment, and from his successful track record in diplomacy. The last of these began during his term in office with such accomplishments as the Camp David accords between Egypt and Israel and has continued through his personal intervention in conflicts throughout the world, including Haiti, North Korea, Nicaragua, Sudan, and Bosnia. Carter is one example of a spiritually motivated citizen-diplomat who understands and practices the principles of CCR. His efforts to understand each side sometimes have led to accusations that he has cozied up to tyrants. Yet his commitment to this basic principle of CCR has led to success in places like Haiti, where others have failed.

57

Although best known for his successful campaign to liberate India from British domination, Gandhi also persevered in efforts to abolish the caste system and reconcile Hindus and Muslims in India. In all these efforts, Gandhi always attempted to treat the opponent as a partner. Boycotts, marches, public disclosure, and civil disobedience were strategies designed to bring one's adversary to the negotiating table where the parties could together find a just and peaceful solution to the problem. Gandhi himself took part in negotiations with the British government in the final stages of Indian independence.[6]

Martin Luther King's six steps for nonviolent social change included reconciliation and negotiation. He even pressed his followers to look for ways in which the opponent could also win.[7] King understood and communicated to his colleagues that civil disobedience is a means to accelerate and strengthen the negotiation process in order for justice to be accomplished peacefully.

Not all successful citizen-diplomats are renowned figures. One illustration of very effective international CCR, performed by persons without fame, took place during the recent war in Bosnia. At the start of Muslim-Croat fighting in central Bosnia, two Franciscans and an imam succeeded in mediating an agreement that kept certain troops on each side out of the fighting. Braving initial threats from both armed forces, they met one another and convinced the two commanders to meet for negotiations. The subsequent agreement lasted throughout the Muslim-Croat fighting, with the result that these particular troops never fought each other.[8]

CHALLENGES, CONCERNS, AND LIMITATIONS

An examination of any conflict situation must consider three factors that have complex interpersonal, cultural, historical, and political dimensions. First, we need to understand the relationships among the people involved in the conflict. Second, we need to understand the sources and dynamics of the particular dispute at hand. Third, we need to understand the social structures—how they continue the conflict and how they offer openings for resolution.

58 CCR has demonstrated much success in addressing the first two factors, interpersonal relations and the dynamics of particular disputes. Some have criticized CCR, however, for lack of attention to the structural dimension; they argue that we need to look beyond the immediate to the broader context in which conflict exists and to the social norms that have contributed to escalation of the conflict. Doing so is likely to reveal an inherent imbalance in the structure of relationships and a complex network of historical, socioanthropological, economic, military, and political factors that shape the conflict.

Does the complexity of this broader context exceed the capacity of CCR? The first answer is that CCR practices are only one part of a just peacemaking approach and cannot be expected to provide answers for all situations. Beyond that, CCR is now being deepened by attention to structural contexts. We will see how by examining five structural issues, beginning with cultural barriers.

Cultural Barriers

Transferring a conflict resolution method across cultural, racial, or ethnic lines may either distort the process or supplant indigenous alternatives that would work better. *Culture* is the system of norms, values, and meanings that help provide identity for a particular society. These boundary markers of group identity are frequently expressed through traditions, stories, rituals, religion, and language. Verbal and nonverbal expression are likely to take on different meanings when crossing cultural lines. How disputants look, stand, move, and position themselves can give mediators diagnostic insight and significantly influence the outcome of a mediation session. These cultural variables are only beginning to be substantively acknowledged and addressed in many European/North American conflict resolution training programs today. Many people who practice mediation in school and community settings are now beginning to look to non-Western practices as resources or models for more culturally literate approaches to mediation.[9] In the transnational arena, an elicitive approach has begun to influence training for conflict resolution in non-Western cultural contexts.[10]

Degree of Damage or Pain

The degree of damage or pain is often much more complex at the intercommunity and transnational levels than it is at the interpersonal level. One must magnify the woes of Job a thousandfold to reach the level of suffering in Bosnia, Cambodia, Rwanda, El Salvador, and countless other war-torn societies. Can one really approach the healing process of whole societies with the same kinds of strategies that can produce reconciliation between individuals? Can expressions of confession, repentance, and forgiveness lead to reconciliation between races or enemy nations? This question is addressed directly in the chapter by Alan Geyer. His call for a better-tutored historical consciousness is echoed by former U.S. diplomat and current theorist of citizen diplomacy Joseph Montville, who calls for acknowledgment of historical guilt as a prerequisite for conflict resolution.[11]

Problems of Scale

Face-to-face problem-solving strategies are said to work best when disputants are few in number, know each other well through daily interaction, and expect to have an ongoing relationship after the dispute is resolved. Close to 90 percent of those involved in school peer mediation, for example, report satisfaction with the agreement and are willing to honor their agreements over time.[12] In contrast, peer mediation with large groups is often less effective. A different kind of training and support might be needed if peer mediators or citizen mediators in national conflicts were to take on the structural issues underlying racial or ethnic clashes and a large number of disputants, as is the case in intercommunity and transnational conflicts.

At the same time, not all aspects of intercommunity or transnational conflict demand working with large numbers of people. For example, persons receiving training in Bosnia will be working in neighborhood facilitation centers, helping specific Muslim, Croat, and Serb people to resolve local interfamily disputes. Ironically, at the other end of the spectrum of transnational negotiations, there is also a strong face-to-face element at work in the process. Official state negotiators often have long-standing relationships with one another. These personal ties do not obscure the fact that large structural issues obviously play an immensely important role. But neither should the interpersonal dynamic be overlooked.

Power Inequities

Political realists contend that an approach based on CCR is likely to fall into the trap of *appeasement,* a negative relational dynamic in which the more powerful party is allowed to dominate. They advocate balancing the power relationship in order to create the conditions in which meaningful negotiation can take place. To accomplish this, they believe the use of threat and coercive force are likely to be indispensable: Only power can effectively confront power. Furthermore, they claim that power asymmetry constitutes the more typical state of affairs. Signs of power discrepancy can readily be found in issues of class, race, gender, age, nationality, and other common indices of social differentiation. The result is dependence on a coercive approach to virtually all situations of conflict, a confrontational stance that utilizes position-taking to address systemic dominance and intransigence.

CCR advocates agree that power relationships must be considered. Yet CCR procedures seek to improve the balance of power by identifying nontraditional sources of power, by providing either party with the option to refuse agreement, and by reaching agreements that include checks against power domination. What we must argue against is reductionism: Traditional power factors, such as economic and military, are not the only factors that shape outcomes. Other structural factors and ways of relating are also important. What CCR can help create is a context where conflict can be resolved without the costs of violence and where solutions depend on the power of persuasion and public opinion as well as on other forms of power.

By using methods of mutual agreement, CCR does eliminate some perceived inequities, but it does not erase them all. Therefore, we must address the place of confrontation. At issue here is the need to unmask the often hidden power inequities and to empower the weaker party so that, in the end, a lasting reconciliation as well as a just resolution of the dispute might be possible. Looking to the New Testament for guidance, we find that, even in situations of significant power inequity, the evidence weighs heavily in favor of first trying a noncoercive confrontation designed to convert or transform one's adversary. First, there is Jesus' call, in the Sermon on the Mount, not to revolt or seek revenge by violent or evil means. Instead, Jesus offers a strategy that biblical scholar Walter Wink interprets as publicly unmasking the oppression and empowering the oppressed in order to shame the oppressor.[13] Second, there is Paul's letter to the slaveowner Philemon, requesting that he take back his runaway slave, Onesimus, and treat him as a brother. Reading this in the context of the first-century Roman Empire, rather than twentieth-century America, biblical scholar John Koenig portrays Paul as one who carefully uncovers each person's misperceptions, empowers Onesimus to view himself as a person of equal worth, and offers to redress Philemon's financial loss in return for Onesimus' freedom.[14] Again to Gandhi, we find a similar nonviolent methodology. Through use of the production of salt, as a metaphor and an organizing tactic, he empowered the Indian people and thwarted British domination of that industry. From each of these examples, we can conclude that persuasion, mixed with confrontation, is well worth an initial attempt to facilitate change in attitude or behavior in situations of power inequity. When the response is positive, adversarial relations can be both unmasked and eliminated without dominance or assimilation by the more powerful. Only when this approach fails should one contemplate coercive means. Yet, even then, some theologians (for example, many within the traditional peace churches) favor persevering with conciliation efforts, based either on the hope of delayed personal transformation or on an eschatological hope of victory over evil.[15]

Irreducible Conflicting Interests

Another realist critique of CCR centers in its conviction that in many conflict situations, especially deep-rooted ones, parties are locked in irreducible conflicting interests that limit them to competing for a zero-sum outcome in which one's gain is always another's loss. The political realist believes that most of the time the pie cannot be enlarged. There is only so much territory in Bosnia, for example. One must attempt to claim one's piece of it, therefore, rather than focusing effort on creating a larger pie. In fact, realists contend that most efforts to discover compatible interests, correct perceptions, brainstorm new options, or promote mutual gain, are terribly naive and, at best, a waste of time. Since, from their perspective, interests are irreducible and the limited number of options are usually well known, they believe that any serious attempt to resolve the conflict in one's favor must rely on firming up a position that will protect one's sphere of interest in the inevitable struggle.[16]

In contrast, the pluralist school of political thought contends that it is usually possible to alter the perceived reality, especially in deep-rooted ethnic and ideological conflicts where one's perceptual lens or viewpoint is all-important. Pluralists view international relations as much more complex than the realist paradigm allows. They expand the number of actors in the international system to include nonstates and maintain that a relationship of interdependence exists among them. Furthermore, they affirm that different parties' basic interests, such as identity and security, do not ultimately conflict because, by nature, they increase in distributable size as each actor has more of them. For example, the real issue at stake in Bosnia, they would say, is not a fixed-sum commodity like territory, but variable-sum entities like identity and security. All this allows for expansion of the pie and adoption of a negotiating style based on interdependence, integration, and cooperation—a stance they claim is much more desirable in a world where the use of coercion and force has become too dangerous as a final arbitrator.[17]

Among theologians, we can also find expressions of both realist and pluralist perspectives. The Christian realism of Reinhold Niebuhr is well known. The challenge to some of his views by his less-well-known contemporary, Helmut Thielicke, deserves more attention. Thielicke's understanding of power in terms of influence rather than coercion and his grounding of this power in the action of God led him to propose an approach to third-party intervention that is very similar to CCR. He calls the conflict intervener to (1) assist the sides to know the real issues by clarifying interests, proposed solutions, and ethical intentions; (2) speak to both sides about ultimate objectives rather than trying to produce a solution; and (3) encourage parties to meet face to face and confront one another as neighbors.[18]

A realist critique often characterizes international relations as similar to the "prisoner's dilemma" in game theory. In the game, two accomplices in a crime are imprisoned and separated so they cannot communicate and cooperate in their defense. Although refusing to betray each other would be in their mutual interest, each calculates that accusing his/her accomplice is the best defense against the likelihood of being accused by the accomplice. The claim is that participants in transnational conflict, like the ones in this game, lack the necessary trusted communication that might motivate them to cooperate.[19]

A closer examination, however, reveals that even in the midst of an intractable transnational conflict, possibilities exist for developing cooperative strategies. First, these chances are significantly enhanced when the parties know they will be interacting repeatedly over the long haul, a factor that is more present in transnational relations than in the single-interaction prisoner's dilemma. Yet due to the lack of communication and mutual distrust that still characterize many transnational conflicts, it may be necessary to involve a third-party mediator who can begin a problem-solving process. If both sides see progress in resolving the conflict, they will invest more trust in the mediator, leading to greater trust and communications between the adversaries.[20]

Second, the likelihood of developing cooperative strategies is enhanced if actors in the conflict become aware of the importance of mutual interests. If a narrow, competitive, individualistic view of self-interest prevails, negotiations inevitably lead to deadlock. But if actors come to see the benefits to themselves in pursuing the common good, this can change. Therefore it is in one's ultimate interest to develop cooperative, rather than competitive, strategies even in the case of prisoner's dilemma.[21] At the very least, this common self-interest can be pursued by announcing and acting on rules of mutual restraint. By eliciting such reciprocity, along with adequate mechanisms for verification, one can affirm mutual self-interest even when there is no friendship.

Third, morality, especially if embedded in a framework of ethics, "can supply additional reasons for restraint."[22] Although realism rightly argues that morality, when it is in strong conflict with self-interest, cannot alone govern transnational relations, it can alter the terms of interaction by encouraging people in conflict to value each other's needs and concerns. Once one engenders a sense of shared morality, affirms mutual collective interests, and builds in repeated interaction between the parties, then the door is open to CCR.

Such a hopeful scenario can be observed in many different conflicts, including those in which governments have been the principal actors. Jimmy Carter's mediation of the Camp David accords between Egypt and Israel is but one prominent example. In this case, the broadening of Israel's understanding of its self-interest, combined with Egyptian reciprocity and Carter's ability to foster communication and trust, paved the way for each "prisoner nation" to free itself from their common dilemma.

The costliness of the opposite scenario is seen in many failures during the Cold War. The pursuit of narrow self-interest spurred many decisions to increase arms rather than negotiate test-ban and arms-reduction treaties. Prior to Gorbachev's initiatives in the late 1980s, the result was continual escalation of the nuclear threat, the wasting of billions of dollars, and the endangering (or even the actual taking) of innocent lives.[23] Again, there is a strong moral obligation for governments to try CCR before embarking on such a costly course. Even if implementing this new paradigm does not always produce the desired result, it is incumbent on governments, international bodies, churches, and all other organs of social power to attempt to resolve the conflict by implementing nonviolent problem-solving strategies.

Churches, because of their moral authority, should take the lead in advocating and modeling noncoercive conflict resolution strategies. From the New Testament to modern-day saints like Doctor King, the tradition provides us with people who have pointed the way. As the agent of God's message of love, healing, and reconciliation for all humankind, the church needs to be in the forefront of the struggle to replace violence with at least a provisional peace and change the adversarial nature of relationships into a partnership approach. This will neither eliminate the need to pursue justice nor usurp the necessity of confrontation, both instrumental to the church's witness. But it can help to transform society's approach to the resolution of conflict, slowly changing it from competitive win-lose to cooperative win-win scenarios.

64

Learning from Peer Mediation

Peer mediation, as practiced in schools and community settings, is based firmly on the principles of CCR. Peer mediators definitely see themselves as partners in a problem-solving process, the aim of which is to achieve a mutually acceptable solution. As third parties entering from outside the conflict, they emphasize their own need to share power with the disputants rather than exercise power over them.

Peer mediation addresses all ten of the criteria we have described for just peacemaking:

1. The process helps each disputant understand the perspective of the other.
2. The emphasis is on active listening rather than on judgment or punishment.
3. The focus is on behavioral change rather than on counseling or changing deep-seated psychological patterns. It helps disputants focus on concrete behavior rather than on sweeping judgments of others.

4. Peer mediators see themselves as members of the community with a role in the history, as well as the solution, of the problem. Therefore, rather than heaping all blame on one person, they help each disputant own or acknowledge her/his role in the problem.
5. The processes of peer mediation are laid out before the actual mediation begins. They are transparent and open to being shaped by the disputants at any time.
6. Rules are established, including rules about the threat of force, in order to create and maintain a safe space for reflection, listening, and resolution. Effective mediators do not seek power for themselves but share the power of the process with the disputants, thereby amplifying the power of peacemaking for all involved.
7. The process seeks and encourages alternatives—devoting a good deal of time to brainstorming possible solutions even when one solution emerges early as a "favorite."
8. All involved in the mediation agree to take a risk in order to seek common ground; the mediators risk failure and in some cases physical threat. The disputants risk by agreeing to let go of

comfortable patterns of conflict (e.g., fight or flight) and by standing against peer pressure to escalate the conflict.

9. The focus is on prevention—on the future rather than the past—and the emphasis is on building a community which supports peaceful conflict resolution.

10. Finally, peer mediation, when it is successful, pays attention to institutional factors that often fuel any individual conflict—for example, unfair or undemocratic discipline policies, the absence of culturally sensitive avenues for dialogue, pedagogy that frustrates students who have different learning styles, and so forth. Without this component, peer mediation programs become tools for the suppression of violence rather than its resolution. Thus, effective peer mediation addresses fairness as well as violence reduction, justice as well as peace.

Peer mediation as an example of CCR also responds to several of the challenges posed by the realist school of thought. Until very recently, the dominant approach to peer mediation in the United States was drawn primarily from an Anglo-American legal framework.[24] In the past decade, however, new models of peer mediation have been evolving that are more culturally literate, reexamining assumptions of universal applicability regarding Western terminology (such as "win-win"), patterns of nonverbal communication, and understandings of conflict and its resolution. New strategies are being developed that will transform conflict instead of merely managing it, so that the results are peace and justice rather than compliance, and empowerment rather than "keeping things under control."[25]

A typical peer mediation case can help clarify the importance of this paradigm shift. Conflict in a high school between a star athlete and a recent Portuguese-Creole-speaking immigrant threatened to escalate into a fight, with classmates taking sides. Crucial to successful resolution were a trained mediator who spoke Portuguese Creole and a prior training program designed to enable the culturally dominant "American" peer mediators to function sensitively with cultural minorities. The use of peer mediators helped to reduce the power inequities so that *power over* the students was replaced by *working with* them. Finally, the goal of the mediation shifted from establishing a judgment of right or wrong to formulating a shared agreement. It then became possible to view the "irreducible conflicting interests" in new ways. Both students were able to save face with peers (rather than having to back down) and agreed to coexist (rather than have to become friends), thereby enabling both to stay out of trouble.

The same principles that enable successful face-to-face resolutions of cross-cultural conflict can also be used with larger groups. As these strategies become even more culturally literate and effective, and as more and more people practice them in their daily lives, people will expect governments to do similarly in intranational and transnational conflict.

Racial Conflict in the United States

CCR strategies have been part of a broader set of strategies to heal and transform American society's historic patterns of racism. CCR can be effective in this context because it integrates personal and institutional change; it emphasizes power *with* instead of power *over*; it recognizes the importance of personal as well as historic pain, transgression, and healing; it opens doors for transformation rather than simply management of conflict; and it includes both peace and justice in its core principles.

Successful CCR depends in part on the development and use of a shared language. Terms like "stereotype," "prejudice," and "racism," for example, mean different things to different people in the United States. Furthermore, terms like "affirmative action," "quotas," and even "multicultural education" have been used by demagogues to obscure rather than inform, divide rather than heal, and incite rather than resolve. At the same time, community workers and even scholars have begun to develop languages and strategies that can help us translate shared ideas across barriers of race, culture, and class. One good example of this progress is the "ten C's" framework, developed by Ulric Johnson and Patti DeRosa in their anti-racism projects.[26]

The ten C's include components that are closely related to our model for CCR. DeRosa and Johnson first identify "five C's of awareness" that help us understand conflict and then begin to resolve it. *Color* they identify as those qualities which "just are," such as race, gender, and age. *Culture* then assigns value to color. For example, in the U.S. culture, men are generally valued more than women, white-skinned more than dark-skinned, adults more than children. *Class* assigns a position or status to both color and culture. Adults have more power than children, baby boomers generally have more power than elders, men more than women, and so forth. *Character* describes those qualities of an individual that make her or him unique. On the one hand, no person is totally defined by color, culture, or class; yet, on the other, individual character in isolation does not help us fully explain or understand conflict. Finally, *context* shapes how the other four C's are enacted. Each of us may function differently in different contexts—including different interpersonal or institutional settings. Therefore, the five C's of awareness help us understand some of the roots of conflict and contribute to each of the ten principles of CCR.

Once we have heightened our awareness, the "five C's of change" then help us develop and carry out strategies to resolve conflict, including interracial ones. *Courage* and *confidence* are required when we recognize our own part in conflict (as noted in CCR principle 4), act honestly and transparently (principle 5), use force or restraint (principle 6), and take risks (principle 8). *Commitment* is demanded when we seek to understand others' perspectives (principle 1), withhold judgment (principle 3), engage in sustainable partnerships (principle 7), and seek long-term solutions (principle 9). *Conflict* itself is reframed in order to depict it as a path toward both peace and justice (principle 10), rather than a problem to be managed or suppressed. Finally, *community* is essential to make all ten criteria effective.

Anecdotal evidence suggests that interweaving the ten principles of CCR with the ten C's helps to sustain lasting change in racially based conflicts at both interpersonal and institutional levels.[27] It can also answer some challenges presented by the realist school of conflict management. One example is a recent intervention into conflict between two schools, one of which was scheduled to be consolidated into the other. The school moving in was comprised mainly of middle-class families. The one losing control over its own space and feeling invaded was comprised mainly of poor and working-class families. Both groups of staff and parents felt unfairly treated by a central administration that seemed distant and manipulative. Both wanted what was best for their children, and both wanted school to open the next fall without major crises. Examining cultural and power differences in a broader institutional context opened doors and helped participants find common ground, overcoming cultural barriers in the process. What looked at first like a conflict of irreducible interests, rooted in racial-cultural barriers, became an opportunity for cooperative effort.

The U.S. civil rights movement and the South African freedom movement are also examples of how CCR can be enlarged from interpersonal and community contexts to national ones. In this way, CCR, as a strategy for transforming racial conflict, also responds to a fourth challenge: the question of scale.

Conflict Resolution Training in the Former Yugoslavia

The carnage, genocide, and cultural destruction in the former Yugoslavia are of such a scale as to challenge any model of conflict resolution. They have taken an immense toll on all levels of society—personal, family, community, national, and transnational. One of the authors of this chapter (David Steele) has been conducting training seminars in community-building and conflict resolution for representatives at the local level, across lines of religion, culture, language, and class, to promote healing and reconciliation as well as social reconstruction. The purpose of these seminars is to encourage people at the grassroots level to work together to overcome the stranglehold of ethnic and religious division on the individual and the collective spirit; to develop constructive ways to handle grievances and differences; to equip people with the tools for promoting healing and social reconstruction; and then to build a critical mass of support for peace-building.

The first-level seminars are focused on building trust through intrapersonal, interpersonal, and intergroup reconciliation. Building toward reconciliation in the aftermath of war requires that special attention be given to the expression and acknowledgment of the others' grievance, and the encouragement of a self-critical honesty. The trainers must themselves listen carefully before judging or offering solutions and distinguish judgments about behavior and actions from those about persons or cultures. Participants must also be encouraged to listen carefully and empathetically to one another's pain. By starting with the common experience of suffering and designing an environment in which each group can begin to feel safe, one begins to see the development of cross-cutting bonds. One of many examples of this phenomenon occurred at a seminar in March 1997 in Vukovar, Croatia, a Serb-occupied city soon to be given back to Croatian control. It was previously the scene of the worst massacre in the war in Croatia. Serb refugees from other regions of Croatia, but now living in the Vukovar region, shared their stories of pain with Croats, some of whom were themselves refugees from Vukovar. Refugees listened and cried with fellow refugees. Though the primary modus operandi in this seminar is storytelling by participants, it is interspersed with interpretive material on the grief process, drawn from Old Testament laments and such contemporary theorists as Kübler-Ross. Biblical laments are used as a ritualized catharsis within a community framework. The expression of contemporary laments like those in the Psalms ensures that the victim is heard and thereby limits vindictive responses.[28] At a seminar in Banja Koviljaca, Serbia (on the Bosnian border), in May 1997, Serbian Orthodox priests, together with Catholics, Muslims, and Protestants, used lament writing to build bonds of trust. In this way, people's deep pain, rather than being a barrier, became a bridge upon which they could engage together in self-critical honesty. It was the beginning of a process that could lead to the training of war-weary people in CCR.

Creative expression of grievance has naturally led to examination of the cyclical relationship between victimhood and aggression. Helping Serbs, Croats, and Muslims recognize that today's aggressors are often yesterday's victims has resulted in a reevaluation of the role one's own people played in both the near and distant past. This walk through history, in turn, has often led to astoundingly open discussion about confession of the sins of one's people. Such discussion needs to be approached carefully, being mindful of the sins of all sides while not assuming equal guilt, being conscious of people's need to protect group identity by refusing to accept false guilt, and distinguishing between admission of collective guilt and feelings of personal responsibility.

Weaving in theological reflection gives added legitimation for religious people. For example, awareness that the later stage of the lament motif in the Old Testament prophets incorporates the confession of sin into the grief process resulted in profound discussion at each of two Serbian seminars held close to the Bosnian border in 1996 and 1997. When Serbian Orthodox priests began discussing the complicity of their church in the Bosnian war, a very big step had been taken toward reconciliation and implementation of CCR principles 4 and 5, acknowledging one's own responsibility and being transparent and honest.

The second-level seminars have continued to focus on attitude change, especially the clarification of perception. Conflict always involves some degree of misperception and, therefore, requires a concerted attempt to understand the perspectives and needs of adversaries (CCR principle 1). In cases of intense conflict, the experience of victimization usually has contributed to such a threatened sense of identity that bias and stereotyping begin to function as a group survival mechanism. These biases become entrenched, distorting and contaminating one group's perception of another. Even in such deep-rooted, identity-based conflicts, it is possible to acknowledge one's own unhealthy prejudices and resulting manipulative behavior. In fact, it is part of the necessary confession of sin, both individual and corporate, as illustrated in the prophetic laments of Jeremiah and Deutero-Isaiah. In order to help correct these perceptual distortions, seminar participants first have received training in communication skills, taking care to be sensitive to cultural differences.

Then they have been asked to step into the shoes of another ethnic, religious, or national group while examining the nature and dynamics of the conflict. When a Croat is asked to describe the tensions as understood by a Muslim and then receives feedback from a Muslim, it usually increases awareness of the need for attitude change and sometimes helps make behavior more inclusive. This is the case even when one is unable to perform the task well, as was the case with some participants in one seminar. By watching others, including members of one's own ethnic group, successfully role-play another persona, the blocked persons started to listen more carefully and began to replace distorted attitudes with accurate perceptions.

In addition, the second-level seminars have introduced participants to problem-solving skills that require acceptance of everyone's basic needs and concerns and creation of alternative approaches to resolving the conflict. It is absolutely crucial to legitimize people's most-basic concerns (CCR principle 1), by which we mean the need for nonnegotiable rights such as recognition, well-being, security, belonging, and control over one's life. Fear that such legitimate needs may be denied creates a desperation, an intransigence, and all too often violence. It is also important to distinguish these basic needs from the positions, demands, or strategies by which a group insists that its needs be met.

Assisting people to look behind their positions to the underlying needs frequently leads to a recognition that the basic interests are compatible, thus providing an element of trust that can become the basis for mutual problem solving. In the seminars, such needs have been identified sometimes by examining the reasons for positions taken; other times by identifying people's fears—naming them, examining their basis in reality, and ensuring that all groups perceive the underlying needs at the root of the fear. For example, in the seminar in Vukovar, Serb refugees living there were able to share openly their fears for safety when the territory would revert to Croatian control. Furthermore, they were able to get a reality check from Serbs already living under Croatian control, hear the empathy of Croats, reflect on the meaning of God's promise of protection and God's call to them, and begin to examine potential cooperative efforts with which to address the deep and often mutual needs of both peoples. In many instances, one could see the profound helpfulness of spiritual disciplines in assisting people to broaden their understanding of others' needs. One very poignant example of this occurred as a Muslim imam from Sarajevo, at a seminar held in 1995 during the war, shared his own soul-searching attempt to comprehend what was happening to his people. During an exercise designed to map the needs and fears that underlay all sides of the war in Bosnia, he shared how he was led, through meditation, to recognize that beneath Serbians' brutal actions lay an understandable fear for survival, a legitimate need based on a history of Ottoman oppression. His moving description of the way God opened his eyes, despite the terrible struggle of his own people for survival, powerfully created trust and opened dialogue, especially with the Serbs who were present. In fact, members of all three ethnic groups were able, by the end of the exercise, to identify numerous mutual needs within their supposedly incompatible entities. This demonstrated that, despite the difficulties still apparent in bringing lasting resolution to the Bosnian conflict, a presumption of completely irreducible conflicting interests is unfounded.

Once people have addressed many of the relational problems and identified compatible needs, they are better able to create alternative solutions for the resolution of conflict. The aim is to generate and support a partnership approach to problem solving (CCR principle 7) that seeks both peace and justice (CCR principle 10). Participants in such a process must be willing to take risks (CCR principle

8) in the search for long-term solutions that will help prevent future conflict (CCR principle 9). After assisting people to identify all the parties to a conflict and to map the needs, fears, goals, power relationships, messages to others, and others' likely response, the task is to reframe the conflict by carefully examining ways to refigure each component of the conflict map. For example, at a seminar in May 1997 in Feketic, Serbia, participants mapped out the conflict over the government's persistent refusal to grant the request of all the religious communities for religious education in the schools. Representatives from Orthodox, Catholic, Protestant, and Muslim communities brainstormed ways to reinterpret the goals of the religious communities, revise the kind of message they would send to the government, deal with internal conflict among themselves, expand the parties involved to include the political opposition, and so forth. Participants role-played state officials as well as the leadership of their own religious communities, one of which was at that very moment making a formal request on this matter to the government. In the end, they arrived at a few feasible suggestions to propose to their own leadership should the state refuse the request, as indeed it was expected to do.

73

A second method of teaching a problem-solving approach is mediation training. As a result of one seminar that focused on this skill, a mediation training program has been established in one church in Zagreb, a group of participants in another city have discussed initiating a similar but ecumenical training program, and a Muslim participant has mediated a dispute between two Muslim men who fought on opposite sides of the war in Bosnia. After being exposed to this problem-solving approach in another seminar, held during the war in 1995, one highly influential participant wrote a book on the subject in the Bosnian language, gave a lecture to the leadership of one of Bosnia's political parties, and was ready to accept an offer to take part in a back channel of communication in order to help negotiate an end to the war. Furthermore, two other participants had already successfully negotiated some very important agreements prior to taking part in the seminars. One Orthodox bishop negotiated the release of U.N. troops who were captured by the Bosnian Serbs, and a Bosnian Catholic priest was one of three clergy who negotiated an agreement whereby two units of the Muslim and Croat armies agreed not to participate in the fighting between their ethnic groups.

These examples illustrate that CCR can be applied successfully to deep-rooted conflicts between large groups.

The third-level seminars, yet to be held, will focus on the systemic challenge of identifying and responding to sources of conflict that lie within the social structures, beyond the immediate dispute. They will be designed to help religious communities develop self-generating local programming that can address directly the power inequities underlying the conflict. In the seminars, participants will be helped to identify specific roles that religious communities can play in the process of social change, to learn to motivate the right individuals or institutions to act, and to build competence in community-organizing skills.

In order to have a lasting effect on structures and interpersonal relationships and on resolving specific disputes, efforts such as this project must develop an indigenous base. Therefore, plans are being initiated to turn over control to local partners in each country. Potential citizen-diplomats have been receiving skills training in communication, problem solving, and mediation and have begun to apply these skills to local disputes. New indigenous institutions with the capacity to implement peace-making projects of their own are being created in Serbia and Bosnia. In Croatia, a new project, focusing on conflict resolution training in religious communities, has been developed in the Center for Peace, Nonviolence, and Human Rights in Osijek. These developments constitute a crucial step toward the development of civil society and the realization of a critical mass of support for peace-building efforts. Interethnic work teams trained in conflict resolution skills will assist in redeveloping both physical and social structures of that war-torn society.

REQUIRED RESOURCES

The above cases are good indicators of the kinds of resources required for the effective practice of CCR. Above all, they reinforce the belief that ordinary citizens can serve as creative problem solvers. In certain limited capacities, they can engender the kind of trust and legitimacy that formal negotiators sometimes lack. For example, while formal negotiators failed to keep Muslim-Croat tensions from escalating into violence, the local Bosnian religious mediators succeeded, on the basis of personal relationships, in negotiating an agreement not to fight. Local citizens and institutions, therefore, should be trained in conflict resolution. A sensitive outside intervener, bringing important skills and a more objective perspective, can play a significant secondary role.

Non-Western practices such as the Hawaiian mediation process called *Ho'oponopono* ("to make something right")[29] also need to be nourished for the sake of both non-Western and Western cultures. The nonlinear processes and the communal (i.e., nonindividualistic) orientation often characteristic of these culturally sensitive models help to undo the misinformation and stereotyping that exacerbate conflict. Furthermore, they are usually preventive in their approach to conflict resolution.

The term "elders," coming primarily from a non-Western context, is an excellent example of an emerging type of intermediary role. Elders preferably have no legal standing or binding preferential affiliation with either party in the dispute. Rather, their influence is based on their ability to lend respect or invoke disrespect and to legitimize or delegitimize particular positions. They may encourage conciliatory actions and discourage premature resort to coercion.

A wisely chosen elder may be able to help both parties find honor in an otherwise unpalatable compromise. As important to those directly involved in the dispute is the capacity of an elder to encourage other stakeholders to accept an agreement. When a resolution to conflict demands legal action or legislative confirmation, the elder's involvement may help the primary leaders hold the support of their constituencies.

Every conflict will offer up a different potential list of relevant elders. The conflict between the Montana Freemen and the FBI found a long list of former military personnel and elected officials who could be heard by both parties. A conflict in Western Africa may find common respect for a Muslim imam with regional followers. One example is Sheik Hassan Cisse, who lives in Senegal but has close ties to Morocco; he is the grandson of a Nigerian cleric regarded as a patriot in somewhat the same way as Gandhi in India. Often the elder will be identified with a religious tradition; for example, Bishop Desmond Tutu is given respect and honor due to both his position and his demonstrated spiritual commitment. In similar manner, on a bloody street in the United States, a local pastor with deep roots in the neighborhood often has the relevant credibility to serve as an elder between gangs and civil authorities.

The role of outside intermediaries also should be given more attention by churches and other religious communities or institutions. As previously suggested, these intermediaries can be individuals, like former president Jimmy Carter, or church service organizations and mission programs that provide humanitarian aid and (re)development. These individuals and institutions, by the nature of their past achievements or their ongoing work, are able to build the needed trust and provide necessary knowledge in conflict resolution. If unable to provide the latter from within their normal programming, they can work cooperatively with persons or organizations that can provide the educational component. Church-related humanitarian aid organizations in the former Yugoslavia (International Orthodox Christian Charities in Belgrade and Ecumenical Humanitarian Services of Novi Sad, Serbia) have provided key linkages for David Steele's conflict resolution projects. Another approach is for a church agency to hire a specialist in conflict resolution. Such has been done by the United Methodist Committee on Relief (UMCOR) for its work in Bosnia.

76

We suggest that churches and religious communities take seriously their potential educational role and develop instrumentalities within their denominations or agencies. The American Baptist Churches did this with Daniel Buttry until they unfortunately shifted priorities. These CCR instrumentalities could become tremendous resources in performing, and even more in training others to perform, effective intermediary roles in conflict resolution. During the past thirty years, American churches have established a strong record of institutionalizing ministries of advocacy for a vast array of peace and justice issues. The need for instrumentalities devoted to the development of mediation, conciliation, and "creative eldership" is equally important.

People of faith must help in the endeavor to exhaust all possible avenues of communication before legitimizing, or allowing a legitimation of, the resort to violence. We should prod governments and citizens' groups to engage in conflict resolution and not to rush to violence. As Dr. Martin Luther King Jr. has said, "We still have a choice today: non-violent coexistence or violent co-annihilation. We must move past indecision to action. Now let us begin. Now let us rededicate ourselves to the long and bitter—but beautiful—struggle for a new world. The choice is ours and, though we might prefer otherwise, we must choose in this crucial moment of history."[30]

4

ACKNOWLEDGE RESPONSIBILITY FOR
CONFLICT AND INJUSTICE AND SEEK
REPENTANCE AND FORGIVENESS

Alan Geyer

Peacemaking, whether in personal, group, or international relations, requires a variety of capacities for self-transcendence:

- Transcendence of one's own interests and perspectives for the sake of understanding the interests and perspectives of the other side, which calls for the virtue of *empathy.*

- Transcendence of one's pride and defensiveness, which inhibit the acknowledgment of injuries done to others—a capacity for *repentance* and perhaps restitution.

- Transcendence of one's own grievances and desire for vengeance over injuries inflicted by others—a capacity for *forgiveness.*

But whatever the personal capacities for empathy, repentance, and forgiveness, is it really possible for nations or their governments to practice such virtues?

SHOULD NATIONS EVER APOLOGIZE?

The authors of this volume have engaged one another in the most spirited disagreements as to how to answer that question, disagreements concerning the very nature of theological discourse about politics. An enduring maxim in "political realism" (of a sort) insists that nations cannot and must not live by such personal dispositions—in particular, that nations should not apologize, lest it be taken as a sign of weakness. Such realism holds further that because nations always seek to maximize their power, expressions of repentance and forgiveness are to be regarded as inappropriate if not irresponsible moralisms.

Politicians and generals are not alone in doubting the place of repentance and forgiveness in political conflict. In his early but still influential writings, the premier American theologian (and also the dominant political ethicist) of the twentieth century, Reinhold Niebuhr, discounted severely the relevance of Jesus' gospel of love and forgiveness to the realities of world politics and even of interpersonal conflict:

> The ethic of Jesus does not deal at all with the immediate moral problem of every human life—the problem of arranging some kind of armistice between various contending factions and forces. It has nothing to say about the relativities of politics and economics, nor of the necessary balances of power which exist and must exist in even the most intimate social relationships. . . . It has only a vertical dimension between the loving will of God and the will of man.[1]

Niebuhr defined political responsibility in terms of a power-compromised ethic of justice which typically has to reject the counsels of love.

But Niebuhr's political and ethical legacy on this matter is ambiguous and even contradictory. For no one has had more to say about the follies of American pride and pretension than Niebuhr, whose works are a constant summons to repentance and humility. His incurable ambiguities are reflected in such statements as "Only a forgiving love, grounded in repentance, is adequate to heal the animosities between nations. But that degree of love is an impossibility for nations. It is a very rare achievement among individuals; and the mind and heart of collective man is notoriously less imaginative than that of the individual."[2] Sixteen years later, in *The Irony of American History*, Niebuhr sounded a similar note, but then qualified it ever so slightly:

> Nations are hardly capable of the spirit of forgiveness which is the final oil of harmony in all human relations and which rests upon the final recognition that our actions

and attitudes are inevitably interpreted in a different light by our friends as well as foes than we interpret them. Yet it is necessary to acquire a measure of this spirit in the collective relations of mankind. Nations, as individuals, who are completely innocent in their own esteem, are insufferable in their human contacts.[3]

These passages from Niebuhr are all from his postpacifist, "realist" years. They were implicitly challenged in the title of a 1953 book by Andre Trocmé, the French Huguenot pastor in the village of Le Chambon whose nonviolent resistance to Nazi tyranny was followed by service as European Secretary of the International Fellowship of Reconciliation. That title, *The Politics of Repentance,* reflected Trocmé's pacifist political witness, similar to that of John Howard Yoder's *Politics of Jesus.* And what to Trocmé is the political relevance of repentance? The repentance of Christians "has very definite consequences in the social and political order. . . . People convinced of their own innocence cannot be reconciled. Only the repentant can. . . . As long as [the State] is abandoned by the church, it knows nothing of repentance. But the church in its midst does know repentance, and it knows *only* that, and it bears witness of that before the State, for the healing of the State."[4] Thus, Trocmé, like Niebuhr, seems to suggest that repentance and forgiveness are unnatural acts for governments, but he holds to the hope that the church may lead the state to repentance and forgiveness.

To regard this as basically a pacifist-nonpacifist controversy, however, would be a mistake. Donald Shriver's groundbreaking 1995 book, *An Ethic for Enemies: Forgiveness in Politics,* puts this issue sharply: "Can whole nations repent? Forgive? Engage in processes that eventuate in collective repentance and forgiveness?" Shriver puts off a theoretical answer in favor of three case studies of twentieth-century conflict, all three involving the United States: U.S. wars with Germany and Japan and the unending struggle for racial justice. But Shriver's book amply vivifies both the needs and the possibilities of political repentance and forgiveness.[5]

This chapter proceeds on the assumption that empathy, repentance, and forgiveness are possible and necessary practices in the work of peacemaking. Moreover, they are unique forms of power rather than expressions of weakness. They may be and have been expressed simply in words or gestures as well as in more substantive forms. In the experience of nations and other social entities, repentance and forgiveness have been and may be the preconditions of reconciliation.

REPENTANCE AS AN ORIENTATION AND ATTITUDE

Repentance and forgiveness share both an orientation to history and an attitude toward the future. The year 1995, punctuated with so many fiftieth anniversaries of the climactic acts of World War II, posed these issues with an emotional intensity that many persons born after 1945 found difficult to understand. In particular, remembrance of the liberation of the death camps of the Holocaust and the atomic bombing of Hiroshima and Nagasaki provided occasions for discussions of repentance and forgiveness.

U.S. Remembrances of World War II

It proved exceedingly difficult for many Americans to acknowledge any national responsibility for the holocaust, Nazism, and the other horrors of history's most terrible war (the so-called "good war" because the Axis enemy was so obviously evil, the American people were rallied to such a high pitch of unity, and the lives of so many Americans were materially enhanced by the wartime economy and its affluent aftermath). Little recollection in 1995 was made of the ways in which the allies' demands after World War I contributed to the ascendancy and aggression of Nazism in Germany and militarism in Japan—or of the likelihood that World War II and the Holocaust could have been prevented, but for American isolationism, repudiation of the League of Nations, the collapse of parliamentary institutions in Germany and Japan in the wake of the North American Depression, Western anti-Semitism, and the racist exclusion of Japanese immigration.

Axis Powers' Ability to Acknowledge Guilt

Some German and Japanese leaders have found it possible to acknowledge their nation's war guilt and to offer words or gestures of repentance. The single most important initiative in German Chancellor Willy Brandt's *Ostpolitik* was the quest for reconciliation with then-Communist Poland. Poland, after all, was the first country to be blitzkrieged by the Nazi war machine and the country with the largest number of Holocaust victims (perhaps three million). In

December 1970, Brandt courageously (with no sure guarantee of parliamentary approval) signed a treaty accepting the Oder-Neisse frontier and therewith the cession of forty thousand square miles of German territory (Silesia and parts of Pomerania and East Prussia)—a decision personally dramatized by his kneeling silently at the Warsaw war memorial as an act of atonement for German offenses against the Polish people. That Brandt, of all people, should assume such a posture of repentance was especially remarkable in view of his own anti-Nazi credentials and his exile in Norway throughout the war. It was an extraordinarily winsome, powerful, long-lasting act of personal leadership. It made peace a human possibility.

Fifteen years later, on the fortieth anniversary of the end of World War II—May 8, 1985—German President Richard von Weizsäcker addressed the Bundestag with one of the most eloquent yet confessional statements of the century. Shriver writes: "The speech achieved international acclaim almost overnight. . . . What impressed the world about this speech was its lengthy, unflinching, excuseless enumeration of Nazi crimes and many degrees of association with those crimes by millions of Germans in the years 1933–45."[6] Among many other stunning passages, von Weizsäcker offered these words:

> We cannot commemorate the 8th of May without making ourselves aware how much conquest of self the readiness for reconciliation demanded of our former enemies. Can we really identify with the relatives of those who were sacrificed in the Warsaw Ghetto or the massacre of Lidice?. . . Who could remain innocent after the burning of the synagogues, the looting, the stigmatizing with the Jewish star, the withdrawal of rights, the unceasing violations of human worth?. . . . As human beings, we seek reconciliation. Precisely for this reason we must understand that there can be no reconciliation without memory.[7]

Von Weizsäcker profoundly understood that conquest-of-self or self-transcendence—whether by victors or vanquished—is the prerequisite of forgiveness and reconciliation.

As the Hiroshima anniversary approached in 1995, the Japanese government officially acknowledged deep remorse for its aggressions in World War II. The mayor of Hiroshima, Takashi Hiraoka, who in 1991 had laid a wreath at Pearl Harbor's battleship *Arizona* memorial, came to Washington to help open a Hiroshima exhibit at American University after veterans' groups had protested effectively the scheduling of such an exhibit at the Smithsonian. Many lively forums were available for reviewing the A-bomb decisions, but the U.S. government made no official statements of remorse or regret.

More-recent Episodes

The issues of war crimes and genocide raised so horrendously by World War II and the Holocaust have been revisited in the 1990s, particularly in the context of escalating ethnic strife in many countries. Former Yugoslavia and Rwanda have presented the most publicized cases, each with hundreds of thousands of victims. At this writing, prospects for acknowledgment of historic responsibility and offers of forgiveness are not promising in either case—but without such actions, peacemaking itself is likely to be thwarted.

South Africa is currently engaged in extraordinary efforts to overcome the brutal legacy of apartheid, notably through the Truth and Reconciliation Commission chaired by Archbishop Desmond Tutu and through the promise of amnesty for the confession of criminal conduct. The moral authority of Desmond Tutu and Nelson Mandela offers a powerful opportunity to confront—and to transcend—the burdens of history. To the extent that it succeeds, this drama of reconciliation in South Africa could transform the political and ethical debates about the appropriateness of repentance and forgiveness.[8]

THE UNITED STATES' INNOCENCE

Repentance may be peculiarly difficult for a country like the United States, which has conceived itself, as Reinhold Niebuhr put it, to be "the darling of Divine Providence." One of the more vicious consequences of such a metaphysical nationalism is a chronic difficulty in viewing history from an adversary's perspective. The naive habit of many, if not most, Americans has been to confront every international conflict reactively, as if it had no history at all, or at least no American implication in it.

This posture of historical innocence helps to explain the insensitivity with which the public has responded to events in Vietnam, Iran, the Persian Gulf, Lebanon, Mexico, Cuba, Nicaragua, and Somalia—

to mention just a few cases. In each case, American power has had a heavy legacy of involvement prior to the eruption of contemporary conflict. A common feature of the peoples of Asia, Africa, and Latin America is a much longer historical memory than most Americans and their leaders possess.

The Gulf War

I regard the Gulf War of 1991, so widely believed to be an exemplary U.S. military triumph, to be largely the consequence not only of Saddam Hussein's dictatorial rule and blundering aggression but also of the United States' lack of meaningful political memory of its past policies and actions that contributed to the hostilities. That past included the CIA's overthrow of Iran's nationalist revolution in 1953; complicity in the Shah's oppressions and corruptions which led to the Khomeini regime, against which the United States then proceeded to help build up the power of Saddam Hussein's regime in Iraq; incoherent U.S. diplomacy vis-à-vis Iraq; a persistent anti-Arab tilt in the Arab-Israeli conflict; an undisciplined energy policy that made the United States excessively dependent on Middle East oil and disposed to intervene militarily for the sake of oil; and a longtime U.S. lack of will to help construct an effective U.N. crisis-intervention force which might have prevented Iraq's invasion of Kuwait.

83

The actual U.S. conduct of the war, moreover, involved the violation of humanitarian laws of war (especially in the pitiless slaughter of retreating Iraqi troops) and enormous civilian casualties and suffering in Iraq. In short, that 1991 war ought to have been an occasion for national repentance rather than triumphalism. In *Lines in the Sand: Justice and the Gulf War*—a case study of the Gulf War that Barbara Green (my spouse) and I coauthored—we devoted special attention to the moral burdens of history as basic to understanding the tasks of peacemaking:

> A truly foundational ethic of war and peace must begin by taking the fullest possible account of the moral burdens of history that weigh upon any conflict within and among nations. Because historical responsibility for the causes of conflict typically is shared, a keen sense of the ambiguities of justice will help prepare conflicting nations for every prospect of peaceful settlement. Such a sense is spiritually

nurtured especially by acknowledging the necessity of repentance as the precondition of reconciliation. The incapacity of nations and their leaders to admit even the possibility of repentance is often more a sign of weakness than of some real strength beneath their proud belligerence. That incapacity may also reflect profound historical ignorance or forgetfulness.[9]

The Cold War

Owning up to the moral burdens of history is also required in coping with the numberless human consequences of the Cold War: a half-century global conflict in which not only the Soviet Union but the United States, the American people, their economy, and all their social institutions were such heavy losers. As Ambassador George Kennan recounts: "Nobody 'won' the Cold War. . . . It greatly overstrained the economic resources of both countries, leaving them both, by the end of the 1980s, confronted with heavy financial, social, and . . . political problems neither had anticipated and for which neither was fully prepared. . . . All these developments should be seen as part of the price we are paying for the Cold War."[10]

Many other countries were dragged into the Cold War, however, and continue to suffer its consequences. One particularly bitter example: While the United States has largely washed its hands of the chaos in Somalia after the October 1993 incident of spray-and-slay gunfire in which U.S. forces killed hundreds of Somalis in Mogadishu (and still suffered eighteen U.S. deaths), the United States showed little memory of the fact that both the Soviet Union and the United States had once sought to make Somalia a client state. In the process, the superpowers bequeathed the heaps of weapons that fueled Somalia's civil violence and the continuing breakdown of that victimized society's basic institutions. U.S.-U.N. intervention, originally a TV-driven humanitarian relief mission in a situation of desperate human need—a mission that undoubtedly saved several hundred thousand lives—climaxed with an unwarranted scorn of the Somalis' capacity for self-government and a continuing presumption of American innocence. On every continent today, the U.N. system and all its works are burdened with the human, institutional, and environmental wreckage of the Cold War.

THE NEED FOR NATIONAL SELF-RESPECT

Whatever the possibilities of repentance and forgiveness as discrete acts in particular cases, they must ultimately be deeply grounded in the dispositions of a political culture and the spiritual resources of a religious faith. American comprehensions of history are more myopic than some nations, less than others. Because of our power and leadership, our responsibility is greater. Our schools, colleges, and churches share with our political leaders a heavy responsibility in cultivating a much better-tutored historical consciousness. That does not mean wallowing in national self-hate and humiliation; it does mean appealing to our national self-respect.

There remain vast treasures of heritage and international policy which must be recalled when the nation needs to summon "the better angels of our nature" in the face of brutal conflict: the foundation of human rights and the vitality of civil liberties; the endurance of democratic, constitutional government; the relentless, if flawed, struggle for multiracial justice and harmony; the overcoming of isolationism in creating and sustaining the United Nations (notwithstanding much backsliding); the Marshall Plan and innumerable other works of relief and reconstruction.

Occasions of U.S. Self-transcendence

Also instructive is to recall those moments, few though they may be, when American leadership has reached for transcendent words and acts expressing (or even hinting at) repentance or forgiveness.

- Abraham Lincoln's second inaugural address, in 1865, which before concluding "with malice toward none [and] charity for all," acknowledged that both sides in the Civil War, while reading from the same Bible and praying to the same God, shared guilt for "the offense" of slavery—and must remember that "the judgments of the Lord are true and righteous altogether."

- President John Kennedy's "Strategy for Peace" address at American University in June 1963 (reportedly inspired by Pope John XXIII's encyclical, *Pacem in Terris*), which confessed "We must re-examine our own attitude" toward the Soviet Union and its legitimate security interests—followed in a few weeks by the Partial Test Ban Treaty prohibiting atmospheric nuclear tests.

- President Gerald Ford's 1976 proclamation revoking Executive Order 9066 (1942) which interned Japanese-Americans in concentration camps. Ford declared that an "honest reckoning . . . must include a recognition of our national mistakes as well as our national achievements. . . . We know now what we should have known then—not only was that evacuation wrong, but Japanese-Americans were and are loyal Americans."[11] More than another decade passed, however, before Congress finally approved twenty thousand dollars in reparations payments to each of the sixty thousand internees still alive in 1988, after protracted lobbying by the Japanese American Citizens league. Two more years would pass before President Bush dispatched letters with the twenty-thousand-dollar checks, acknowledging: "A monetary sum and words alone cannot restore lost years or erase painful memories. . . . We can never fully right the wrongs of the past. But . . . in enacting a law calling for restitution and offering a sincere apology, your fellow Americans have, in a very real sense, renewed their traditional commitment to the ideals of freedom, equality and justice."[12]

- President Bush's 1991 address on the fiftieth anniversary of Pearl Harbor, speaking to an audience largely of Pearl Harbor survivors and their families: "I have no rancor in my heart toward Germany or Japan. . . . This is no time for recrimination. World War II is over. It is history. We won. . . . We reached out, both in Europe and in Asia, and made our enemies our friends. We healed their wounds and in the process, we lifted ourselves up."[13]

WHAT IF REPENTANCE HAD BEEN ENACTED?

This study concludes with a "what-if" case: What if acts or signs of repentance had been forthcoming in a severe foreign-policy crisis in 1980 that virtually destroyed a presidency and thereby contributed to a perilous breakdown in U.S.–Soviet relations and nuclear diplomacy? This case remains controversial in participants' memories, including my own, as I was recruited to assist in its hoped-for resolution.

The context was the U.S. hostage crisis in Iran, which lasted 444 days from November 4, 1979, until inauguration day 1981. In February 1980, there was an unpublicized effort to signal a penitent U.S. attitude as a step to facilitate the release of the sixty-three U.S. hostages. The effort eventually failed, not because of intransigence in

Iran but because of White House rejection and bureaucratic resistance within the churches. Yet many elements of potential success were present and, if allowed to be put into action, might have had profound effects not only in U.S.–Iranian relations but in Presidential politics and across the entire agenda of both domestic and foreign policy.

Throughout 1980, Jimmy Carter's presidency was traumatized and increasingly enfeebled by apparent American impotence in the face of the captivity of the Americans in Tehran. However, within weeks of the militant Muslim students' seizure of the U.S. embassy, there were intimations that they wanted a face-saving way out of their unanticipated difficulties in managing prolonged belligerent operations. But the militants clearly saw themselves as defenders of a nationalist revolution, which, first, had been overthrown by a U.S.-engineered coup in 1953 and, second, had been brutally repressed by the corrupt tyranny of the Shah, whose military and secret police were regarded as extensions of American power.

An American Methodist leader, John P. Adams, was on temporary service in Tehran to help facilitate a mail-exchange project for the 87 hostages, a project led by John Thomas of the International Indian Treaty Council. Adams, a resourceful specialist in conflict resolution employed by the United Methodist Board of Church and Society, sent word to me from Tehran that the militants would probably respond favorably to a high-level (preferably presidential) U.S. acknowledgment of the legitimacy of Iranian grievances. Preparation for such a statement might include expressions of repentance by American churches. The Adams initiative was strongly backed by the United Methodist Bishop of Washington, James K. Mathews.

Adams's presence in Iran was cut short by apprehensive board members in Washington and by the advice of U.N. Secretary General Kurt Waldheim to the National Council of Churches that nongovernmental efforts might hamper U.N. negotiations. (Waldheim's personal diplomacy in this case ended with a highly publicized, hapless trip to Tehran, from which he hastily departed.) A denominational staff colleague of Adams opposed his initiative, citing a recent passage from denominational editor Arthur Moore, who had taken the "realist" line that repentance was inappropriate for a government. Moore insisted: "We should always be re-examining the results of our foreign policies whether they turn out well or ill, but to call such an examination national repentance is extremely poor theology. . . .

The concept of *metanoia* [repentance], of turning about, rightly applies only to religiously committed individuals, as it does in the New Testament. It is a religious, not a secular, experience."[14]

However, Adams and I had received alternative counsel from two veteran professionals in the field of conflict resolution, Roger Fisher of Harvard Law School and James Laue of a conciliation center in St. Louis. Their advice was precisely that an unofficial channel might be just the key to ending the crisis, and they doubted Waldheim's capacity to do so. Their advice was seconded by a former U.S. delegate to the United Nations.

Accordingly, the Adams initiative proceeded on two tracks. At the request of Bishop Ralph T. Alton, president of the United Methodist Council of Bishops, and Bishop Mathews, Council secretary, Ash Wednesday, February 20, 1980, was widely observed as "a day of repentance and intercession" for the United States and Iran. A background paper on U.S.–Iranian relations was prepared to be distributed at Ash Wednesday services and throughout the churches. That piece concluded: "Our deepest concern for the welfare and release of American hostages, as well as for the principle of diplomatic immunity, is not likely to find effective expression unless and until those Iranian grievances are better recognized and understood."[15]

But the prospect for success of this unofficial initiative ultimately depended upon official words from the U.S. government. Meanwhile, the Iranian government was also publicly seeking a signal of contrition as a catalyst to end the crisis. On January 29, 1980, the Iranian ambassador to the United Nations, Mansour Farhang, had urged President Carter to say something like this: "Yes, we made some policies in Iran that were not in the interest of the Iranian people. . . . We want to change that perspective, and we are sorry for the mistakes or misperceptions or the wrongness of the past."[16]

"A proposal for a Presidential Statement on U.S.–Iranian Relations" was drafted in consultation with Fisher, Laue, and Bishop Mathews and also with Congressional leadership and interested officials of the State Department. The majority leader of the House of Representatives forwarded it to the White House with his endorsement. That draft statement said, in part:

> We are eager to restore our friendship with the Iranian people. We know that grievances on both sides must now

be heard. As Americans, we cannot accept the seizing of hostages as an act of social justice, whatever the record of wrongs in years past. . . . Wherever our own policies may have given offense, even when their purpose has been our mutual peace and security, we shall seek to understand and to rectify.[17]

No such statement was ever made by President Carter or any U.S. official. When Carter was asked at a press conference whether some acknowledgment of the U.S. role in overthrowing the nationalist government in 1953 might help resolve the crisis, he dismissed the reference as "ancient history." The weeks went by. Carter was under mounting pressure to do something forceful to save the hostages. On April 24, 1980, an ill-conceived and ill-fated military rescue effort ended at Desert One south of Teheran. The effort was abandoned after mechanical failures and the deaths of eight Americans, with five more wounded and with good reason to fear discovery by Iranian personnel. As all the months of that national election year passed, President Carter seemed increasingly powerless to cope with either Iran or double-digit inflation. His presidency was overwhelmingly repudiated in the Reagan electoral vote landslide, 489 to 49. When the hostages were finally released on Reagan's inauguration day, Carter's humiliation was compounded. Yet the defeated president was justifiably commended for his protracted restraint in favor of negotiations—that is, after the disaster at Desert One.

As it happened, the 1980 election led to momentous changes in American politics, both domestic and foreign policy, and the public role of the churches. The Iranian hostage crisis offered one of the more important "what-if" moments in the late twentieth century. Now there is no way to know whether words of repentance and forgiveness might have made all the difference—but history shows time and again that the lack of such expressions merely sows the seeds of future conflicts.

89

PART TWO

justice

5

ADVANCE DEMOCRACY, HUMAN RIGHTS, AND RELIGIOUS LIBERTY

Bruce Russett

As World War II drew to a close, leaders of the great powers drew up
a set of documents, including the Charter of the United Nations and
the foundations for the Bretton Woods financial institutions. The
inspiration for these documents stemmed primarily from the democracies, notably the United Kingdom and the United States. They were
determined to do what they could to avoid repeating the causes of
World Wars I and II. To do so, they created new international institutions which would potentially have the military means to restrain
aggressors. But more than military strength was at issue, and the
new structure for international relations encompassed much more. It
promoted trade, economic assistance, and foreign investment, both
as direct means to prosperity and indirect means to a peace resting
on prosperity and economic interdependence. It also promoted
democracy and human rights as expressed in the Universal
Declaration of Human Rights and advocated by instruments of cultural influence like the U.S. Information Agency and the BBC. A key
feature was that it was not a unilateralist policy, but multilateralist.
Its multilateral instruments ranged far beyond NATO and the rest of
the alliance system to depend heavily on regional trade arrange-
ments like the OECD, the World Bank, the IMF, GATT, and many
U.N. specialized agencies. Central U.N. institutions were also vital.

Initially, the hope was that the Soviet Union would be fully inside this structure. But the rise of the Cold War meant that some of the institutions were ineffective and many operated without the active participation of the Soviet Union. Thus, it was only in part a fully global structure and, in important ways, principally a structure for managing and strengthening relations among the Western allies. For that purpose, on the whole, it worked well. Now, with the end of the Cold War division of the world, we see an opportunity to broaden the earlier structure to encompass a much larger proportion of the earth.

Contemporary policy formulation needs a similar central organizing principle. To promote its acceptance, that principle would be best rooted in the earlier experience. It should build on the tripod of principles which underlay the rhetoric and much of the practice—principles rooted in beliefs about the success of free political and economic systems. The first of these principles is democracy and institutionalized respect for human rights. The second (now buttressed by increasing evidence that economic interdependence promotes peace as well as prosperity) is free markets. The third is international law and organization. These ideas remain as strong as ever.

Consider a puzzle about the end of the Cold War. The question is not simply why did the Cold War end, but rather, why did it end before the drastic change in the bipolar distribution of power, and why did it end peacefully? In November 1988, Margaret Thatcher proclaimed, as did other Europeans, that "the Cold War is over." By spring 1989, the U.S. State Department stopped making official reference to the Soviet Union as the enemy. The fundamental patterns of East–West behavior had changed, on both sides, beginning even before the circumvention of the Berlin Wall and then its destruction in October 1989. All of this preceded the unification of Germany (October 1990) and the dissolution of the Warsaw Pact (July 1991). Even after these latter events, the military power of the Soviet Union itself remained intact until the dissolution of the USSR at the end of December 1991. None of these events was resisted militarily.

Any understanding of the change in the Soviet Union's international behavior before its political fragmentation, and in time reciprocated by the West, demands attention to the operation of the three principles.

1. Substantial political liberalization and movement toward democracy in the Soviet Union, with consequent improvements in free expression and the treatment of dissidents at home, in the East European satellites, and in behavior toward Western Europe and the United States.

2. The desire for economic interdependence with the West, impelled by the impending collapse of the Soviet economy and the consequent perceived need for access to Western markets, goods, technology, and capital, which in turn required a change in Soviet military and diplomatic policy.

3. The influence of international law and organizations, as manifested in the Conference on Security and Cooperation in Europe (CSCE) and the human rights based on the Helsinki accords and their legitimation and support of dissent in the communist states. Whereas the United Nations itself was not important in this process of penetrating domestic politics, the CSCE as an international organization most certainly was, as were the many citizens' groups and international nongovernmental organizations devoted to human rights.

A vision of a peace among democratically governed states has long been invoked as part of a larger structure of institutions and practices to promote peace among nation-states. In 1795 Immanuel Kant spoke of perpetual peace based partially upon states sharing "republican constitutions." His meaning was compatible with basic contemporary understandings of democracy. As the elements of such a constitution he identified freedom, with legal equality of subjects, representative government, and separation of powers. The other key elements of his perpetual peace were "cosmopolitan law," embodying ties of international commerce and free trade, and a "pacific union" established by treaty in international law among republics.

By the twentieth century, some progress had been made in actualizing these principles. Woodrow Wilson expressed the vision forcefully. In his famous Fourteen Points, he did not explicitly invoke the need for universal democracy, since not all of America's war allies were democratic. But his meaning is clear if one considers the domestic political conditions necessary for his first point: "Open covenants of peace, openly arrived at, after which there shall be no private international understandings of any kind but diplomacy shall proceed always frankly and in the public view." Point three demanded "removal, so far as possible, of all economic barriers and the establishment of an equality of trade conditions among all the nations consenting to the peace and associating themselves for its maintenance." The fourteenth point was "A general association of nations must be formed under specific covenants for the purpose of affording mutual guarantees of political independence and territorial integrity to great and small states alike."

The Wilsonian application of this vision failed, but later in the twentieth century it was picked up again. Konrad Adenauer, Jean Monnet, and other founders of the European Coal and Steel Community (now the European Union) sought some way to insure that the great powers, who had repeatedly fought dreadful wars over the previous century, would finally live in peace with each other. To do so, they supported restored democratic institutions and protections for human rights in their countries, built a network of economic interdependence to make war unthinkable on cost/benefit grounds, and embedded their relationships in new structures of European organization.

DEMOCRACIES RARELY FIGHT ONE ANOTHER

The following discussion will necessarily be merely an overview with references to detailed research. I will discuss evidence supporting all three elements of this vision here, although I focus more on democratization than on the other two elements. That is also appropriate because the most solid, extensive, and elaborated evidence is for the proposition that democracies do not make war on each other. Much of it is addressed in my book on this topic, although far more has accumulated since then.[1] In the contemporary era, "democracy" denotes a country in which nearly everyone can vote, elections are freely contested, the chief executive is chosen by popular vote or by an elected parliament, and civil rights and civil liberties are substantially guaranteed. Democracies may not be especially peaceful in general (we all know the history of democracies in colonialism, covert intervention, and other excesses of power). Democracies may be nearly as violent in their relations with some authoritarian states as authoritarian states are toward each other. But the relations between stable democracies are qualitatively different.

Democracies are unlikely to engage in militarized disputes with each other or to let any such disputes escalate into war. In fact, they rarely even skirmish. Since 1946 pairs of democratic states have been only one-eighth as likely as other kinds of states to threaten to use force against each other, and only one-tenth as likely actually to do so. Established democracies fought no wars against one another during the entire twentieth century. (Although Finland, for example, took the Axis side against the Soviet Union in World War II, it engaged in no combat with the democracies.)[2]

The more democratic the states are, the more peaceful their relations are likely to be. In their disputes with each other, democracies are more likely to employ democratic means of peaceful conflict resolution. They are readier to reciprocate each other's behavior, to accept third-party mediation or good offices in settling disputes, and to accept binding third-party settlement. Democracies' relatively peaceful relations toward each other are not spuriously caused by some other influence such as sharing high levels of wealth, or rapid growth, or ties of alliance. This has been established by statistical analyses of the behavior of pairs of states in the international system since World War II.[3] Pairs of states that are democratic are more peaceful than others, even controlling for these influences. The peace between democracies is not limited just to the rich industrialized states of the global North. It was not maintained simply by pressure from a common adversary in the Cold War, and it has outlasted that threat.

The phenomenon of democratic peace can be explained by the pervasiveness of normative restraints on conflict between democracies. That explanation extends to the international arena the cultural norms of live-and-let-live and peaceful conflict resolution that operate within democracies. The phenomenon of democratic peace can also be explained by the role of institutional restraints on democracies' decisions to go to war. Those restraints insure that any state in a conflict of interest with another democracy can expect ample time for conflict-resolution processes to be effective, and that the risk of incurring surprise attack is virtually nil.

Nonindustrial societies, studied by anthropologists, also show restraints on warfare among democratically organized polities that typically lack the institutional constraints of a modern state. Despite that absence, democratically organized units fight each other significantly less often than do nondemocratic units. And political stability also proves an important restraint on the resort to violence by these democratically organized units. Finding the relationship between democracy and peace in preindustrial societies shows that the phenomenon of democratic peace is not limited to contemporary Western democracies.

The end of Cold War ideological hostility is particularly significant because it represents a surrender to the force of values of economic and especially political freedom. To the degree that countries once ruled by autocratic systems become democratic, the absence of war among democracies comes to bear on any discussion of the future of international relations. By this reasoning, the more democracies there are in the world, the fewer potential adversaries we and other democracies will have and the wider the zone of peace.

The *possibility* of a widespread zone of democratic peace in the contemporary world exists. To bring that possibility to fruition, several fundamental problems must be addressed: the problem of consolidating democratic stability, the interaction of democracy with nationalism, the role of economic development and interdependence, and the prospects for changing basic patterns of international behavior.

STRENGTHENING DEMOCRACY AND ITS NORMS

The literature on the conditions under which democracy can develop and flourish is vast. Most but by no means all of the influences on the successful consolidation of democratic transitions are largely domestic, within states. Some of the international influences, along with the domestic ones, can have a great effect.

Among the international influences that played significant parts in producing the latest wave of recent transitions to democracy, Samuel Huntington notes changes in some religious institutions (including transnational ones) that made them less defenders of the status quo than opponents of governmental authoritarianism; a more activist policy by states, international organizations, and nongovernmental agents to promote human rights and democracy; and snowballing or demonstration effects, enhanced by international communication, as transitions to democracy in some states served as models for their neighbors.[4] Among his list of conditions that favor the consolidation of new democracies is a favorable international political environment, with outside assistance. While internal influences are certainly prominent, the international conditions are impressive also. Favorable international conditions may not be essential in every case, but they can make a difference and sometimes a crucial one when the internal influences are mixed.

Citizens' groups and nongovernmental organizations have often been vital to this process. For example, in the Helsinki negotiations, human-rights organizations prodded Western governments to insist on the human-rights plank. The resulting agreement put a strong lever in the hands of many different movements in Central Europe and the Soviet Union, who pushed for actualization of the guarantees that had been officially endorsed. The Solidarity movement in Poland, the nonviolent "revolution of the candles" in East German churches, the Czechoslovakian human-rights movement led by Vaclav Havel, all were human-rights movements that added pressure for democracy. They were, in turn, part of a larger international movement for human rights and democracy which changed almost all the military dictatorships in Latin America into various stages of democratization. Their efforts were echoed with substantial success in South Korea, Taiwan, South Africa, and Zimbabwe. The indigenous movements were aided by a shift in U.S. government policy, beginning with the Carter administration, to monitor human-rights performance and require governments to show progress in observing those rights as a condition of economic assistance. They also drew on transnational support from churches, groups like Amnesty International, labor movements, cultural leaders, the influence of the U.S. civil rights movement, and the impetus for human rights reflected in the international conventions adopted on various human-rights and nongovernmental organizations' participation in U.N. conferences.

The culture of human-rights organizations and their allies requires a network of persons who are ready to serve as independent and articulate reporters of abuses perpetrated by governments and who have confidence in others' reports. They must be ready to engage in protests and collaborative action; to spend considerable amounts of time, energy, and money to gain public attention for their protests and for the people they are trying to protect; and to incur the risk of retaliation by their governments. Human-rights organizations require from their members compassion for the victims and toughness in the face of the practices relied on by governments and groups that routinely violate human rights.

With economic conditions still grim in much of the developing world and in former communist countries, and the consequent dangers to the legitimacy of new democratic governments, external assistance is especially important. New democracies will not survive without some material improvement in their citizens' lives. As a stick, aid can surely be denied to governments that regularly violate human rights, for example of ethnic minorities. Clear antidemocratic acts, such as a military coup or an aborted election, can be punished by suspending aid. As to the carrot of extending aid on a conditional basis, broader goals of developing democratic institutions require creation of a civil society and are less easily made conditional. Recipients may see multilateral aid, with conditions of democratic reform attached, as a less blatant invasion of their sovereignty than aid from a single country.

100 | ETHNIC CONFLICT AND THE HUMAN RIGHT TO CULTURAL EXPRESSION

A special complication, hardly unique to the current era but felt acutely now, is ethnic conflict. With its lines of inclusion and exclusion, nationalism readily conflicts with the quasi-universalistic ethos of "democracies don't fight each other." Hatreds, long suppressed, emerge to bedevil any effort to build stable, legitimate government. An irony is that the initial creation of democratic institutions can contribute to the explosion of ethnic conflicts by providing the means of free expression, including expression of hatred and feelings of oppression. People who have long hated each other now can say how much they hate each other.

Even if stable and established democracies are generally at peace with one another, the process of democratization is not always a peaceful one. A brand-new democracy may be unstable and may face fierce problems of restructuring its economy and satisfying diverse interests and ethnic groups. Under these perhaps temporary circumstances, nationalism and domestic problems may sometimes lead to conflicts with neighboring states. Nearby autocracies may attack them because they see their shift to democracy as endangering the legitimacy of authoritarianism, or their period of transition as a moment of potential weakness to be exploited. But, importantly, only those democracies that have autocratic states as neighbors are most likely to get into military conflicts. One piece of good news is that democratizing states from the former Warsaw Pact have been substantially peaceful with democratic or democratizing neighbors. Furthermore, transitions from autocracy to democracy are no more dangerous to international peace than are failed democracies that revert to autocratic rule. The problem is one of instability and transition in both directions, not just of new democracies.[5]

Any solution does not lie in less democracy. Rather, it requires measures, including external assistance and protection, to assist and speed the transition. It also requires attention to devising institutions, and nurturing norms and practices, of democratic government with respect for minority rights. Countries that have a history of racist practice and present struggle, including the United States, need to pay attention to racism both domestically and in their foreign policy. The United States can project racial bias outward while hardly noticing it or it can use its own struggle to help it understand and offer help in international struggles against racism.

Minority rights are rightly thought of largely in terms of the rights of ethnic, racial, and linguistic minorities. More broadly, however, they reflect tension between the legitimate needs of the state to build common loyalties to a nation versus the basic rights of individuals and groups to the preservation and expression of cultural diversity. In this respect, rights to religious liberty, as specified in the U.N. Charter and the Universal Declaration of Human Rights, are central and often help define ethnic identity.

Current Western principles of religious liberty did not, of course, evolve quickly or easily even in the West. Catholics and Protestants learned painfully the costs of trying to impose their beliefs on each other, coming belatedly to see freedom of religion not merely as a matter of prudence but as an essential moral and ethical principle. That principle still is strained by some fundamentalist groups in democratic countries and is highly contested in countries not sharing the Western experience of difficult learning about democracy and religious liberty. The alternatives, however, are either civil war and attempted secession of minorities or vigorous repression of them.

The creation of institutions, norms, and practices to protect minorities and human rights has never been easy. If democratization is temporarily a problem, the establishment of stable democracy is vital to the solution. But it presents the fundamental challenge of world political development in this era. It is worth remembering that the most terrible acts of genocide and state-sponsored mass murder in this century (from Turkey's slaughter of the Armenians through Hitler, Stalin, Pol Pot, and others) have been carried out by authoritarian or totalitarian governments, not democratic ones.[6]

ECONOMIC INTERDEPENDENCE AND INTERNATIONAL ORGANIZATIONS

Ties of economic interdependence—international trade and investment—form an important supplement to shared democracy in promoting peace. Here is the second leg of the tripod for peace, representing the role of free trade and a high level of commercial exchange. Economic interdependence gives countries a stake in one another's well-being. War would mean destruction, in the other country, of one's own markets, industrial plants, and sources of imports. If my investments are in your country, bombing your industry means, in effect, bombing my own factories. Just the threat of war inhibits international trade and investment. Economic interdependence also serves as a channel of information about one another's perspectives, interests, and desires on a broad range of matters not the subject of the economic exchange. These communications form an important channel for conflict management. Interdependence, however, is the key word—mutual dependence, not one-sided dominance of the weak by the strong.

Interdependence in the last fifty years has importantly contributed—above and beyond the influence of joint democracy, wealth, and alliances—to reducing conflict among states so linked. When countries' trade with each other constitutes a substantial portion of their national incomes, violent conflict and war between them are rare. Democracies trade more with one another than with nondemocratic countries. The combination of democracy and interdependence is especially powerful. States that are both democratic and economically interdependent are extremely unlikely to initiate serious military disputes with one another.[7]

New democracies and freer markets should be supported financially, politically, and morally. Successful transitions in some countries can supply a model for others. A stable and less menacing international system can permit the emergence and consolidation of democratic governments and peaceful economic growth and interchange. International threats—real or only perceived—strengthen the forces of secrecy, authoritarianism, and autarky in the domestic politics of states involved in protracted conflict. Relaxation of international threats to peace and security reduces the need and the excuse for repressing dissent and centralizing control of the economy.

Reliance on international law and institutions, and the need for strengthening them, constitutes the third element of this structure for peace. As expressed in Secretary General Boutros-Ghali's *An Agenda for Peace,*[8] the United Nations has a new mission of peacebuilding, attending to democratization, development, and the protection of human rights. It is newly strengthened and, paradoxically, also newly and enormously burdened.

International organizations, like other institutions, may serve a variety of functions. Their occasional role in coercing norm-breakers (e.g., by the Security Council) is only one. In addition, they may mediate among conflicting parties, reduce uncertainty in negotiations by conveying information, expand material self-interest to be more inclusive and longer term, shape norms, and help generate narratives of mutual identification among peoples and states. Some organizations are more successful than others, and in different functions. But overall, as Michael Smith will demonstrate in chapter 8, they do make a difference.

An extension of the quantitative empirical analyses referred to above makes the point. The same kind of analysis that first established an independent and significant influence of democracy in reducing conflict among countries, and then added evidence for an additional meliorative influence of economic interdependence, has been carried out on the effect of international organizations. We have collected information on the number of intergovernmental organizations (IGOs) in which both of any pair of countries are members. This "density" of IGO membership varies from zero for some countries to over one hundred for some pairs of European states. Adding this information to the previous analysis, we find that it too contributes an additional, independent, statistically significant effect in reducing the probability of international conflict. The thicker the network, the fewer the militarized disputes. We still need to know more about how this effect works and under what conditions. But these results represent good evidence for the third and final leg of the structure underlying peaceful international relations.[9]

DEMOCRATIZATION AND THE ROLE OF INTERNATIONAL ORGANIZATIONS

Understanding that democracies rarely fight each other, and why, has great consequence for policy in the contemporary world. It should affect the kinds of military preparations believed to be necessary and the costs one would be willing to pay to make them. It should encourage peaceful efforts to assist the emergence and consolidation of democracy. But a misunderstanding of it could encourage warmaking against authoritarian regimes and efforts to overturn them—with all the costly implications of preventive or hegemonic military activity that such a policy might imply.

The post–World War II success with defeated adversaries can be misleading if one forgets how expensive it was and especially if one misinterprets the political conditions of military defeat. The Allies utterly defeated the Axis coalition. Then, to solidify democratic government, they conducted vast (if incomplete) efforts to remove the former elites from positions of authority. The model of "fight them, beat them, and then make them democratic" is no model for contemporary action. It probably would not work anyway, and no one is prepared to make the kind of effort that would be required. Not all authoritarian states are inherently aggressive. Indeed, at any particular time, the majority are not. A militarized crusade for democracy is not in order.

External military intervention, even against the most odious dictators, is a dangerous way to try to produce a democratic world order. Sometimes, with a cautious cost-benefit analysis and with the certainty of substantial and legitimate internal support, it might be worthwhile—that is, under conditions when rapid military success is likely and the will of the people at issue is clear. Even so, any time an outside power supplants any existing government, the problem of legitimacy is paramount. The very democratic norms to be instilled may be compromised. At the least, intervention cannot be unilateral. It must be approved by an international body like the United Nations or a regional security organization. When an election has been held under U.N. auspices and certified as fair—as happened in Haiti—the United Nations has a special responsibility, even a duty, to see that the democratic government it helped create is not destroyed.

Under most circumstances, international bodies are better used as vehicles to promote democratic processes at times when the relevant domestic parties are ready. Peacekeeping operations to help provide the conditions for free elections, monitor those elections, and advise on the building of democratic institutions are usually far more promising and less costly for all concerned than is military intervention.

With the end of the Cold War, the United Nations has experienced highly publicized troubles in Somalia and the former Yugoslavia as it tries to cope with a range of challenges not previously part of its mandate. Nonetheless, its successes, though receiving less attention, outnumber the failures. It emerged as a major facilitator of peaceful transitions and democratic elections in such places as Cambodia, El Salvador, Eritrea, and Namibia. Its Electoral Assistance Unit has provided election monitoring, technical assistance, or other aid to electoral processes in more than sixty states.

105

Economic interdependence is also supported by international organizations. Increasingly, economic development is seen as dependent on open markets for goods and capital. Without the network of regional and global institutions to promote liberalized and expanding trade, much of the world could readily slip back into protectionism and trade wars. Chapter 7, by Paul Schroeder, adverts to this, and chapter 6, by David Bronkema, David Lumsdaine, and Rodger Payne, discusses the problems of sustainable development more extensively. Sustainable development requires not only freedom of individual initiative and expression but some protection of basic human rights to employment and decent living conditions.

The demands of growth and equality are not always well reconciled. The IMF and the World Bank often have been rightly criticized for applying to their loan policies economic and fiscal criteria that neglect equity, political liberties, and the rights of minorities such as indigenous peoples. Recently, however, those institutions have given greater attention to criteria of political responsibility, transparency, and good governance (close synonyms for democracy), and have become instruments not just to create and strengthen free markets but also to ease transitions to democracy and to rebuild societies shattered by civil war.

THE EMERGING ORDER

Democracy and international peace can feed on each other. An evolutionary process may even be at work. Because of the visible nature and public costs of breaking commitments, democratic leaders are better able to persuade leaders of other states that they will keep the agreements into which they do enter. Democratic states are able to signal their intentions in bargaining with greater credibility than are autocratic states. Democracies more often win their wars than do authoritarian states—80 percent of the time (remember that the coin-flip odds would be only 50-50). They are more prudent about what wars they get into, choosing wars that they are more likely to win and that will incur lower costs. With free speech and debate, they are more accurate and efficient information processors. Authoritarian governments that lose wars may be overthrown and replaced by democratic regimes, as was the Argentine junta after the Falklands/Malvinas war. States with competitive elections generally devote lower shares of their national products to military expenditures, which in relations with other democracies promotes cooperation; as democracies' politically relevant international environment becomes composed of more democratic and internally stable states, democracies tend to reduce their military allocations and conflict involvement.[10]

The modern international system is commonly traced to the Treaty of Westphalia and the principles of sovereignty and noninterference in internal affairs that it affirmed. That settlement affirmed the anarchy of the system, without a superior authority to ensure order. It also was a treaty among princes who ruled as autocrats. Our understanding of the modern anarchic state system risks conflating the effects of anarchy with those stemming from the political organization of its founding units. When most states are ruled autocratically, then playing by the rules of autocracy may be the only way for any state, democracy or not, to survive.

But the increasing if uneven spread of democracy over the past two centuries, along with the slow emergence of new international norms and institutions, now presents an opening for change in the international system more fundamental even than at the end of other big wars—World Wars I and II and the Napoleonic Wars. For the first time ever, in 1992 a virtual majority of states (91 of 183) approximated the standards for democracy that I employed earlier. Another 35 were in some form of transition to democracy. Democracy will not be consolidated in all these states. A subsequent report notes some backsliding in the number of people living in democracies, though still an increase in the number of democratic governments. Yet states probably can become democratic faster than they can become rich. Some autocratically governed states will surely remain in the system. In their relations with states where democracy is unstable or where democratization is not begun at all, democracies must continue to be vigilant and concerned with the need for military deterrence. But if enough states become stably democratic in coming decades, then among them we will have a chance to reconstruct the norms and rules of the international order. We already have come a long way from 1648.

In time, the current quasi-hegemony of the United States and its allies will fade, giving way to a more diffused distribution of global power. That diffusion will occur across some very different national cultures and experiences, in Asia, Latin America, the Middle East, and perhaps Africa. It could give rise to a highly fragmented, competitive, and dangerous international system or to one in which conflicts of interest can be managed without an excessive frequency and severity of violence. In order for the less-fragmented and less-violent system to emerge, agreements to disagree peacefully and protections for minority needs and cultural distinctiveness—centrally associated with concepts of democracy—will have to be built into the structures of nation-states and into relations between states. Those relations will need to be further buttressed by linkages of economic interdependence and mediated by international and perhaps supranational institutions. Wide implementation of this vision offers the opportunity to manage global power changes in constructive fashion. Its elements have the ability to feed on one another in a dynamic system of reinforcing virtuous circles. Just as democracy, interdependence, and international organizations support peace, each in turn is supported by peace, and they support one another.

This vision can be and has been held by government leaders. But to achieve it in practice, among diverse countries and peoples, requires constant effort by individual citizens and by private national and transnational organizations as well as by governments. The sacrifices needed to support democracy at home and elsewhere, to share the costs of global economic interdependence, and to strengthen international organizations must constantly be renewed. These elements can be lost, as they were in the 1930s. A placard on the wall of one of my colleagues' offices warns, "Every good thing has to be rewon each day."

These practices may well be the only alternative to disaster. The extreme "realist" precept to treat all states as potential enemies is untenable. Worse, in Michael J. Smith's words, "To treat all politics as inexpiable struggle is to propound a self-fulfilling prophecy."[11] I would go further. Except as a self-fulfilling prophecy, it is empirically erroneous. It is therefore a poor guide to practical action, and it is also therefore immoral. While we always acknowledge that some states remain outside the system of peace and thus are dangerous, we must recognize that many, while remaining self-interested actors, nonetheless can be stable and reliable partners in cooperation. That's not "idealism"; that's life.

6

FOSTER JUST AND SUSTAINABLE ECONOMIC DEVELOPMENT

David Bronkema
David Lumsdaine
Rodger A. Payne

This essay reflects on the role of sustainable development in making and maintaining a just peace. "Sustainable Development" is an attractive term, conjuring up a picture of continual, yet environmentally friendly, increases in material welfare that are locally generated and controlled. Yet we should be careful when we invoke such hopes: Processes of economic and social change and aspirations to improve standards of living in poor countries and regions are complex, and catchwords which seem to embody aspirations often can prove misleading.

WHAT IS SUSTAINABLE DEVELOPMENT?

As anybody with experience at the local level can attest, the poor, while working hard to better their lot themselves, also clamor for "development" projects from the state and from international agencies.[1] Yet well-intended development schemes have often worked out badly, frequently by failing to heed local insights and needs. Useless or destructive projects often have been undertaken on expert advice against the protests of ordinary people. Wholesome "development," then, might best be defined as "processes of change in peoples' relationships to their environment which increase their well-being, standards of living, or quality of life."[2] Increasing material welfare means changes in relationships, and working with people to help improve their material situations involves a relationship that can draw those involved together into a kind of community working toward a common goal.[3]

The Idea of Development

The words "sustainable development" have been used in many ways. "Development" generally describes a process of material and social progress; this usually leads to wider involvement in the world economy, and cultural adaptation to modern world customs. Some criticize development generally as an imposition of "modern" standards and values on non-Western countries. But in poorer, Southern countries, many people live in abject poverty, lacking adequate food, shelter, medical care and clean water; and evidence suggests that this poverty most affects women, children and all with meager political and economic power. We may not ignore the urgent, unmet, basic human needs of the earth's many peoples. Desires for material development are more than the imposition of an outside, Western standard: People in such circumstances, in almost all cultures, consistently try to become more economically prosperous; others want to try to help them; and both parties refer to this as "development."[4]

Development should not be understood, however, primarily as material accumulation, or as acquisition of the equivalent in skills ("human capital"), though those goals may often be important. Rather, at base, this aim should be thought of literally as *development*, the growth and flourishing, the cultivation, of the human person. Such human development is both the ultimate purpose, and the practical foundation, of other development objectives. Thus, concerns about modernization have an important point. Our age characteristically and easily presumes that "modern," more-affluent (often American or Western) ways are the best, or the only good and acceptable ones, even though explicitly it believes the very opposite; and it tends to assume implicitly, too, that increasing material wealth and pleasure is life's chief purpose. Development needs to be concerned with building up and cultivating human persons and communities as wholes. Preserving the past and local culture and stability, limiting desires, and respecting ancient ways are not just important ends to be balanced against the ends of development (though balancing may be needed) but vital sources and constituents of human virtue, growth, and satisfaction—that is, of development.

The Idea of Sustainability

The term "sustainable" was early used to indicate people being able to improve their material welfare on their own steam and subject to their control; the term is still frequently used this way.[5] As the poor, with some help, obtain the ability to make use of local resources and local, regional, national, and international institutions in ways they weren't able to before, they are able to sustain their economic development in this first sense.

The term "sustainable" has also taken a second, "green" sense, especially since the 1987 report of the World Commission on Environment and Development (also known as the Brundtland Commission). This report, *Our Common Future,* emphasizes the need for development to include protecting the environment and natural resources for future generations.[6] Preventing economic activity from irrevocably sullying the environment is, in any case, a necessary part of living in peace, in harmony with the world of nature, and is part of the biblical mandate to "tend and dress" the land we have been given. Sustainability in either sense—enabling the poor to earn a better livelihood or meeting today's needs without threatening the needs of tomorrow—entails significant changes in the economic activities as ordinarily undertaken by individuals, transnational corporations, and nation-states. In sum, those whose needs are currently met should regulate their resource use so as to prevent exhaustion or other threats to current or future resource availability; while those who do not have adequate material and economic resources must somehow gain access to them.

These two senses are often related. Ecological destruction often threatens poor people's basic needs; poor communities often have an interest in long-term, ecologically sustainable development; and in any case, both involve a humane commitment to permanence and human flourishing. Commitment to the sustained well-being of human beings everywhere, and of their local, regional, national, and global communities, is vital to justice and peace and to care of the creation. The capacity-building and ecological aspects of sustainable development hint at a third element: the place that politics, power, justice, and peace have in development.

Sustainable Development and a Just Peace

Sustainable development is integral to making peace and to maintaining justice for several reasons. First, peace is not only an absence of war, violence, and hostility; it is also a state of reconciliation, human flourishing, and natural beauty. Severe privation and want require our response. A world where many are trapped in dire poverty while others have an abundance, or in which nature is destroyed, unnecessarily crushes the spirit and offends justice. Active concern for those in need and for the environment is, simply in itself, a part of living in peace. Further, developing human powers and capacities, allowing people to exercise their gifts and talents, and doing useful work and improving our surroundings are a part of any just order. Thus, sustaining, community-building, useful livelihoods are, by definition, part of a just order. A just order is organized to favor making useful and beautiful, well-made and long-lasting goods rather than meretricious, shoddy, short-lived ones.

Second, human need and the absence of a chance to earn a useful livelihood, if unaddressed, lead to despair, societal disorder, and even war. An unjust order violates the proper patterns of human life and can erupt in open violence, especially as people find their lives futile or deteriorating.[7] Similarly, economic development that is not ecologically sustainable will cause unexpectedly worsening patterns of human life which may well lead to violence in the long run. Again, a process of sustainable development will enable people of all sectors of society to participate in governing themselves more fully than many of them are now able to do. Sustaining a just order, besides its intrinsic value, is therefore a crucial foundation for peace and justice.

Third, the absence of sustainable development, and impediments to it, are often bitter fruits of human greed, sin, violence, and injustice. That is, lack of sustainable development may be a result as well as a source of an absence of justice and peace. An inability to earn proper livelihoods in useful work often arises from ongoing abuses of power, perhaps even from open violence. Working for justice—including securing property rights—for peoples unable to defend themselves can be a prerequisite of their gaining opportunities for productive work and sustainable development. War and violence, too, are major causes of environmental deterioration and of people's losing control over their own lives and communities. Thus, sustainable development is also a result or fruit of justice and peace.

Thus, in sum, justice and peace are closely bound together with sustainable development. Basic development goals—providing all people with access to resources and opportunities necessary to full human flourishing, and protecting the rights of weaker people who may face opposition as they try to escape situations of dependence and poverty—are also central elements of a just and peaceful order. The absence of peace and justice undermines development and sustainability, and vice versa; justice and peace tend to foster development and sustainability and vice versa; and both areas are inherently linked concepts, even apart from their many causal connections. Together, then, the words "just and sustainable development" highlight the several crucial pillars of ethically faithful social conservation and change: preserving nature and helping the needy—in relationship and community—to preserve their rights and attain a fruitful life.

THE RECORD OF DEVELOPMENT

Broad goals of sustainable development have, in principle, been widely embraced by many individuals, nongovernmental organizations (NGOs), and governments. They were embraced, for instance, in the *Agenda 21* report of the United Nations Conference on Environment and Development, produced and accepted by a large gathering of countries and NGOs.[8] Sustainability understood in "green" terms can also be important because resource scarcity, ecological deterioration, and relative deprivation might contribute to violent conflict. Positively, peace embraces as well as depends on a wholesome and ecologically aware economic order that allows human flourishing and good working relationships.

How is sustainable development related to peace? Where do issues of justice come in? What can be learned from recent efforts to take the preservation of natural resources seriously? What can be learned from efforts at development? How can peacemakers be most effective?

In understanding the implications of sustainable economic development, it may help to distinguish two levels. "Microdevelopment" refers to efforts made by local people on their own behalf and that of their communities, and also to nongovernmental agencies and governments targeting small-scale efforts and the poor. "Macrodevelopment" refers to efforts by governments and international agencies to increase production or decrease poverty by broad national policies and projects. Such efforts often seek to increase a country's overall production of goods and services by linking to the system of global trade. But the global system is mostly fashioned by states and international businesses, which create the economic opportunities and barriers weaker actors face. Thus, these two levels are intertwined, and the interlinkages are important.

Microdevelopment

At the micro level, the most successful development assistance taking place locally in communities has been carried out by NGOs.[9] The successful and sustainable projects are those that respond directly to the material needs identified or "felt" by the people.[10] These projects can "listen" to people, incorporating indigenous knowledge about the environment instead of assuming that the outside experts can devise the solutions unaided. Particularly important for sustainability is forming organized groups in the community that can take charge and assume leadership of projects.[11] This contributes towards "ownership" of the project by the community and also builds up the capacity to increase problem-solving skills by pooling the physical and mental resources of the community in a coordinated way. Development at this level is a slow and painstaking process, requiring a long-term committed relationship with the community in order to encourage change in the multiple areas of income-generating projects, health, agriculture and education. The Grameen Bank in Bangladesh is a well-known example of an agency employing such practices.

Even the best of agencies cannot be assured of success (however that may be defined), and the specter of "unintended consequences" rears its head often here as well. Cooptation of the projects by elites is not the only way things go awry. Often, the political consequences of the change that begins to happen—whether within the community itself or in its relationships with elites outside the community—can bring a quick halt to the process.[12]

Macrodevelopment

Explicit macrodevelopment approaches and policies are the province of the state and international assistance agencies. The history of macrodevelopment strategies since decolonization and independence of the Global South gives at best a mixed picture of the governmental success as a vehicle for development.[13] Some developing nations, notably in East Asia, have grown rapidly by building a dirigiste economy (directed or guided by the central government);

yet most others, especially the countries of Latin America and Africa, have fared poorly.

Differences in degrees of inequality may well be an important factor. In successful East Asian economies, especially Taiwan and South Korea, major land reforms occurred prior to the market opening and state protection of infant industries, and these countries have continued to have among the world's best (least uneven) patterns of income distributions.[14] This somewhat reduced the coercive and economic power of the local elites and gave the majority of the population access to productive resources, creating a thriving domestic market for goods produced by the national industries.

There are both theoretical and historical reasons to suppose that greater equality may promote human development and welfare, human rights and democracy. For instance, one may argue historically that Thomas Jefferson's aim and accomplishment (wrongfully achieved, to be sure, because at the expense of the Indians) of making citizens small farmers was an effective "land reform" for citizens which led to a historically high wage share, many small propertyholders, economic growth, and more-effective citizen democracy. Similar, the U.S.-mandated reforms in Japan after World War II may have contributed to the success of that country as markets took off. Generally, historical evidence suggests that the formal conditions of markets and elections are difficult to institute and probably less important to vital and free development than widespread citizen participation in the economy, society, and politics. As a matter of theory, if one assumes capital (including control of economic processes) is most efficient when mixed relatively equally with labor, then there is every reason to suppose that a relatively equal distribution of resources, as of political power, will utilize those resources most efficiently. Furthermore, insofar as a main mechanism of efficiency in markets and of good government is accountability, a wider distribution of economic and political assets works to balance power and thus to hold wielders of economic and political resources more accountable. Principles of provision for the poor, relationship, nonmaximization, land lying fallow, and preserving family and historic preservation of assets with relatively equal distribution may be found in the biblical Jubilee legislation (Lev. 25). In the Jubilee (fiftieth) Year, slaves were to be freed, land was lie fallow so it could be renewed, and property that had been sold returned to the original owner, so that the poor would not lose ownership permanently.

In Latin America, by contrast, land reforms occurred in name only. Land tenure was very—perhaps increasingly—skewed, and most people had resources barely sufficient for living. Therefore, no strong internal market developed. Control over land often let power-brokers dominate state programs aimed at modernizing agriculture. They consolidated their excessive power, including illegal land acquisitions that poorer people were unable to resist or protest effectively. In Africa, state power and bureaucracies were often used to extract resources from poorer and weaker groups (as also occurred in Eastern Europe and the Soviet Union). Rapid "privatization" can risk further consolidating these "kleptocratic" takings as the powerful take state holdings as their personal property without paying fair amounts.

The questionable history of macrodevelopment strategy also includes a variety of unpleasant consequences resulting from actions of international assistance agencies. The World Bank—arguably the most important and powerful development institution of the past few decades—has an extensive track record of financing large capital projects that have proven environmentally destructive, socially irresponsible, and economically unproductive.[15]

Finally, the open global trading system mostly rewards those wielding the greatest economic resources and power. This is true within countries as well as among countries. Over time, many Southern nations have developed crippling levels of foreign debt—a legacy of borrowing by previous governments for unproductive development projects, corruption, and precipitous drops in the prices of primary commodities, their main exports. The interest and principle payments on the debt drastically curtail the government funds available for social goods such as education, health, environment, and infrastructure. As a result, poorer countries have to depend on international finance and development agencies like the IMF and the World Bank to keep their economies afloat. Moreover, it means that the South must toe the line of the development strategies and focuses of the international finance agencies, leaving these states with very little opportunity to devise and implement their own development strategies. They are required by the banks to open up their economies to foreign investment and capital, doing away with tariffs and other protectionist measures, curtailing their public sectors and expenditure, reducing government involvement in the economy, and promoting agricultural exports—all measures that go under the name of "structural adjustment" or "neo-liberal programs." This strategy is designed to take advantage of the cheap labor of the South. Yet this "comparative advantage" is a meaningless one for long-term development in the global economy.

While the transnational companies that have set up assembly industries in the South have provided thousands of sorely needed jobs, it is not at all apparent that they will provide a solid and sustainable industrial base for the future. A reliance on cheap labor means few if any incentives to develop domestic industries that might eventually compete internationally, reinvest many of their profits, and produce sorely needed foreign exchange to take care of debt payments. It reduces the priority of developing a highly educated population, including scientists and engineers, crucial to developing domestic industries.[16]

In sum, the claims of "injustice" in the global economic system from the South revolve in large measure around the structure of debt that requires the South to transfer immense amounts of money each year to the North, forces it to open its economies to Northern companies, and relegates it to being a source of cheap labor, limiting the development of its own industrial base while allowing consumers in the North to enjoy cheap prices for their goods.

There are strong indications that link this neoliberal model to an increase in poverty and polarization of income in Latin America, although there are variations among countries.[17] Each country has distinctive sets of circumstances and implements technical models in different ways. Therefore, given past experience, one should expect a variety of results. Macrodevelopment rarely works out in the way one expects.

What is most troublesome about all macrodevelopment approaches is the fact that the poor are rarely seen as productive agents, while the wealthy are treated as the privileged catalysts to economic growth. Returning to the cases of Taiwan and South Korea, the single most important common factor in their success was the land reforms that gave the poor access to resources and educational opportunities. This provided a solid base for the internal economy. Yet even in those cases, there were unexpected consequences. In both countries, rapid industrialization has led to serious problems of environmental destruction and pollution.

Conflict and the Environment

To highlight some of the most recent thinking on these problems, consider more carefully possible links between environment and resource issues and conflict.[18] First, resource scarcities might provoke war. Presumably, states might be short of resources because of their pursuit of unsustainable economic practices. Even realists in international relations concede that states might use violence to assure access to vital raw materials. The Persian Gulf war, for example, was in large part a result of overarching conflicts about the control of oil. Additionally, the 1967 Middle East war was at least partially motivated by concerns over water resources, and water remains one of the most potentially conflictive problems in that area.[19]

Other sources of conflict come from a combination of local politics and power structures, ethnic diversity, population growth, and environmental distress. Wealthy landowners and skewed land tenure, along with a high population growth rate, have pushed peasants to the ecologically fragile and unproductive slopes of hills and mountains. This has led to insurgencies in many places including the Philippines and Mexico and to ethnic conflict in countries like India, where millions of neighboring Bengali poor have fled to the state of Assam, triggering serious intergroup conflict. However, Homer-Dixon's wide review of the empirical data finds absolute scarcity the least significant cause of environment/resource conflicts.[20]

A second cause of conflict comes from a combination of local politics and power structures, ethnic diversity, population growth, and environmental distress. For instance, poverty and social turmoil in Bangladesh, related to high population growth, flooding, and land scarcity, have led millions of people to flee to neighboring India, "trigger[ing] serious intergroup conflict" in the state of Assam.

Third, people impoverished by environmental calamities may become increasingly exasperated by their plight, leading to "deprivation conflicts," which result from the gap between actual and expected living conditions. This pattern may underlie recent insurgencies in devastated rural uplands in the Philippines and in Mexico. As wealthy landowners turned to cash crops requiring fewer workers, for instance, Filipino agricultural laborers and farmers were forced to less-productive uplands or to urban shantytowns, resulting in a cycle of low food production, clearing of new lands (often by burning forested areas), and further land degradation.

Some problems display multiple conflict elements. A look at water resources in the Middle East suggests why former U.N. Secretary General Boutros-Ghali, serving earlier as an Egyptian minister of state, predicted that "the next war in the Middle East will be fought over water, not politics," and why Anwar Sadat said in 1979 that "the only matter that could take Egypt to war again is water." For instance, Ethiopia and neighboring central African states have announced plans to divert Nile waters for development. But, according to Robert Engelman, director of the population and environment program at Population Action International, "there is ... not enough water in the Nile basin for all these countries to develop the way they want."[21] Egypt, a downstream nation almost totally dependent on the Nile, could suffer serious water shortages as a consequence and has threatened to respond to such acts with violence. Similarly, Turkey has planned hydroelectric projects that would reduce the Euphrates River's downstream flow to Iraq, and by one-third or more to Syria, which has a rapidly growing population (3.5 percent annually) and few alternative supply options. Intermittent talks about water rights over the past thirty years have not produced any lasting agreements (although there are a few limited bilateral agreements among the three nations). Thus, unsustainable and conflicting development plans may wreak havoc or even provoke violent conflict, perhaps exacerbated by conflict over the status of Kurds along joint borders.

119

Similarly, the Jordan River is shared by Jordan, Syria, Israel, Lebanon, and the West Bank, all of which have vital needs for its water.[22] Jordan's rapidly growing population (3.5 percent per year) will have fully used all known water sources by 2015. Israel's steadily growing population (1.7 percent annually) has exceeded its sustainable annual water yield since the mid-1970s. Water tables are dropping in the West Bank, where one-third of Israel's water originates, and Palestinians have been allocated far less water than Israeli citizens.

Many fear that one or more of these disputes over water could lead to internal conflict or war. Yet these experiences from the Middle East are not unique: All over the world, environment and resource disputes hold the potential for igniting violent conflict.

DEVELOPMENT LESSONS AND PRINCIPLES

Based on historical experience with development and on ethical teaching, this section sets out some essential principles for attempts at peacemaking in the area of sustainable development:

- The focus of development is the needs, dignity, and productivity of the poor.
- Efforts to assist development must be based on lasting relationships with poor communities.
- A relational approach also leads us to the national and international political side of development.
- Development must be sustainable, in being directed toward holistic, environmentally sound, balanced development.
- It must also be sustainable in giving the people and nations being helped effective control and ownership.
- Development efforts must take into account human fallibility: ignorance, lack of complete control, desire for power and wealth, and abuse.

120

The Poor

The focus of development on social and economic relationships emphasizes the importance of making provision for the weak, the defenseless, the needy, the poor. This challenge is to institutionalize access to immediate provisions, resources for long-term productivity, and just institutions that defend against possible oppression. We must see poorer people not as the hapless recipients of our generous concern or pity but as fully human, dignified, responsible persons, with much to contribute. Development efforts should focus on the dignity, insight, and energy of poorer people and the value of bringing these assets to common tasks of development rather than assuming any kind of superiority. At the same time, assisting the poor with immediate help and longer-term, institutionalized access to resources is the priority in development. Much experience and development thinking suggest that this is a practical, effective, long-term approach to development and growth as well as an approach that is most just.

Recognizing the worth, intrinsic value, and contributions of poorer people—quite apart from any (also important) questions of their rights and needs or of our obligations—is an important place to start in development. People know a great deal about their own lives and what is appropriate to their specific context, and their values and practices—whether rooted in universal principles or chosen customs—have much to teach us. They have a right to their choices and ways, and often these are wiser than plans imposed by others. Subsidiarity—leaving people to do as much as possible for themselves—is also in itself a part of their development of self and of skills and of their dignity.

With specific regard to economic activities, in general poor people are often highly productive when given the resources to be so. John Farrington and Anthony Bebbington note that in several countries in Latin America the peasants produce up to 60 percent of the food consumed nationally with very limited resources. Joe Remenyi and Bill Taylor, in a study of creditworthiness of the poor in developing countries, show how the poor have astoundingly high repayment rates and use the credit productively.[23]

Some writers on development suggest that "cultural" factors make the poor generally unproductive or even focus on how bad habits—laziness, improvidence, drunkenness, ignorance—can impede development, casting some of the poor as the sole authors of their own troubles.[24] Yet the evidence tends to show the reverse: the ability and eagerness of most poor people to be very creative in finding and utilizing good opportunities. Indeed, simply to survive, most poor people must be strongly entrepreneurial, as much research has shown.[25] This is not, however, to say that the poor do not need or want to learn from others, even as others need to learn from them.[26]

Poorer people do, however, need significant transfers of material resources, in the context of thoughtful community relationship. Globally, foreign-assistance levels do not approach the stated goals for most affluent nations (0.7 percent of GNP for members of the Development Assistance Committee) and should be substantially increased, with most assistance channeled to projects involving the poor directly.

Relationships

Human beings are not isolated individuals. Facilitating and transforming relationships is at the heart of sustainable development.

First, development requires attention not only to many basic material needs but also to how poor people can identify, manipulate, and create resources—including political, social, and cultural resources—in new ways. Forming long-lasting associations and organizations with particular development projects and efforts has often proved to be of utmost value toward this end. Second, development work is likely to be more effective and helpful where there is an attempt to foster community responsibility for, and ownership of, development projects. (Many times, in fact, one of the most difficult challenges faced in development efforts is to get a large number of people from the community involved.) Development is not just a matter of individuals prospering, but of a community working together. Material improvements depend upon human skills and cooperation; and just, balanced, sustained local cooperation requires attention to and support from the communities in which it takes place.

Finally, development work is unlikely to be helpful, and may do real harm, unless efforts to help poor people and communities are based on a sustained relationship with them. Before one can offer effective assistance, one must learn about people, listen, know their situation, and develop relationships of trust. This approach is well suited to the resources of the NGO community, including churches, with their local networks and affiliations, and possibilities of relationships between individuals and organizations from rich and poor areas, in which each can learn from the other. Of course, governments play an important role in creating and maintaining the political and social opportunities in which NGOs can act.

Political Environment

Sustainable development requires a political and legal environment that will protect the rights of the poor to carry out their process of development. Rule and authority are properly part of human society; however, in a badly distorted world, they are of further importance since without just rule and institutions there will be bad, abusive rule. It is difficult to specify the role of the state in setting the economic environment, because experience has shown that while at times state planning and intervention in the economy have been disastrous, at other times they have yielded impressive results. What can be said with confidence is that the state should ensure that poor people have access to sufficient resources, such as land, technical assistance, credit, health, and education to give these people an opportunity to be productive and, above all, that the rights of the poor—including their property rights—are protected against the more powerful.[27]

Creating such a political environment includes working toward an international economic structure that will enable poor nations to seek paths of development that have their own welfare as a priority. One example is the debt problem. Debt has relegated many of the poor countries to a situation analogous to the odious debt peonage suffered by some of their own poor citizens. This situation can force countries to adopt development models favored by international capital, international banks, and the wealthy nations. A country's decision to follow a particular development model—while undoubtedly a complex one—remains better subject to that country's control; this requires that international debt problems be solved in such a way that the countries feel free to adopt, modify, or reject development models presented to them.

Sustainability

Permanence and sustainability are core moral values as well as vitally practical requisites of successful development efforts. Often, in the past, hasty consumption of resources, creation of hazards, degradation of land, and the like have led to long-term losses rather than gains; care must be exercised to see that the creation is preserved and that development can be maintained long-term. To tend and dress the garden, to care for the earth and its many creatures, species, habitats, and wonders, is part of the human mandate, a duty, and a part of what makes life interesting, beautiful, and worthwhile.

To be lasting and peace-sustaining, development must also be sustainable in the sense of giving access to resources to ordinary local people able and committed to keeping the processes going. Projects that are not locally supported are likely to decay and not be maintained, even if they were not initially ill-conceived. Thus, giving people ownership of their communities and processes of development and the skills to further those processes is an essential part of sustainable development.

Local responsibility and ownership are also logically related to environmental sustainability. Where development consists of projects not rooted in local communities, those undertaking development have little incentive to make sure that social and physical environments are protected in the long-term. Alternatively, people who live in a community have a great interest in preserving their surroundings, especially its resources and natural beauty.

The question of sustainability also raises a set of ethical issues: Development, realistically understood, needs to be seen as a social, spiritual, and political issue, and not just an issue of material productivity. One reason for this is that the infinite multiplication of physical consumption is not a realistic possibility: In a world of limited resources and expanded population, part of sustainability is learning to make a good life and an improved life without ever-growing resource consumption. Moreover, the possibility of effectively maintaining development efforts rests upon community and local involvement, civil society, and opportunities in the international arena, and thus upon healthy political and social development and relationships. The ability of poorer people to prosper, to lead good lives, depends upon cultivating right skills and attitudes in people at all levels. Thus, issues of simple living, such as learning to do more with less, are part of the worldwide efforts needed for sustainable development. In addition, sustainable development requires a holistic understanding of the social and political processes that bear upon people's lives; for often poverty and environmental degradation are results of unjust power structures, or arrogant quick fixes.

Human Fallibility and Sin

Two related points should be noted here. First, development needs to be seen with full awareness of political and economic structures and their potential for violence and oppression. Poverty is often an outcome of subjugation. People who are poor are easy targets for abuse by economically powerful persons and institutions, especially where there are not strong traditions of government and law. In a rapidly changing economy, powerful domestic or foreign interests may seek to expropriate the property of small cultivators or to capture and abuse government power for their own purposes. This is often particularly easy since traditional property rights of poorer parties may not be well documented. Governments and public officials can also take advantage of their positions of power, at the expense of weaker parties. The weakest and most vulnerable are the least able to resist. Again, traditional societies may keep women or other poor people dependent by charging exorbitant rates of interest and discouraging or prohibiting access to capital or property. Unfettered markets may, perhaps inadvertently at times, lead to similar results. As poor people start to acquire more resources, this itself may be seen as a threat by powerholders, who may respond by disrupting and repressing community building and development. Thus sustainable development often requires defense of the rights of the poor—both human rights and economic and property rights—and is thus often inseparable from legal and political development and other elements of just peacemaking.

Second, even under the best of circumstances and without any wrongdoing, the ability to forecast the future is quite limited. This is especially true of large-scale development plans. Development plans have often failed and done harm, despite overall good intentions, through planners' overconfidence in their ability to engineer large social changes and projects or even some permanent state of growth and utopia. Peacemakers must remain humble, aware of their limits and ignorance, and not suppose that they are capable of completely controlling the future of projects. Thus, macrodevelopment strategies are not simply prescribed. It is easy to be mistaken about their conception and their implementation, even for technical experts; and an emphasis on grand plans often ignores the needs of poor people.

Our ignorance accompanies our lack of control over the process of sustainable development. This point, supported by past experience, is also an acknowledgment that human beings are not omnipotent. In efforts to bring about material or spiritual change, an attitude that claims certain and superior knowledge is both mistaken and counterproductive. In sustainable development activities, the strategies by which social change is sought must acknowledge the relative contributions of various local, national, and foreign actors. They must begin with a humble acknowledgment that knowledge and capability do not lie with any particular actor. Much-lauded development experts, pundits, and aspiring prophetic voices have frequently given unwise prescriptions that ended in disaster. Wise development requires robust respect for the lack of control anyone has over the results of social engineering. A closely related principle is the full valuation of all people involved and of the relationships among them.

STRATEGIES OF SUSTAINABLE DEVELOPMENT

The poor have, for the most part, received only the crumbs from development projects, which are often aimed at large infrastructure or economic reforms. Affluent people are often able to capture many development resources intended for the poor. Yet poorer people are not helpless; they are resilient, resourceful, and worthy of great respect. They are great, productive "engines of development" when given access to resources. Thus, advocacy of sustainable development should emphasize both the moral need to place the poor first and also the great losses society incurs when a lack of access to resources keeps poor people from their productive potential. Peacemakers must make the poor a focus of their efforts, entering into community in an attempt to help them.

What are tangible ways in which this can be done? First, agencies that carry out development by working directly with the poor should be supported. These should be agencies that establish long-term relationships with the poor, acknowledging that development is an extended process, while at the same time being aware of the dangers of creating dependency. In addition, the development work they carry out should be a holistic work, focusing on the community's many areas of need, and not just a "specialized" approach of engaging in one particular type of enterprise, such as well-drilling, which ends the relationship upon the project's conclusion. A commitment to a community requires spending a lot of time getting to know it and working with it in all aspects. (This is not to say that agencies that engage in mostly specialized projects are bad. Rather, it is to point out that those agencies that have a holistic approach are almost forced to establish a stronger bond with the community.) Peacemakers should support agencies that have an obvious respect for the poor and have established structural channels for the opinions of the poor to be incorporated into the planning, management, and execution of the projects. In addition, these should be agencies that place the responsibility for planning, direction, and implementation of development approaches in the hands of nationals. Among other things, this contributes toward building the capacity of the developing nations to manage their own development.

Second, peacemakers need to support the creation of community ties with the poor, the establishment of relationships that will allow them to learn more about peoples living in the developing world and ways of supporting them, even as the latter learn more about the peacemakers. This can be done in a variety of ways. Many agencies are already engaged in small efforts at "development education," sharing information with their donors about the people with whom they work.[28] Perhaps even more important is the promotion of trips and visits by donors to specific communities in the Global South. Visits by as many people as possible to the developing world and to communities of the poor are crucial for creating opportunities to learn from one another and for keeping alive the concern for others which is so valuable. Agencies should be doing more to promote these kinds of visits, incorporating work opportunities for the visitors in the projects themselves. One way to institutionalize this is to create official links among churches, NGOs, and/or local communities in the North and South.[29]

Third, peacemakers should support networks of agencies that work toward protecting the legal rights of the poor. This creates a political environment that will allow poor people to participate fully in development. International networks of agencies plugged into NGOs working alongside the poor have been active for many years in bringing pressure on governments to enforce respect for the property rights of the poor and for their right to organize into groups to change their situation. They, along with some of the Northern governments, have also been working to press for the creation of independent judicial systems, to eliminate the favoritism shown to those who have more resources and can either bend or break the rules with impunity. It is also important to create or support organizations in the North that can monitor the situation in the various developing countries through contact with partners working directly with the poor. Such organizations can lobby the Northern governments to lend their weight to policies that will protect the poor and let the poor have access to resources that will secure their autonomy and rights.

Fourth, helping the world's neediest people will likely require substantially increased transfer of material and natural resources. The poor's needs are not currently being met, as evinced by morbidity and mortality statistics, and their desperation contributes to the exhaustion of natural resources and the degradation of the global environment. Wealthy states should increase their foreign-assistance programs and work to transform bilateral and multilateral development institutions into agencies that:

- Are relatively autonomous and apolitical.

- Target the poor directly.

- Have multiyear budget appropriations to reduce the pressure to move money and treat development as a rapid process.

- Adopt a program methodology that incorporates the poor and NGOs at each stage into the decision-making processes on projects in which they are involved.[30]

Fifth, sustainable development requires ecologically sensitive practices by individuals, organizations, businesses, governments, and international aid institutions. It should encourage the economic, social, political, and cultural conditions necessary to carry these out. Rather than clear-cutting or burning tropical forests, people and companies should harvest primarily renewable products from the trees, including natural wax, resins, dyes, rattan, and even medicines. For citizens of the North, these practices can be extended to consumers. Individuals and private organizations can largely determine the demand for goods produced by sustainable or unsustainable means. Consumers might choose to purchase only paper products made with recycled materials. They could prefer rattan baskets to plastic containers, natural to chemical dyes, and solar water heaters to more-conventional ones. Surveys have found that individuals are willing to pay a bit more for "green" products.

Instead of taking as many fish from a coastal area as possible and thereby threatening the future of the stock, individuals (and perhaps states or international organizations) should manage the total catch to assure long-term supply. In the case of both forest logging areas and coastal fishing zones, securing and maintaining indigenous ownership rights might be an important prerequisite to embracing sustainable practices.

Governments, of course, can do a great deal to encourage sustainable development practices. First, rather than finance and build large capital-intensive projects like hydroelectric dams or coal-fired plants that flood valuable forest areas or pollute the air, leaders should develop a greater number of small, nonpolluting energy-generating facilities for communities in the developing world. Impoverished and rich states alike should stop rewarding unsustainable activity.

"Full-cost pricing" would be one mechanism. Rather than leasing water, land, timber, or mineral rights for arbitrarily low rates, assessments should reflect the ecological harm done by lessees like energy firms, farmers, ranchers, loggers, or miners. At minimum, states should charge market rates.

Governments are also consumers of many products (energy, paper, water, etc.). Regulations could mandate purchases from companies or states that utilize renewable resources, sustainable practices, or recyclable materials.

Finally, governments and their international institutions should set regulations when necessary to limit harm to the environment. The Convention on International Trade of Endangered Species in Fauna and Flora (CITES) and the Montreal Protocol ozone accord are good examples of interstate regulatory practices that seem to be working toward desired ends.

Interstate agreements are also proving indispensable in the Middle East water contexts discussed above. For example, Sudan and Egypt signed the Nile Waters Agreement in 1959, which resolved many potential disputes between these two neighboring states. Basically, the parties agreed to allocate fixed quantities of water, thereby creating a framework for sustainable development. Unfortunately, no other states in the region, including Ethiopia, are party to the agreement. Consequently, the treaty does not provide for a fixed allocation of Nile waters to these other states. However, there is hope for sustainable development via an extension of the Nile Agreement. Representatives from ten Nile Basin states have met annually since 1993 to try to monitor and share the river's resources.

Additionally, the recently agreed-to peace treaty between Israel and Jordan addresses some of their mutual water concerns. Under the agreement, a pipeline has been constructed that transports water from Israel to Jordan. Furthermore, Jordan is receiving external assistance to build a dam on the Yarmouk River, a tributary of the Jordan, which will limit water to Israel, and a storage facility on the

129

Yarmouk/Jordan confluence.[31] These measures could be interpreted as cooperative practices for sustainable development. Almost certainly, water rights will need to be addressed in any comprehensive political settlement involving the West Bank.

CONCLUSIONS

Advocating just and sustainable development means recommending a change in relationships that will bring about new opportunities for the poor. A peacemaker works alongside the poor, establishing direct relationships with them, advocating an increased access to resources that will allow them to flourish, and working with them to protect their property and human rights from control by the powers that would keep them in their present trap.[32] The weight of the literature and development experience shows that not only are the majority of the poor extremely creative and entrepreneurial in eking out a living from the few resources to which they have access, but also that giving them access to resources, information, and opportunities yields impressive results.[33]

love and community

7

WORK WITH EMERGING COOPERATIVE FORCES IN THE INTERNATIONAL SYSTEM

Paul W. Schroeder

This chapter aims to correct certain widely held ideas about the international system and its connection with wars and international conflict. It has less to say than other essays in this book about concrete actions to take and particular strategies and tactics to follow in peacemaking. Yet like the other chapters, it seeks to promote a perspective so that just peacemaking can extend to the widest areas.

Not that every prevalent impression is incorrect. For example, the roots of international conflict do indeed lie deep in the very nature of international politics and therefore cannot be wished away or abolished by adopting certain rules or persuading states and peoples to be nicer to one another. In contrast, the common notion is wrong that the international system itself is the problem. I will argue that since the seventeenth century the international system (that is, the system of rules and practices governing relations between states) has represented a series of attempts at solving or at least managing an inherently insoluble problem, that of unavoidable clashes between independent states over claims, rights, and goals. While these systems have seldom met the problem of recurrent wars durably and satisfactorily and have sometimes broken down completely or made the problem worse, overall they certainly have produced more peace and less war than would have occurred without them.

The most important thing to understand about the international system is that its basic rules, institutions, and procedures do not, as some believe, stay the same forever; rather, they develop, grow, and change like other social institutions. This growth and change are unprecedentedly rapid and widespread at the present time. Fundamental changes in society and dramatic developments in international politics have combined to make the old, perennial, and apparently insoluble problem of preserving general international peace at least manageable, if not soluble.

This insight should translate into action: On one hand, peacemakers can recognize and understand the major institutions, forces, and trends working internationally toward peace as resources to encourage, support, and use. On the other hand, if would-be just peacemakers do the opposite—treat the system and its institutions not as a resource to be used and reformed but an evil to be fought or overthrown—then however well-intentioned their activities may be, they are likely to do more harm than good. The message could be put in the words, "Be wise as serpents and harmless as doves" (Matt. 10:16b). For purposes of just peacemaking in the international arena, one needs to be wise as a serpent—that is, aware of the nature of the current international system, cognizant of its possibilities for good and harm, ready to sustain it where it is vital and valuable for peace, ready to try to reform and develop it where it is inadequate or corrupt and to oppose it where it is actively evil or dangerous. Only by being wise as a serpent in this way can one be harmless as a dove—that is, engage the system for good ends without harming it, others, or ourselves.

I cannot make this case in a scholarly fashion here as I would like, but will only offer a series of propositions as guidelines for thinking about international politics in terms of just peacemaking.

1. The current international system (meaning the overall pattern of relations between international actors, mainly independent states) should not be thought of either simply as a competitive struggle for advantage based on relations of power, or as a set of relations that can and should be governed by mutual obligation, fixed norms, contract, and law. The best way to think about the system as it has evolved over centuries is to see it as an anarchic society.[1] That is, it is anarchic not in the sense of being totally chaotic or without rules but in the sense of having no recognized lawgiver or law-enforcing authority. At the same time, it is a society in the sense of having many

members who are in permanent, inescapable contact with one another, who normally recognize and deal with one another as legitimate members of the group, who engage in mutually necessary and potentially beneficial transactions, and who need rules by which to regulate and carry on these transactions.

2. This concept of the international system as an anarchic society defines what a just peace means in international relations: the best practical system of rules, norms, practices, and institutions for reducing the anarchic (conflictual, violent, destructive) elements and promoting the societal (legal, cooperative, and normative) aspects of this anarchic society, while recognizing that for profound reasons it will remain an anarchic society for the foreseeable future (in my view, for any conceivable or desirable one). Just peacemaking does not require one to be a realist in some senses of that much-abused term (e.g., to believe that international politics reduces to power politics, that there must always be great wars, that war is rooted in human nature, or the like). It does require realism in the sense of acknowledging the nature and limits of the system.

3. The root cause of destructive competition and conflict in international affairs is not simply that the various actors are competing over scarce goods (scarce in the sense of being limited, not infinite, so that one can always desire more at someone else's expense). Undoubtedly, competition over such scarce goods as territory, natural resources, wealth, trade routes, strategic positions, and the like has been a prominent cause of war and still is. More fundamental still, however, is an inherent tension within the goals to which individual governments aspire—the fact that the very aims they pursue in the international system are in a sense self-contradictory. All governments and organized societies basically need three things to survive and prosper: order (rule of law, sanctity of contract, predictability of obligations and performances, and so forth), welfare (enough material and psychic well-being among the inhabitants to sustain domestic peace), and legitimacy (a broad acceptance of governmental authority as legitimate, so that domestic law and order can be sustained with a minimum of overt force). Governments pursue these goals of domestic order, welfare, and legitimacy also, inevitably and necessarily, in international politics.[2] That is, they defend and advance their interests with regard to their borders, territory, citizens' rights, trade, governmental authority, and intangibles like their

political systems, religious and cultural values, and ethnic and national honor. This frequently breeds international conflict not only because it involves scarce resources and competing claims and rights, but above all because in simultaneously pursuing these three goods in the international arena, governments and peoples are demanding two contradictory things at once: order and freedom. All governments (and governments are still the dominant actors in international affairs) want to enjoy order (sanctity of contract, performance of obligations, respect for their rights and status, and the like). But they want order without sacrificing freedom—that is, independence and sovereignty, being their own source of law and authority for themselves. The deepest root of conflict in international affairs is therefore the tension and contradiction between two equally vital goals, order and freedom, within this anarchic society.

4. The contradiction has a further dimension: the free-rider problem. Most international relations theory and practice rests on rational choice theory—basically, that governments make rational choices on the basis of cost-versus-benefits utility analysis (e.g., they decide whether to make war or how to respond to a neighbor's challenge on the basis of a calculation as to the likely costs and benefits of various responses). Scholars of course debate whether governments really do act in this manner and recognize also that, even if they do, such supposedly "rational" calculation provides plenty of room and occasion for miscalculations, misperceptions, and faulty strategies, leading to conflicts and destructive consequences. Beyond these, however, there is a deeper problem with "rational choice" as the model for state action in international affairs. It involves a concealed contradiction between the "good" of the individual state or unit and the "good" of the system as a whole. Like every other society, international society, to survive and function, requires certain public goods—that is, goods that all members need and enjoy but whose costs cannot be easily imposed on individual consumers or apportioned among them. Everyone benefits in international society from general peace, freedom for trade, freedom of the seas, free exchange of information, and the like. Yet these goods all have costs attached, sometimes high ones. Who is to pay? More important still, a rational method of payment in terms of the whole system (that every member pay its fair share for these collective goods by individual restraint and performances) clashes with the most rational

choice for each individual member (to make others obey the rules and pay the costs while one's own state breaks the rules and gets the benefits free). Here lies the classic clash between rational individual state morality (raison d'etat) and rational international morality.

To this point, the analysis seems wholly pessimistic. It apparently suggests what many idealists, reformers, and peacemakers historically have believed—that controlling or eliminating the root causes of international conflict and war requires radically changing or eliminating the whole system, perhaps through world government or international law enforced by some supranational authority. I will not attempt to explain here why this supposed way out seems to me futile and desperate, a Utopian or rather Dystopian dream, promising far worse conflict, tyranny, and war than the present system. Instead, in what follows I want to argue that the problems and contradictions within the anarchic society of international relations, though real and ineradicable, are not fundamentally insoluble or unmanageable—at least not any longer. Rather, the current system contains trends, developments, and institutions that potentially can enable governments and societies to pursue their basic goals (order, welfare, and legitimacy) in the international arena without causing general systemic conflict, thereby managing and partially transcending the contradiction between order and freedom. Moreover, I will try to persuade readers that in conceiving the task of just peacemaking as one of encouraging and promoting these positive trends and institutions, we make it both a practical way of dealing with the realities of international politics and, at the same time, a fully justifiable one morally and ethically. This is a tall order; I can try to fill it only with some more briefly stated propositions.

5. While the anarchic society with its inherent contradictions accounts at the deepest level for international conflict and war, it also accounts for international cooperation and peace. The simultaneous, self-contradictory pursuit of order and of freedom never fully succeeds and sometimes spectacularly breaks down in great wars; but it also never totally or finally fails and often succeeds to a remarkable degree. More peace has always prevailed and still prevails in international relations than war—more peace than one should expect, given the multitude of causes and conditions making for war, and far more peace than one could explain without the existence and operation of the international system.

6. International politics furthermore is not static but rapidly changing. Four separate but interrelated trends in international history, marked since the early nineteenth century and increasingly powerful and accelerating in the latter twentieth century, have sharply altered the nature of the international system. These are:

A. The decline of the utility of war, that is, a steep rise in the costs and dangers of major war as a tool of statecraft, and a corresponding decline in the applicability and potential benefits of even a successful use of large-scale military force as a way of solving major problems, securing either order or freedom.

B. The rise of the trading state, that is, the priority now placed by most modern states on success in trade and the economy, as opposed to success in war, as the key to domestic order, welfare, and legitimacy.[3] Where it used to be said that war made the state and the state made war, it is now becoming more true to say that trade makes the successful state and the successful state makes trade or promotes it.

C. A dramatic increase in the volume, density, and speed of international exchanges, communications, and transactions of all kinds and the increasing integration of these exchanges into organized, complex, international, supranational, and transnational networks, corporations, and other institutions. This has now developed to such a degree that the domestic economics, politics, and culture of individual states cannot be isolated from them or do without them. Along with this has gone an equally startling increase in the number, scope, durability, and effectiveness of international organizations of all kinds, both governmental and nongovernmental, to which both modern governments and nongovernmental groups must pay attention and must use for their particular purposes.

D. A gradual, uneven, but unmistakable ascendancy of one form of government, liberal representative democracy, as the dominant legitimate form of governance of modern states and of one kind of economic system, market-oriented capitalism (whether of the welfare-state or a more laissez-faire variety), as the dominant form of modern economic development.

7. These four trends combine not to insure general international peace (nothing can do that) but greatly to enhance the possibilities of just peacemaking within the existing system. Some of the ways they do so are fairly obvious and frequently discussed—for example, the great rise in costs and risks of large-scale war or military coercion and decline of its perceived benefits, together with the greater importance of non-zero-sum commercial competition in comparison to zero-sum military and power-political competition. Mature democracies seem to show less willingness either to fight one another or to resort to force generally. The dramatic rise in international transactions and organizations means far greater interdependence among states and at least potentially greater incentives for cooperation and disincentives for overt conflict. All these arguments, it must be conceded, are disputed by some observers; yet at least these trends represent potential openings for peacemakers to exploit.

8. More important and less obvious, these trends indicate how the central contradictions in international politics (that is, the contradiction between international order and freedom and the tension within rational decision making between "egoistic" raison d'etat morality and "altruistic" international morality) can be, if not eliminated, nonetheless sufficiently transcended or bridged so that, for most practical purposes, they no longer will be decisive. The theoretical answer to both these core problems has long been apparent: the principle of voluntary association. Every great peace plan from the Middle Ages onward, every scheme for so-called collective security from Cardinal Richelieu's to George Bush's, has called in different ways for a voluntary association or league of like-minded "peaceful" states formed to secure for all its members the common benefits of peace and to share among them the costs and burdens of defending the association against aggressors or lawbreakers. It is easy to see, purely in principle and theory, how such voluntary durable leagues for peace could solve the problem of reconciling order and freedom. Since the norms, principles, rules, and sanctions in such associations would all be decided and enforced jointly and the benefits and burdens of the association shared in common, no one's freedom or rights would be sacrificed. Even the problem of imbalances of power and weight within the association and related dangers of hegemony or domination theoretically could be managed. What weaker members would lose in decision-making power and

influence they would gain in concrete protection, security, and guaranteed juridical independence, security, and voice. And since the common, shared goods would also be defined by the whole association and only available within it, the tension within rational decision making between the good of the individual state and that of the whole association would tend to disappear.

It is even easier, however, to see why such schemes and such actual associations in history (the Holy Roman Empire, various leagues of German and Italian states, the Concert of Europe, the League of Nations, the United Nations, among others) have had only partial and temporary success, and often broken down disastrously. Historically, one can list at least six reasons:

1. Not enough carrot in the associations in the form of concrete payoffs to prevent defections or discourage free riders.

2. Not enough stick in the form of force- and cost-effective sanctions against the same.

3. No adequate mechanisms to distribute the costs, burdens, and benefits of the association equitably or to settle quarrels over them.

4. No assurance that in critical circumstances the costs and risks of maintaining the association will not exceed its benefits (e.g., that the association can only be saved by a great war that will destroy some of its members).

5. Insufficient unity in the form of common purposes, beliefs, and goals of members within the association, so that individual aims outweigh the common ones and internal rivalries outweigh common ties.

6. Insufficient adaptability of the association and its goals to changing needs, circumstances, and aims of its members, so that on balance it hinders their pursuits rather than advancing them.

But while it is easy enough to explain why voluntary associations for peace have not worked regularly or well in the past (though they were almost always better than nothing), the point to emphasize here is that these basic obstacles no longer have the same force today. The four trends mentioned earlier have altered the conditions and practices of international relations so much that it is possible now, as it was not possible earlier, to form and sustain voluntary associations for peace and other related useful purposes that avoid or overcome the fatal weaknesses of former ones. That is, they prove to be so beneficial, cost-effective, durable, united, and adaptable that members are dissuaded from defection and outsiders discouraged from aggression, new members are attracted, and new aims and purposes developed to replace obsolete ones and to meet new challenges. This is not just theory; it is happening. The continued existence and success of organizations like NATO, the European Union, the United Nations, and many others go a long way to make it demonstrable fact. To argue that voluntary associations for peace cannot work better today than in the past seems to me a bit like arguing that manned heavier-than-air flight is not possible for the same reasons it was impossible before 1903.

Yet, of course, none of this will happen or has happened automatically. If the system can and does work for good, as I claim, where it does and to the extent that it does it is because people— leaders and followers—make it do so. All these useful societal trends and potentially valuable peacemaking and peacekeeping organizations and developments can readily be corrupted for wrong purposes, defeated or overwhelmed by new challenges, or so stultified and confined that they become useless for meeting the emerging problems of peace today and in the future. This makes just peacemaking into a task for action—a process in which ordinary citizens individually and in groups work to sustain, criticize, goad, influence, reform, and lead the many kinds of voluntary associations—governmental and private—that can contribute to transcending the contradictions and managing and overcoming the conflicts of an anarchic international society. In other words, it means exploiting, encouraging, and strengthening the concrete world trends that enable cooperation to fly: the decline in the utility of war; the priority of trade and the economy over war; the strength of international exchanges, communications, transactions, and networks; and the gradual ascendancy in the world of liberal representative democracy and a mixture of welfare-state and laissez-faire market economy. Citizens, intermediate associations, and governments should act so as to strengthen these trends and the voluntary associations that they make possible.

To make this a bit more practical and down-to earth: In seeking to avert a crisis that could lead to war, as well as in noncrisis actions, governments should seek the counsel and the mediating help of parties that represent these international networks. And in both crisis and long-range actions, they should seek to act in a way that strengthens these networks and associations when they can assist practical problem solving. As the realist Reinhold Niebuhr observed, institutions of international cooperation are not created out of nothing by fiat or wish, but built bit by bit as nations act day by day in ways that strengthen their usefulness.

This method of building peace through durable voluntary international association both between governments and nongovernmental actors is applicable far more widely and effectively today than previously. However, it is, as noted earlier, not new, but it has much historical precedent and evidence in its favor. As I have argued elsewhere, one cannot adequately explain the course of international politics in earlier centuries by a version of realist theory that places all the emphasis on state security, power, and the balance of power within the system. Instead, scholars have to pay attention to transnational forces in the international system, prevailing rules and norms, and the different functions and roles filled by different kinds of states within the system in order to understand the actual historical behavior of states in international relations. For example, the long period of peace under the Concert of Europe (1815–1853) resulted not from a balance of power but from the influence of transnational ideas and forces; agreements carefully worked out among governments on a practical definition and structure of peace; a system of benign hegemonies or spheres of influence mutually agreed upon or shared; a consensus on norms and rules, rights, and the rule of law; and finally, a sense that Europe constituted a community of nations with shared responsibility to preserve the system.[4]

As Aaron Friedberg argues in a recent article, something similar but more profound is developing today. The likelihood of war in Western Europe has been reduced by "the existence of recognized rules of international conduct" and "the evolving character of the economic, institutional, and cultural inter-connections among" European states, where "barriers to the free movement of people, goods, capital, and technology have now been drastically lowered."

European states have become "enmeshed in a dense web of institutions, . . . 'a thick alphabet soup of international agencies.' International institutions help to promote peace by assisting in the resolution of disputes and by easing all forms of mutually beneficial interstate cooperation. . . . Joint participation in international institutions can breed mutual understanding and an important measure of trust." In addition, growing cultural linkages increase mutual understanding and transnational loyalties; "slowly and with some difficulty, that web has begun to extend from Western to Eastern Europe." His argument posits the value of transnational linkages also where they are much less fully developed, including Africa and Latin America, but he concentrates on Asia since economic and military power are growing there with dramatic speed, remarking, "The ties among Asian states are, by comparison, much less fully developed, . . . and the possible obstacles to their growth more readily apparent." It is crucial for world peace, he concludes, that the United States and other nations contribute to strengthening the ties or linkages among nations in order to overcome instabilities that may erupt during the critical next few years as the post–Cold War world takes shape.[5]

Critics, of course, disagree. Many contend that dramatic events since the end of the Cold War—in Somalia, Chechnya, Rwanda and Burundi, the Persian Gulf, the former Yugoslavia, especially Bosnia, and elsewhere—prove clearly that conciliation, persuasion, and the influence of transnational linkages and pressures do not work in cases of real conflict. Power remains the main denominator of international politics, force the main instrument of deterrence and compellence; and an unwillingness to use force where necessary, or the failure to use it wisely and persistently, remains an invitation to failure and defeat. The argument goes beyond the bounds of this essay, and a reply could be better given by a political scientist or contemporary historian than by me, whose expertise lies in the history of international politics from the mid-seventeenth to the mid-twentieth century. Yet one might observe that the argument here is not that nonviolent strategies and tactics (which include coercive devices of various kinds, diplomatic, economic, political, and cultural) always work. To claim this would be absurd. It is only that such strategies and tactics can work far more widely and durably than they used to, or than many think; that where they do not work, often nothing else will work either; and that plenty of evidence from recent peacekeeping and peacebuilding illustrates their value. Not all leaders, governments, and peoples can be convinced through the kind of persuasion and pressure discussed earlier that they must adopt certain rules of conduct if they hope to have a decent future, but some can. This sort of pressure and persuasion, and not just the intervention of American troops, led to the surprising American success in ousting the military leaders in Haiti and restoring President Aristide, for example. Radovan Karadzic and Ratko Mladic in Bosnia are no doubt immune to such influences and considerations; but Franjo Tudjman in Croatia and Slobodan Milosevic in Serbia—both of them authoritarian, nationalistic politicians, are not immune—and their peoples, including their own followers, are even less so. Whatever success the peace process has had to this point in Bosnia and can hope for in the future rests at least as much on these kinds of pressures as on NATO military intervention.

This essay, as noted, can say little about the concrete, particular ways of doing this kind of peacemaking. It will close only with another reminder of the priority of practical consequences and results, and of appraising them in terms of the whole system.

Two quotations seem to me appropriate. In a recent book, William L. Kissick writes, "As a medical student I learned an important lesson: when a patient has a host of pathologies or multi-organ-system disease, selective therapeutic strategies are critical. Any attempt to treat everything at once risks a confluence of physiological and pharmacological side effects that could overwhelm the patient; one has to address specifics and to anticipate consequences. . . . Comprehensive reform, while attractive in theory, is a high-risk venture."[6]

What Dr. Kissick says about critical patient care and the whole health-care system applies also to peacemaking and the whole, complex international system. Precisely because there are so many sources of conflict and war, so many ways for peace to break down or fail to emerge, it is essential to concentrate on doing practical good, such as saving and strengthening the system and solving or managing immediate problems, sometimes even simply limiting the damage and binding up the wounds, rather than seeking a comprehensive solution. We need a kind of Hippocratic oath in peacemaking: First, do no harm.

The second quotation comes from James Goodby, both an excellent scholar and an outstanding diplomatic negotiator for the American government in various capacities, whom I came to know at the United States Institute of Peace in 1993 to 1994. In one seminar, he remarked (I quote him from memory but accurately, I think) that he had often encountered three kinds of persons in negotiations: the "realists," for whom the essence of the question was the clash of interests, the relations of power, and the struggle to win, gain the advantage; the "idealists," for whom the vital question was a matter of principle, the vindication of a claim or the attainment of a just outcome; and finally, the problem solvers, for whom the central concern was to try to understand the problem and figure out what, in practical terms, could be done about it. As Goodby remarked, his sympathies were on the side of the problem solvers. I responded then, and remain convinced now, that history (and real morality) are also, in the long run, on the side of the problem solvers.

8

STRENGTHEN THE UNITED NATIONS AND INTERNATIONAL EFFORTS FOR COOPERATION AND HUMAN RIGHTS

Michael Joseph Smith

For those engaged in constructing a just peace paradigm, the traditional model of self-contained nation-states—sovereign, secure, distinct—will no longer do. Realists and just war casuists alike love to think of the world as made up of states (countries or nations with their governments). But the world has changed too much for this so-called Westphalian model to guide our ethical inquiry. The end of the Cold War, the rise of a genuinely global economy, the increased salience of human-rights norms, and the growing demands for democratic participation have created new opportunities for non-nation-state actors—most prominently the United Nations—to develop policies and practices that can moderate conflicts and enhance respect for human rights. An approach to just peacemaking must encourage these international developments for the pacific settlement of a whole range of conflicts. In the most basic terms, this means support for the United Nations and associated regional international organizations so that, collectively, we can develop the capacity to identify, prevent, and, if necessary, intervene in conflicts within and between states that threaten basic human rights.

THE POST–COLD WAR ENVIRONMENT

What kind of international system do we now live in? Perhaps symptomatic of a major period of change and confusion is the absence of anything approaching consensus on what to call this new international system: unipolar? balance of power? globalist? new world order? We agree only on the term "post–Cold War" and that any historical analogy is deeply flawed at best. Let us examine the new environment from two perspectives: first, a "structural" perspective that emphasizes power and institutions; and, second, a "juridical" perspective that emphasizes changes in prevalent norms.

For historians and political scientists, the traditional place to begin an analysis of the international system is with power: Who has it, and who uses it for what purposes? According to the long-dominant theory of international affairs, realism, the international system is a milieu of states, who, by their very nature, are locked in an unending and always potentially murderous competition. States seek to increase their power, and they try to prevent the rise of rivals or "hegemons" through unilateral moves as well as through balances of power. And for their survival and success, they depend above all on military might and its economic underpinnings. War is always possible, and the restraints of international law and organization can always be swept aside in the name of the "national interest."

On this view, throughout the Cold War, power was concentrated in two "poles," the United States and the Soviet Union—hence the prevalent characterization of the international system as "bipolar." The collapse of the Soviet Union and the end of the Cold War led to a "diffusion of power." But where has power gone? Here, we must make an important distinction between two arenas of simultaneous interaction—the arena of traditional military security and the arena of economic interdependence.[1]

The traditional realm of security remains relevant and potentially quite destructive: States have not dismantled their armies and weapons. But new threats to security come at least as much from internal conflict as from external aggression.

In the modern arena of economic interdependence, state actors remain relevant and important, but the character of their goals is quite different and their capacity to control events is increasingly limited. For one thing, they live in a world economy whose continuing growth is in their common interest. Competition is not "zero-sum": My gains may well require that you make some yourself. Moreover, the stakes of competition clearly differ: physical security and the control of territory in the first arena; market shares, the creation and expansion of wealth in the other. Nor are the necessary ingredients and possible uses of power the same.

In the arena of military-security and strategic-diplomatic interaction, we have moved from bipolarity to a complex and unprecedented situation. Here, the main actors are still the states—though, even in this realm, states find themselves challenged from above and below. During the Cold War period, the security arena proved most recalcitrant to U.N. operations when the superpowers were themselves directly involved. Until 1989, the most powerful interstate institutions were the rival alliances. Now, one of these, the Warsaw Pact, is defunct, and the other, NATO, finds it difficult to define new purposes even as it expands its membership. The United States remains the most important player in terms of global military power, and the United States and Russia still hold the capacity to destroy the planet several times over. But Russia's economic weakness and political turbulence have reduced its ability and will to be a worldwide challenger. The number of other active players has increased and is likely to increase still further: The proliferation of military technologies—nuclear and conventional—makes this possible.

In the new, post–Cold War world, the security worries of states are more likely to be internal and regional than global. Negatively, this means that local tyrants may try to become regional bullies; but positively, it opens a space for international and regional organizations to develop capacities and norms to damp down and even to prevent conflicts. The examples of Rwanda and Bosnia are daunting because they demonstrate the rudimentary and imperfect capacities of such organizations to deal with deep-seated conflicts. And yet they have also pointed up the urgent necessity to develop such capacities.

In the realm of international economic interdependence—a huge subject that defies brief summary—two broad trends bear emphasis. First is the emergence of what Susan Strange has called a new "international business civilization"—a term that suggests a kind of supranational capitalism of banks, large corporations, and enterprises. This international business civilization operates beyond national borders in search of opportunities for investment and profit, and it limits the "operational sovereignty" of nation-states, who no longer can control many of the decisions that most assuredly affect them.[2] More and more of the important decisions about the direction of the global economy are made by private firms or markets, and states are left to react to these decisions.

Second, the rise of this international business civilization has meant effectively a change in the structure of the international system. In this realm, as opposed to the security realm, states jostle with other actors that in many cases have greater power and influence than they do. Nongovernmental actors and institutions make possible transnational coalitions of, say, environmentalists or mining interests. These coalitions in turn seek to influence the policy of their own nation-state. On this model, states are less like hard-boiled eggs than they are like the partial ingredients of a vast and complex global omelet.[3] Thus from a structural vantage point, the post–Cold War international system combines national sovereignty and global interdependence in a quite unprecedented way.

Beyond international structure, an understanding of the contemporary international system requires us to examine the juridical or normative environment. Here again I emphasize two broad trends. The first (rather inchoate) trend is demand from below for what might be called autonomy—in the sense of greater economic security and a greater degree of political participation and accountability. Various analysts have called this trend a demand for democratization, but this strikes me as too specifically political. Perhaps the best way to encapsulate what I am calling autonomy in the sense of security and independence is to invoke Henry Shue's notion of "basic rights." People throughout the world are demanding the rights "without which the enjoyment of any other right is impossible."[4] These are rights of security and subsistence, and the demand for these rights can be witnessed in places as diverse as China, the Philippines, or Haiti. Both nation-states and international institutions such as the International Monetary Fund have had to take note of these demands and to modify policies and practices because of them.

For states, the demand for basic rights has meant a move away from the traditional realist goals of statecraft—territorial conquest and coercive political control. The long-term trends identified by Immanuel Kant in 1795—the increased destructiveness of war and preparations for it, the attractions of "greed" or commerce, combined with the spread of popular participation and "republican" forms of government—seem now to be joining to make traditional war if not obsolete at least highly dysfunctional.[5] This does not mean that peace is spontaneously breaking out all over the world; but it does suggest that the normative legitimacy of war, imperialism, and conquest has markedly declined. Thus, states now increasingly define their goals in terms of creating wealth and welfare in the context of an interdependent global economy. Even the most jingoistic American does not propose to close our trade gap with Japan by declaring war.

This redefinition of the traditional goals of states follows a long-term decline in the legitimacy of colonialism. Here, the effects of World War II were reinforced by the ideological convergence of the United States and the Soviet Union against imperial rule of the nineteenth-century style. Early in its history, the U.N. General Assembly effectively stripped colonial powers from exercising "domestic jurisdiction" over their colonies. The United Nations also declared that apartheid in South Africa and the unilateral declaration of independence by Rhodesia were threats to peace. In this way the U.N. brought about a gradual expansion of legitimate international concern in matters that states had traditionally treated as domestic affairs.

The Holocaust and the atrocities of World War II awakened a vital concern for human rights and resulted in the Universal Declaration on Human Rights and gave rise to the notion—ultimately quite subversive to traditional conceptions of state sovereignty—that egregious human-rights violations could be considered as a legitimate matter for international action.

The growth of international consciousness about the limits of sovereignty and the deficiency of a legal order dedicated primarily to its preservation has accelerated since the end of the Cold War. There is increasing awareness of the dangers that a variety of domestic policies may create for other states, in areas as diverse as the production of weapons of mass destruction, drugs, or the training of terrorists. We also witness a triple evolution of the idea of human rights. In particularly serious cases, the protection of basic human rights can now override the traditional norm of nonintervention (as in the case of sanctions against Iraq and the famine in Somalia). In addition, the protection of minorities—neglected after the failure of the post-Versailles attempts after World War I—is again a major concern. Given the impossibility, in most cases, of producing "ethnically pure" nation-states, protecting minorities is a major focus of international attention. Finally, there is what has been called "the emerging right to democratic governance."[6]

What has this "triple evolution" of human rights meant? More and more, individuals are seen as having not merely a right to a state providing a modicum of law and order, but also a right to a nation-state providing that sense of community and togetherness which is national consciousness, and, finally, a right to democratic government. In practice, of course, there are striking tensions, and even contradictions, among these rights; but together they challenge a traditional conception of state sovereignty that regards forms of government as opaque to international scrutiny. The universal norms of human rights try to make the behavior of states toward their citizens transparent to all the world and subject to criticism and direct action.[7]

If this first set of normative developments—toward the achievement of basic human rights—seems cosmopolitan in its effects, a second trend appears to contradict and work against it. I refer here to demands for national and cultural self-determination, to demands for ethnic particularity in the face of an apparently homogenizing global economy. The human costs of these demands can be devastating—as events in Chechnya, Rwanda, or Bosnia demonstrate. In the wake of the collapse of the Soviet empire, several national minorities have demanded states of their own. We also witness many examples of weak, postcolonial regimes that have failed to establish substantive legitimacy and have never solved issues of ethnic autonomy and meaningful political participation. Profound religious, ethnic, and ideological differences characterize a range of states in Africa and Asia, and when these differences are combined with widespread poverty and predatory rule by self-interested elites, horrendous conflicts can result.

These conflicts present daunting challenges to all who would manage conflict and seek peace. After this sketch of the contemporary international system, let us turn now to the developing and potential international practices that aim at establishing at least the preconditions of a just peace.

COLLECTIVE INTERNATIONAL ACTION FOR HUMAN RIGHTS

Perhaps the first step in considering any international action for humanitarian purposes is to recognize the vital role of the United Nations, both as an actor itself and as an agency to coordinate the efforts of international humanitarian relief agencies. American citizens should urge both the Congress and the president to pay U.S. arrears for past U.N. operations and to pay currently assessed dues. Repeated polls have demonstrated that the American people believe the United Nations to be the most appropriate agency for peacekeeping and, despite some notable U.N.-bashing from American politicians, hold the U.N. in much higher regard than the U.S. Congress.[8]

Citizens should urge their governments to create and support collective mechanisms for the management of conflict and the construction of peace both within and between states. Collective action for purposes of peacekeeping, humanitarian aid, conflict management, and even "peace building" are increasingly necessary as we approach the turning of the centuries than perhaps at any time since World War II. U.S. citizens should press their government to act in small and large crises in ways that strengthen the effectiveness of the United Nations, of regional organizations, and of multilateral peacemaking, peacekeeping, and peace building. Many multilateral practices are building effectiveness to resolve conflicts and to monitor, nurture, and even enforce truces. They are initiating cooperation where violent conflict has occurred or is threatened. And they are organizing to meet human needs for food, hygiene, medicine, education, and economic interaction.

Why emphasize the United Nations? Perhaps most obvious is that, despite some well-publicized failures, it has responded to the human needs presented by conflicts throughout the world. In the period from 1988 to 1994, the U.N. initiated nearly twice as many peacekeeping missions as it had in its entire history until then.[9] The budget for peacekeeping operations rose from $230 million in 1988 to $3.61 billion in 1994. In 1994, seventy-six countries contributed police and military units for seventeen peacekeeping operations that involved some 75,500 persons.

At the same time, it is widely recognized that the capacities of the United Nations are in no way equal to the magnitude of the needs. Without going into great detail, there is a whole range of proposals to improve the ability of the U.N. to identify, seek to prevent, and, if necessary, to move on to intervene in areas where humanitarian disasters are unfolding.

Three kinds of international forces have been identified as necessary:

1. Unarmed or lightly armed peacekeepers deployed after an agreement by all the parties has been reached.

2. Peace-enforcers, whenever there is no genuine consent of all the parties and the operation, or the execution of the agreement reached under international jurisdiction requires the use of force to protect the international contingents from attack and to allow them to carry out their mission.

3. Genuine war-fighting forces under Article 43, "useful . . . in meeting any military force" other than that of a major modern army. Such forces ought to be capable of resorting to air strikes against military targets in a variety of "domestic" cases (genocide, dangerous nuclear build-ups, state terrorism, etc.).

A recent detailed study by Carl Kaysen and George Rathjens, "Peace Operations by the United Nations: The Case for a Volunteer U.N. Military Force," makes specific suggestions along these lines. They conclude that a volunteer force, though "requir[ing] a mobilization of political will in a way that goes against the current tide," could enable the international community to respond quickly in ways that could save human lives, reduce human suffering and facilitate political settlements between contestants. Moreover, "it would also have a broader deterrent effect, which in some cases would make diplomatic intervention alone effective in preventing armed conflict, and give a weight to the resolutions of the Security Council that they now lack."[10]

Perhaps a more basic question for those seeking a just peace is, simply, "When is humanitarian intervention justified?" I would suggest an answer that, in principle, is relatively straightforward. Collective intervention is justified when the condition or behavior of a state results in grave threats to the peace and security of other states and peoples, and in cases of egregious violations of human rights— even if those violations occur entirely within the borders of a given state. A genocide is no less "a common threat to humanity" (the characterization of former U.N. Secretary-General Boutros Boutros-Ghali) if it occurs within borders than if it crosses them.[11] The basic principle that should guide international intervention is this: Individual state sovereignty can be overridden whenever the behavior of the state, even within its own territory, threatens the existence of elementary human rights abroad and whenever the protection of the basic human rights of its own citizens can be assured only from the outside.

153

State sovereignty, in short, is a contingent value: Its observance depends upon the actions of the state that seeks its protection. Members of the international community are not obliged to "respect the sovereignty" of a state that egregiously violates human rights. Why "egregiously"? The sad answer is that the world presents a far-too-rich array of human-rights violations that might justify outside intervention. We must choose among the evils we seek to end. For much of the world, for example, capital punishment violates human rights. Yet few disinterested observers would urge or welcome the forcible landing of an international military force to prevent Virginia's next execution. However one regards capital punishment after due process of law, it cannot compare with the scale of violations that occurred in Rwanda or in the Cambodia of Pol Pot. As one analyst has observed, we currently possess "neither the capabilities nor the willingness to right all wrongs, even the relatively small number of wrongs that are deemed to warrant international action." But as President Clinton expressed in his speech justifying the NATO action in Bosnia, "We cannot stop all war for all time. But we can stop some wars. . . . There are times and places when our leadership can make the difference between peace and war."[12] Thus, some judgment must be made about the scale of evil and the capacity we have to end it.

This process of judgment should, in my view, be multinational. For all the flaws of the United Nations, it does provide a forum for international debate and for the emergence of consensus. An insistence on collective, multilateral intervention—or, as in Haiti, collectively approved unilateral action—can correct for self-interested interventions thinly cloaked in humanitarianism. At the same time, it may be just or necessary for a state to declare its intention to act on its own; if the cause is truly just, this declaration may make collective action more possible. And the intervention may still be just even if its motives are mixed. For example, India's intervention in the former East Pakistan and Tanzania's in the Uganda of Idi Amin are often cited as unilateral interventions that nevertheless ended humanitarian disasters.[13]

CONCLUSION

An approach to just peacemaking must include a willingness to abridge the sovereignty of states in cases where human rights are egregiously violated. Given the values ideally protected by nation-states—self-determination, cultural and historical autonomy, rudimentary international order—we should not be cavalier about violating sovereignty, but neither should we respect sovereignty at the cost of wholesale injustice and of ignoring grievous violations of human rights. Certainly there is an obligation to develop what might be called instruments of rescue, so that a disaster like Rwanda need not occur for want of a capacity to intervene. Waging peace, no less than waging war, requires us to combine capability with intention. Although the obstacles are formidable, a revitalized United Nations equipped with a standing volunteer military force seems a minimum goal for those who would seek to wage peace in a world of states.

9

REDUCE OFFENSIVE WEAPONS
AND WEAPONS TRADE

Barbara Green
Glen Stassen

The practice we advocate is reducing offensive weapons and the weapons trade. We focus on two parts of the practice: first, reducing nuclear weapons and combating their proliferation, and when possible, reversing it; second, reducing the weapons trade, including a ban on the production, sales, and transfers of antipersonnel land mines. Both parts of the practice significantly reduce the dangers of war; both need active support by U.S. citizens and informed citizens' groups. First, we present briefly our underlying rationale.

REDUCING OFFENSIVE WEAPONS REDUCES INCENTIVES FOR WAR

International-relations scholars regularly note that one factor making war less likely in many areas is that war is no longer worth the price. The enormous destructiveness of the retaliating force, with modern weaponry, means it makes no sense, by any rational calculus, to initiate a war. The offensive weapons are unable to destroy the defensive response, and the likely defensive or retaliatory response is simply too enormous to risk. It was unthinkable for the United States to initiate war with the Soviet Union or for the Soviet Union to initiate war with the United States; to do so would have been to commit national suicide. Hence, both were very careful not to enter into battle where the other was engaged. The Soviet Union stayed out of

Korea and Vietnam, and the United States stayed out of Czecho-slovakia and Afghanistan. Robert Jervis has argued cogently that the destructive response would be so thoroughly devastating that, even when it is not guaranteed but only a significant probability, deterrence still occurs. When losing the gamble would mean nuclear destruction of one's whole nation, one does not enter into the gamble. This logic applies also to conventional, or nonnuclear, weapons because these weapons, too, are enormously more destructive than they were a century ago.

The war in Bosnia is the counterexample that proves the rule: Because the Serbians controlled the former Yugoslavian army and kept the army's weapons, they had the offensive capability to initiate a war without much fear of a powerful Muslim counterattack. Because of their offensive weapons, they thought war would be worth the price. They did not count on NATO intervention.[1]

Another example is the Gulf War. Iraq had built up a large offensive capability. (The United States had assisted Iraq in this build-up in an effort to counterbalance Iran, whose large offensive capability under the Shah the United States had also built up, selling Iran more weapons in ten years than it sold to all of NATO combined in the same ten-year period.) Next to Iraq's offensive capability, Kuwait had little defensive capability. Saddam Hussein calculated he could occupy Kuwait with little damage to Iraq from Kuwait's military. He was right. What he had not been told was that international forces would intervene and cause his troops great damage. And subsequently, the international forces, led by the United States, used international sanctions to reduce Iraq's offensive capability—chemical and biological weapons, Scud missiles, and potential nuclear weapons. They did not want Iraq tempted again by its large offensive capability to attack an oil-rich neighbor or Israel.

The logic that war is not worth the price when the offense cannot destroy the defense suggests a change toward defensive force structures. Nations can adopt a force structure designed to defend against attack more than to initiate an attack. With less offensive than defensive capability, initiating a war is even less attractive. For example, Gorbachev removed half the Soviet Union's tanks from Central Europe and all its river-crossing equipment, thus reducing the Warsaw Pact's ability to make a sudden offensive attack; but the USSR retained its defensive capability. This reduced the likelihood of war, and the West realized it. Previously, NATO had worried about a possible blitzkrieg attack by Soviet tanks and so was not willing to get rid of medium-range and shorter-range nuclear missiles in Europe. But after observing the new Soviet force structure, oriented more toward defense, the West agreed to a mutual disarmament of all medium- and shorter-range nuclear missiles (the zero solution). This was the first major disarmament step toward ending the Cold War peacefully.

The practice of reducing offensive weapons has two additional advantages. If, in spite of the practices that widen the zone of peace, war nevertheless occurs, then there is less killing if there are fewer offensive weapons to do the killing. Let us state this carefully: The difference is not between enormous destruction and minimal destruction; modern weapons are too destructive for that. The difference is between unimaginably horrible killing and somewhat less killing. But the magnitudes are so great that merely "somewhat less" may mean a hundred thousand lives, or in the case of nuclear weapons, hundreds of millions of lives. The picture is hardly rosy, but the difference is significant for the lives of millions of potential victims.

158

The other advantage is the reduction in monetary cost of weapons build-ups, and therefore the ability to spend the money for real human needs that are going unfulfilled. This advantage is in fact causing almost every nation in the world to reduce the percentage of its GNP that it spends for military weapons because it makes sense to realistic decision makers.

Nevertheless, there are forces of resistance—powerful forces that block sensible reductions. Offensive weapons are still in enormous oversupply in the world. Costs are still enormously destructive to many nations' economies and to human needs. Therefore, there is a need for people who want peace to come to the aid of their countries' security and the security of all countries.

The Case of Nuclear Weapons

A dramatic case in point is the reduction of nuclear weapons by the Soviet Union, the United States, and NATO. The break came with "the zero solution": NATO and Gorbachev agreed to destroy all medium- and shorter-range nuclear weapons. Then U.S. presidents Reagan and Bush negotiated START I and START II to reduce the combined nuclear warheads of the United States and the former Soviet Union from 47,000 to 15,500. Agreements have been reached to ban the production of chemical and biological weapons and to destroy their stockpiles. The Comprehensive Test Ban Treaty will impede the development of new types of nuclear weapons. Russia and the United States no longer aim their nuclear missiles at each other. These dramatic reductions in offensive weapons increase our security significantly.

The practices of citizen pressure for reductions, independent initiatives, and negotiations, have shown that they can make the world safer. They have also shown the practical possibility of further reductions, which will remove offensive threats that can still cause war and unimaginable destruction by accident, by escalation, and by proliferation of weapons to other countries.

When the START II treaty is implemented, the world will still have approximately 20,000 long-range and short-range nuclear weapons, with an explosive power of 400,000 Hiroshima-sized bombs. Enough bombs will remain to destroy civilization as we know it several times over.

A National Academy of Sciences study signed by a broad array of scientists and national-security specialists who have been engaged in advising governments of both parties on national security policies recommended a first-step reduction to 3,000 long-range warheads and then to 1,000 for the United States and Russia each if they need two warheads per target (or 1,500 if they want three warheads per target).[2] The first step has been taken, down to 3,000. We should now push for the second step, down to 1,000. Then we should focus on the third step of further reductions.

Security Advantages for Reductions

The security advantages of the United States and Russia reducing to one thousand warheads each are many.

1. The fewer nuclear weapons there are, the fewer there are to threaten an adversary with a Pearl Harbor-like, surprise, first-strike attack. For many years, nuclear war has not been likely to be initiated intentionally, since starting a nuclear war makes no sense when retaliation would be so devastating. The far greater danger all along has been a panicked response to a false warning of a disarming first-strike attack in a time of tension. As the National Academy of Sciences study

pointed out, if nuclear powers fear that a first-strike attack could destroy most of their missiles, submarines, and bombers, thus crippling their ability to retaliate, they are pressured to launch their missiles if their sensors or computers give them a false warning of attack. Decreasing the number of warheads on each side greatly decreases the ability to launch a disarming first strike and thus decreases this pressure.

A study for the Union of Concerned Scientists argues, as many others do, that we should reduce to one thousand warheads:

> By virtue of their small size, dispersal, and inherent invulnerability to attack, these forces would pose little risk of accidental use, generate no pressures to launch promptly in a crisis, and would be too small in size to make a first-strike feasible or conceivable. This would in practice eliminate the capability of the Soviet republics to make a deliberate nuclear attack on the United States. Such reductions would in one stroke . . . sharply diminish the chance that Soviet instability could lead to inadvertent nuclear war.[3]

160

2. The fewer nuclear weapons we and other nations have, the fewer there are to be fired in an unauthorized launch that would start a nuclear war.

3. Reducing the numbers of nuclear warheads will remove surplus weapons for which there are no urgent military targets. That will provide incentives for obeying the rule against intentionally bombing noncombatants. "An adversary would thus not be able to use available weapons against civilian targets without leaving important military targets uncovered."[4]

4. The fewer nuclear weapons we and Russia have, the fewer a Zhirinovsky will have if he should become president of Russia. The Union of Concerned Scientists study by Dean and Gottfried states the reality perceptively: "It may be possible to avert emergence of right-wing governments in the nuclear weapon successor states (of the former Soviet Union). . . . But if it does occur, the dangers to the outside world are so great that it would be a serious error to leave a large arsenal of strategic-range nuclear weapons" in their hands.[5] The study goes on to say that "Even if current political trends do not culminate in authoritarian regimes, chronic economic difficulties will make it impossible for the Russian Federation . . . to sustain the enormously

costly, complex infrastructure needed for firm control over the huge strategic arsenals that will remain . . . after START reductions."[6]

5. The fewer nuclear weapons there are, the fewer there are for terrorists or other nations to steal or purchase. This threat is especially real in Russia, where many nuclear weapons still remain. A global crime network is growing in strength. And economically threatened scientists, military personnel, members of the control network, and politicians may be readily tempted by offers of money for their weapons, their plutonium or uranium, and their scientific skills. Faced with this threat of anarchy, we have enormous incentives for reducing the numbers of weapons available for theft.

6. If the United States and Russia agree to reduce to one thousand nuclear weapons each, they will have a much stronger case for persuading other nuclear powers to reduce and restrict their arsenals. The problem is especially acute in the Middle East, where Israel has an undeclared arsenal of over two hundred weapons, and where this fact, combined with the intense rivalries and hostilities of the region, fuels pressures for Iran, Libya, Syria, and Iraq to go nuclear.[7]

7. The fewer nuclear weapons we and other nations have, the millions or billions fewer people will be killed if they are used, and the less radiation will be spread throughout the world to make life miserable for those who survive.

The end of the Cold War and the reductions we have achieved are causing overconfidence that we have eliminated the probability of nuclear war and thus need not be concerned about reducing the millions or billions likely to be killed if nuclear war does occur. People have had the false perception that the nuclear threat arose because of a hostile Kremlin that might make war on us. That was never likely; the Kremlin knew better than we the destructive consequences of nuclear war because they had vivid memories of losing twenty million lives—10 percent of their citizens—in World War II. Furthermore, Russia and the United States had little incentive to make even conventional warfare to change the status quo, since they already had the hegemony and the territory that were most important to them. The realistic threats were always the seven we have enumerated above, and those threats still menace us after the Cold War. We still need mutual reductions in a big way.

For example, the more we reduce the level of nuclear weapons worldwide, the safer we are. In December 1996 General Lee Butler, former commander-in-chief of the U.S. Strategic Command, and sixty-one other retired generals and admirals called for the step-by-step abolition of nuclear weapons, arguing that they have no use except to endanger our lives. The generals also know that the United States has such a preponderance of conventional weapons that it would be safer and actually stronger if nuclear weapons are eradicated. The peace movement has adopted the same goal, with Peace Action of Washington, D.C., being the largest group working on abolition. As we approach zero, solutions to the problem of verification are likely to become clearer, and each step of multilateral reductions toward zero will make our lives safer. We need to embark on the journey toward complete abolition of nuclear weapons.

REDUCE AVAILABLE PLUTONIUM AND URANIUM FOR BOMBS

Another important step is to ban any more production of nuclear bomb fuel: the fissile materials plutonium and highly enriched uranium (Pu and HEU). We can press Congress and the president to begin talks on a fissionable fuels production ban.

162

We already have a huge surplus of bomb fuel, increased daily by the Pu and HEU removed from decommissioned nuclear weapons. We do not know how to store what surplus we have. Nor does it wear out; its half-life is 2,400 years. There is no immediate need for more until at least 4,800 years from now. Our strong concern about the spread of fissionable fuel for nuclear weapons to North Korea, Libya, Iraq, Iran, etc., supports the need to achieve a worldwide fissionable fuels production ban; more fuel is an invitation to proliferation.

President Clinton has canceled the breeder reactor, the advanced liquid metal reactor (ALMR), which would have bred more plutonium. Furthermore, "for environmental and safety reasons the U.S. has ceased producing Pu for military purposes and is not reprocessing civilian reactor fuel for recovery of Pu."[8] It has also ceased producing highly enriched uranium. In September 1993 at the United Nations, President Clinton announced a new nonproliferation policy, which includes a proposal for a multilateral ban on the production of new fissile material for nuclear weapons and international monitoring of all production of fissile material. "In addition, the U.S. pledged to remove the fissile material it considers excess to its nuclear-weapon needs from military stocks and place it under international safeguards" if Russia will do the same.[9] "A multilateral, nondiscrim-inatory, and effectively verifiable fissile material production ban would strengthen substantially the nonproliferation regime by re-straining the unsafeguarded nuclear programs of certain non-NPT states for the first time. It would also halt the production of separated plutonium and highly-enriched uranium for nuclear explosives in the five declared nuclear-weapon states."[10]

A crucial covenant that has been unexpectedly effective in halt-ing the spread of nuclear weapons for twenty-five years is the Nonproliferation Treaty (NPT). This has just been renewed and signed by most nations. Since 1990, twenty-eight more states have joined the NPT. "More countries have joined the NPT than have joined any other arms control treaty in history."[11]

Article VI of the NPT commits each of the parties to the treaty "to pursue negotiations in good faith on effective measures relating to cessation of the nuclear arms race at an early date and to nuclear disarmament, and on a treaty on general and complete disarmament under strict and effective international control."

Obstacles

The corrupting force of money on U.S. politics, which distorts deci-sion-making processes on the weapons trade, also distorts decisions on nuclear weapons. The profits are very large. The United States still plans to spend $35 billion for nuclear weapons each year for the next decade, amassing another $350 billion indebtedness—the inter-est on which (at 6 percent) causes it to double every eleven and a half years even if no more were spent. Another enormous cost is the loss of jobs due to the transfer of $35 billion from more-labor-intensive economic sectors to the highly capital-intensive nuclear weapons industry, which produces far fewer jobs per $35 billion investment than money invested in roads, bridges, schools, health care, and so forth. It takes money away from jobs programs, neighborhood pro-grams, drug clinics, educational improvements, help for the working poor, and health care that are necessary to alleviate root causes of gun violence and structural violence, destroying many young people in this generation.

Combining savings proposed by the Center for Defense Information and the Congressional Budget Office indicates that the United States can save $0.7 billion by canceling the Trident II D-5 missile, $1.8 billion by halting B-2 bomber production, $3 billion by decreasing work on new nuclear weapons, and $3.3 billion by limiting the Star Wars program to theater defense programs. Total savings equal $9.5 billion. These are *annual* savings; over ten years they would total something like $95 billion, and *much more if you take into account the interest paid on the national debt.* Permanently halting production of plutonium and highly enriched uranium and not restarting Tritium production would result in further savings. Halting nuclear bomb testing and the accompanying development of new types of nuclear weapons would save further billions.

There are also the bureaucratic influences and momentum of those engaged in nuclear weapons development. The distortion of the decision process by financial and bureaucratic interests is evidenced in the ten-month review of nuclear policy, studying whether to negotiate a reduction of nuclear weapons from the presently agreed 3,500 to 1,000 each for the United States and Russia. Defense Secretary William Perry announced that the United States would cut Trident subs from eighteen to fourteen, and B-52s from ninety-four to sixty-six, but would not propose cutting the warheads from 3,500 to 1,000. Pentagon officials said they want "a strong capability to respond if a hostile government took power in Moscow—something Pentagon officials stressed was unlikely."[12] It does not take extensive thought to see through this argument. Suppose a Zhirinovsky did come to power in Russia: Would we be more secure if he had 3,000 nuclear weapons or if he had 1,000? The specter of a hostile, authoritarian, nationalistic, and militaristic government in Russia gives significant added impetus to negotiating reductions to 1,000 now, without tarrying for the time when he might be the other party to the negotiation.

The Need to Slow Proliferation

The lameness of the argument begs for analysis. Why would highly intelligent Pentagon officials put forth such a transparently illogical argument? There are two potential explanations. The decision may have been made on the grounds of not wanting to offend military and industrial interests and because the political climate for further reductions had not been created; such grounds could not be admitted in polite discourse. Alternatively, it may have been made because the decision-makers were still living in the ideological inertia of the Cold War, which brought us a many-times-overkill capacity. The accurate conclusion is that we need reductions now while the Russian parliament is dissatisfied with leaving the numbers where they stand and thus is hesitant to ratify START II unless a process begins for further reductions. It is not logical to wait for the Russian climate to change. We need to create the climate in the United States for reductions that increase our security more.

Concern about nuclear build-ups by China or other nuclear states is legitimate. At this point, other nations have far smaller nuclear arsenals than the United States and Russia. It should be possible to include them in negotiations and set mutual limits that include them. That will increase our security and theirs.

A major concern is proliferation of nuclear weapons to nations that presently do not have them. Setting reduced limits for the nuclear nations sets the example for nonproliferation; it increases the persuasive power of arguments that other nations should not proliferate; and it moves toward fulfilling the agreements in the nonproliferation treaty that others will not obtain nuclear weapons and that the nuclear nations will reduce theirs.

SUPPORT THE CODE OF CONDUCT FOR CONVENTIONAL ARMS TRANSFERS

The practice of reducing the weapons trade is already being carried out by many of the purchasing nations themselves. As nations turn toward democracy and respect for human rights, their governments have less need for a military to keep them in power by threat of force. As their neighbors turn toward democracy, they feel less threat and less need for weapons. As they struggle with their deep indebtedness, they have less ability to buy weapons. Furthermore, the International Monetary Fund is now requiring big reductions in expenditures for weapons if nations are to receive loans or aid. For these or other reasons,

> the real news from the 1996 Congressional Research Study released in August by Richard Grimmett is that selling arms to the third world is a dead-end market economically; at $15 billion for 1995, the developing world's arms imports dropped to just one-quarter of their peak in 1988. . . . We should recognize that the shrinking demand for high-tech armaments represents an unprecedented opportunity for controlling the arms trade.[13]

One step in the practice of reducing the arms trade is the growing support for the Code of Conduct for Conventional Arms Transfers. The Code of Conduct Bill was introduced in the Senate by Senator Mark Hatfield (retired 1996) and in the House by Representative
Cynthia McKinney in 1993; it has been growing in support since then.
It says:

> U.S. military assistance and arms transfers may not be pro-
> vided to a foreign government. . . unless the President cer-
> tifies to the Congress for that fiscal year that such govern-
> ment meets the following requirements: promotes
> democracy; respects human rights; does not engage in
> armed aggression; fully participates in the U.N. Register of
> Conventional Arms.
>
> The prohibition . . . shall not apply . . . if the President
> submits a request for an exemption [based on] a determina-
> tion that it is in the national security interest of the U.S. to
> provide military assistance and arms transfers . . . and the
> Congress enacts a law approving such exemption request.[14]

The provision that no nation will be eligible for arms transfers if
it does not fully participate in the U.N. Register of Conventional Arms
serves several purposes. Transparency is a deterrent against secret
arms build-ups, and a partial deterrent against arms build-ups that
earn opposition and/or hostility from other nations. It is also a confi-
dence-building measure for neighbor nations, enabling them to know
the limits on their neighbors' weapons and thus to constrain their own
expenditures for weapons build-ups. Furthermore, it is a step in
strengthening the United Nations and the cooperative forces in the
international system.

The United States should pass the Code of Conduct, and seek
acceptance of these rules of conduct by the other major weapons-sup-
plier nations, especially Russia, France, China, Germany, and Great
Britain. The Center for Defense Information says "the six largest
traders control over 90 percent of the arms transfers to the developing
world," which is the most unstable region and which can least afford
to be spending its countries' limited incomes on arms races. The U.S.
peace movement is pushing hard for the Code of Conduct bill. On
June 10, 1997, the code passed the House of Representatives by a
voice vote as an amendment to the State Department Authorization

Bill. McKinney's long and valiant efforts had finally been rewarded, to her great satisfaction. Representative Dana Rohrabacher's (R-CA) impassioned support made a big difference. As of this writing, the bill still has a long way to go, especially in the Senate, before becoming law. Actions like this, which can make a major difference in many countries suffering from poverty, military spending, and a military-supported authoritarian regime, depend on church members and other citizens expressing encouragement to legislators. People need to be a part of a peace and justice group or alert network to be effective, as the dramatic victory in the House shows we can be.

Many arms sales are based on U.S. subsidies to purchasing nations (which cost U.S. taxpayers heavily) and on offsets, which are agreements to transfer U.S. manufacturing jobs to other nations in exchange for their agreeing to purchase U.S. weapons. The United States' agreement to the Code of Conduct should include agreement to disclose the nature and value of such offsets that accompany sales; legislation has been introduced to implement this.

Poor nations whose governments spend large amounts on military weapons are being deprived of much needed money for the necessities of life and are likely to have their human rights breached by a government that relies on military weapons to dominate its people. Foreign aid should be contingent on a recipient nation holding its military spending below a set percentage of its income. The precedent is straightforward: President Carter's encouragement of human rights became far more effective once U.S. foreign aid was made contingent on assessment of the human-rights record of recipient nations. Arms sales undermine human rights and distribute weapons that often boomerang, being used against the seller's troops, as happened to the United States in Somalia and Iraq.

Another part of the practice of reducing the arms trade is a ban on the production, sales, and transfer of antipersonnel land mines. In 1992, Senator Leahy and Representative Evans introduced the Landmines Moratorium Act, imposing a moratorium on the sale and export of antipersonnel land mines. People rallied in its support, and the moratorium passed and has since been renewed. In response to extensive public pressure and endorsement from many top U.S. military leaders, General Shalikashvili, Chairman of the Joint Chiefs of Staff, ordered a review of U.S. policy and indicated that he was "inclined to eliminate all antipersonnel landmines."[15] The Clinton administration almost agreed to a ban on land mines, but then refused (perhaps in the process of defending its military flank against anticipated election politics). The United States should lead other nations to a worldwide ban. Insisting on an exception for itself legitimizes refusals by other nations. Land mines are made to hide in fields, paths, and travel routes and to kill, amputate, or maim for life whoever passes—child, adult, soldier, civilian. They are killing eight hundred people per month, far more than the total deaths from chemical, biological, and nuclear weapons. They are maiming another twelve hundred per month. They are cheap, easy to acquire, and devastating; they are very expensive to remove. They have been used most in developing countries. Banning them is a key step in reducing the arms trade. The U.S. military is ready to do it; what is required is for political leaders to sense that the people want it and that, thus, it would be politically advantageous. Senator Leahy announced a new bill on land mines at a press conference on June 12, 1997. It would mandate a permanent ban on U.S. land mine use starting in 2000, with an annually renewable exemption for Korea. It helped pressure the administration to join the Ottawa process (the Canadian proposal that successfully led to an international treaty banning land mines). Leahy rallied fifty-seven cosponsors before introducing the bill. Church groups and peace and justice groups have been exerting strong pressure to ban land mines, and it is getting results. The treaty allows twelve years for compliance—time enough to develop alternative solutions for Korea. The United States needs to sign the treaty, not only to ban its own land mines, but to support the ban for other nations.

Obstacles

We have already mentioned causal factors for the weapons trade in purchasing nations: authoritarian governments, influence of the military in national security states, fear of hostile neighbor nations. These factors can be reduced by practices described in other papers: support for action to push for human rights and democratization; support for cooperative forces in the international system, including the United Nations; encouraging the U.S. government to support requiring dramatic reductions in military expenditures before aid is approved by its own aid policies and by IMF policies.

Another causative factor of the arms trade is large contributions of money to political candidates from weapons manufacturers. When the United States exports $30 to $50 billion in weapons annually, weapons manufacturers can contribute millions to politicians—a major factor for political campaigns but a small investment for manufacturers as a percentage of their huge profits. The Center for Defense Information presented this table from data of the Federal Election Commission:[16]

Selected Military Contractor Political Action Committee
Contributions to 1994 Congressional Campaigns

General Electric	$328,300
Lockheed	$315,891
Martin Marietta	$285,160
General Dynamics	$258,263
Textron	$243,460
Boeing Corporation	$173,745
Northrop	$164,068
Rockwell	$160,020
McDonnell Douglas	$153,200
Loral Systems	$144,400

To correct this distortion of the decision process that determines how tax money is spent, we must curtail contributions from political action committees of arms manufacturers and others. Many are pushing for limits on political contributions from all sources and on campaign spending, including soft as well as hard money. Until the power of money to corrupt the decision process is curtailed, it will be hard to make the process peaceable.

Another cause is the United States' subsidies of weapons exports to other nations and of weapons manufacturers' foreign-sales efforts. While Congress drags its heels at paying the United States' share of U.N. peacekeeping costs (as well as its assessed dues!), the U.S. government and commercial manufacturers fan the flames of regional conflicts by subsidizing arms sales abroad.

Russia, China, and France are competing ferociously for shares in the global arms market, with Britain, Germany, Israel, Italy, and the Czech Republic claiming niches for themselves. The 1996 Congressional Research Study by Richard Grimmett, cited above, shows that for 1995 Russia surpassed the United States in arms sales to Third World countries. But the Grimmett report shows all sales by other countries, but only country-to-country sales for the United

States, leaving out commercial sales. The larger point it makes is that the United States has dominated the global market since the collapse of the Soviet Union.

Implications of Inaction

Consider several of the implications for not overcoming these obstacles. First, federal subsidies for arms exports have climbed from $7.0 billion in fiscal year 1994 to $7.6 billion in 1995, an increase of 8.5 percent. This represents the second-largest subsidy program for business in the entire federal budget, after agricultural price supports.

Second, the U.S. government is the world's largest arms broker, spending over $450 million and employing nearly 6,500 full-time personnel to promote and service foreign arms sales by U.S. companies. The Pentagon alone has a full-time arms-sales staff of 6,395, an increase of 7.5 percent since the Clinton administration took office.

Third, federal government expenditures on promoting weapons at international air and trade shows now average over $26.5 million per year. The Pentagon actually receives a 3 percent commission for every foreign arms sale it negotiates.

Fourth, U.S. arms exports in 1995 totaled an estimated $12 billion. Of that sum, $7.6 billion was paid by taxpayer subsidies—more than one-half of all exports.

BREAK THE ARMS-EXPORT PEACEKEEPING CYCLE

U.N. peacekeeping operations have cost roughly $3 billion annually in recent years. The U.N. currently has thirty-one thousand peacekeeping troops deployed in seventeen missions around the world. This represents a 42 percent drop from recent years due to the closing of UNPROFOR and UNCRO missions in the former Yugoslavia. Those operations were replaced by the U.S.-led operation currently in place there. In support of U.S. contributions to peacekeeping operations, Secretary of State Warren Christopher told Congress, "millions spent now on multilateral preventive diplomacy, emergency refugee support, and peacekeeping may save hundreds of millions in defense and international relief later."

Restraining arms exports would likely lessen the need for preventive diplomacy, refugee support, and peacekeeping missions in the first place. Arms exports (for example, to Angola, Somalia, and Iraq) in the 1970s and 1980s greatly increased the level of violence and chaos which led to current U.N. peacekeeping operations.

In fiscal 1993, the U.S. government approved nearly $60 billion of weapons exports to 145 countries. Some of these weapons may necessitate future peacekeeping operations. The U.S. joint chiefs of staff stated in their 1992 Joint Military Net Assessment that instability arises "in areas where nations are acquiring increasingly sophisticated and expensive military equipment and large armed forces. This tendency undermines regional stability and the balance of power and defers economic growth." Very few developing countries produce any, let alone all, of their own armaments; they import weapons from the same countries that are ostensibly working to develop international peacemaking and peace-enforcing mechanisms.

Regional Arms Races

Under the excess-arms programs, the Army, Navy, and Air Force are transferring relatively sophisticated systems. Following the Gulf War, the Army gave Israel surplus Apache attack helicopters, Blackhawk transport helicopters, multiple-launch rocket systems, and Patriot tactical antimissiles. In 1995, four M-1 Abrams tank turrets were provided to Egypt as excess defense articles. (Egypt is building 535 M-1A1 tanks under license from General Dynamics.)

Even older equipment, like M-60 tanks and F-4 aircraft purchased in the 1960s or 1970s, can remain quite formidable through regular upgrades and modifications. While these weapons seem dated to the U.S. armed services, they often become the centerpiece of foreign militaries. A discarded U.S. Navy ship, for instance, will serve as the flagship of Bahrain's navy. Similarly, Greece, Turkey, Egypt, and Morocco have each received hundreds of used M-60 tanks for free, creating large modern tank armies which they otherwise could not afford.

The executive branch claims to consider thoroughly the implications of surplus transfers on the regional balance of forces. For example, as a condition of the transfer of M-60 tanks to Egypt in 1990, the U.S. government required that Egypt retire one older tank for each M-60 received. Although this transfer resulted in no quantitative increase, it did result in a qualitative upgrade, since the new tanks are more effective.

In other cases, American surplus arms seem to be fanning regional rivalries, as excess weapons are sent to both sides of several ongoing arms races. Significant quantities of surplus arms are going

171

to Argentina and Chile. The two are embroiled in a nascent arms race and ongoing border disputes. In the Middle East, American surplus arms are flowing to both Israel and Egypt, engaged in a cold peace. Most notable is the vast amount of arms that the United States has given to hostile NATO partners Turkey and Greece.

In 1994, Admiral Edward Shaefer, director of naval intelligence, called Turkish-Greek animosity "among the most worrisome situations developing in Europe, and the one most dangerous to NATO as an institution." In February 1996, this long-simmering tension boiled over. President Clinton had to intervene to head off a military confrontation over a disputed island. Shaefer said that "The Greco-Turkish dynamic has been exacerbated by a continuing Aegean naval buildup prompted by Western naval surplus disposals. Greece has acquired virtually a completely modernized surface force from the United States, Germany and the Netherlands. . . . In order to redress the naval balance in the Aegean, Turkey has found it necessary to accept U.S. Navy offers for eight Knox-class frigates." The United States has transferred more than sixteen warships to this antagonistic pair and large quantities of tanks, aircraft, and artillery as well.

172

Off-budget Procurements and Downstream Costs

As Admiral Shaefer noted, the United States is not the only country getting rid of surplus arms and contributing to regional arms races. The Federal Republic of Germany inherited—and has been selling off—the armed forces of the German Democratic Republic. Russia has been demobilizing troops in large numbers, creating an enormous surplus which it is seeking to sell, and the Netherlands has marketed abroad its older ships, aircraft, and army vehicles. Other governments, too, can be expected to follow America's lead with respect to disposing of their surplus military stocks. Indeed, Eastern European countries sought to export tanks and other combat equipment limited by the Conventional Forces in Europe Treaty, much as the United States did. Poland and Czechoslovakia marketed their surplus weapons in Syria and Iran, causing great alarm in Washington.

Particularly dangerous in this respect is an Air Force initiative to sell old weapons to fund the procurement of new weapons. In early 1994, the U.S. Air Force disclosed plans to finance the purchase of up to 90 new F-16C/D aircraft through sales of some 360 older model F-16A/B fighter jets. Air Force Vice-Chief of Staff Michael Carns, an architect of the plan, said the scheme would give him "brand new war-fighting planes at no cost to the taxpayer." Lockheed Martin, manufacturer of the F-16, is lobbying hard for the hundreds of millions of dollars in upgrade work and new Air Force orders.

To overcome arms control opposition, the Air Force put a Madison Avenue spin on the sales plan, repackaging it as "coalition force enhancement"—a way to strengthen friendly militaries. Over a dozen countries have been briefed on the availability of the cheap F-16s (at $9–14 million per plane). Potential customers include Argentina, Chile, the Czech Republic, Egypt, South Korea, Malaysia, Morocco, New Zealand, the Philippines, Poland, Singapore, Thailand, and Tunisia.

There is precedent for this sort of off-budget procurement, although not to the magnitude envisioned here (the Air Force plan would involve $5 billion of aircraft sales). In the fiscal 1993 Defense authorization bill, Congress permitted the Army to use $197 million from the sale of excess M-48 and M-60 tanks for the M-1 Abrams tank upgrade program. The act also allowed the use of $15.2 million from M-113 sales for the procurement of Bradley fighting vehicles. And in the fiscal 1994 Department of Defense bill, the House Armed Services Committee suggested that the Navy sell excess Mk-46 torpedoes and use the proceeds to offset buying the Mk-50 advanced light-weight torpedo.

Again, the potential downstream costs of this practice are considerable, especially if other exporters follow our lead and seek to fund their weapons procurement through arms sales. In fact, the U.S. government has protested vociferously in the past when other governments pursued such a policy.

In 1991, China's practice of buying new weapons with the proceeds from weapons exports generated outrage in the Western press. Similarly, U.S. government officials heavily denounced a Russian plan in the early 1990s to finance arms industry conversion through arms sales. In both cases, U.S. officials criticized the creation of a dangerous and short-sighted bureaucratic interest in selling weapons abroad.

TIE SURPLUS ARMS TRANSFERS TO HUMAN RIGHTS

Several of the countries receiving large quantities of U.S. arms through surplus programs are engaged in conflict or have poor human rights records. In cases where government repression or other abuses are prevalent, transfers of small arms, light weapons, ammunition, bombs, and missiles are of primary concern, as these are the implements that actually kill people. In addition, so-called nonlethal equipment—such as observation and transport planes and helicopters—is also of concern, as it is used to locate targets and deliver soldiers to those targets.

The Turkish government has a well-documented record of abysmal human-rights performance. According to the State Department, in 1995 "police and security forces often employed torture during periods of incommunicado detention and interrogation." In addition, the government is cited as being responsible for so-called mystery killings, disappearances, and political repression.

Most abuses center around Turkey's repression of its Kurdish population and war against Kurdish militants. Police and military forces have destroyed some two thousand villages, killed tens of thousands—primarily civilians—and displaced millions in its twelve-year-long war. The State Department acknowledged in a report in June 1997 that Turkey was employing American-supplied weapons in attacks on noncombatant populations. In particular, the report noted that Turkey has used M-113 armored personnel carriers and Cobra and Blackhawk helicopters in indiscriminate attacks on Kurdish villages. Turkey received 250 free M-113s as a result of the CFE Treaty limits, and twenty-eight free Cobra helicopters under Section 516 of the Foreign Assistance Act. In addition, the United States has sent Turkey hundreds of howitzers at no cost.

In Bahrain, government forces have fired live ammunition and tear gas into crowds of demonstrators demanding a restoration of the parliament, which the ruling al-Khalifa family dissolved in 1975. Antigovernment demonstrations and bombings broke out in early January 1996, after several months of calm, and continued through May. In addition to some measure of representative democracy, the protesters are demanding jobs, freedom of speech, the release of political prisoners, and the return of deported dissidents. The State Department has stated that "the United States supports expansion of political participation for all Bahrainis."

Nevertheless, during 1993 to 1995, but principally in 1995, the United States gave the ruling clique two C-130 military transport planes, six observation/light attack jets, twenty-two Cobra attack helicopters, two thousand .38 caliber pistols, and 120 grenade launchers. In addition, the Pentagon transferred sixty M-60 tanks under a lease arrangement.

Morocco is governed by a highly repressive monarchy which has illegally occupied the western Sahara for twenty years. In 1991, the United Nations brokered a fragile peace agreement between Morocco and Polisario Front guerrillas of the western Sahara, who are seeking independence. However, Morocco has obstructed the peace process, and the resumption of fighting appears likely.

The United States has a long history of quiet but close military and intelligence ties to the Moroccan monarchy. In the past five years, Morocco has taken delivery of significant quantities of U.S. surplus small arms, tanks, and attack aircraft.

A MODEST BEGINNING

The United States and other peacekeeping participants should restrain arms exports to national governments. If they are going to indulge in the arms trade at all, they should instead supply weapons primarily to international regional security organizations. The U.N., NATO, Organization of African Unity, and Organization of American States are currently on the United States' list of approved arms customers.

Global restraint in arms production and exports would make a true contribution to global and regional peacemaking and peacekeeping. Pursuing peace with one hand while doling out weapons with the other is cynical and counterproductive. We have described practices that reduce offensive weapons and have demonstrated that, in spite of powerful obstacles, these practices are bringing significant reductions. They need the support of people who care about the peace of the world and who see a major opportunity as well as great danger at this turning point in world history.

10

ENCOURAGE GRASSROOTS PEACEMAKING GROUPS AND VOLUNTARY ASSOCIATIONS

Duane K. Friesen

As the United Church of Christ document "A Just Peace Church" states: "Just peace requires peacemakers."[1] A just peacemaking theory presupposes not only individual peacemakers but a community of peacemakers. It requires groups of citizens who take peacemaking initiatives themselves and who encourage governments to do so. Individuals should form or join such groups; governments should support freedom of assembly, freedom of information, and the right to petition the government. And in situations where governments resist democratic institutions and democratic change, nonviolent movements and organizations have been formed and have been effective in helping create peace with justice.[2]

The ten practices of just peacemaking theory are already implicitly shared by a network of interlocking groups of people at a grassroots level. The relatively new phenomenon in history of a network of peacemaking groups can be seen in the following developments, among others:

1. A growing knowledge, awareness, and experience (recently evident in the collapse of the Soviet Empire) of nonviolent movements for social change in the traditions of Gandhi and King.

2. An interlocking network of NGOs and INGOs (nongovernmental organizations and international nongovernmental orga-

nizations, such as church organizations, Amnesty International, Peace Action, United Nations/USA, etc.) which bring pressure to bear on governments all over the globe on everything from human rights to arms control and reduction.

3. An increasing networking and cooperation worldwide of people across confessional and religious boundaries and barriers.

4. The coming together of these people into clusters of local organizations, just peace and justice groups in churches, and interfaith committees—not just isolated individuals.

5. A strengthening of international governmental organizations that may be able to work more effectively on common human problems, and perhaps the emergence of a United Nations World Disaster Relief Force (UNWDRF).

6. Increasing awareness and study of the vast repertoire of processes and skills by which most people make peace most of the time, and with that knowledge the possibility of extending those processes to an ever-wider sphere of human interaction.

Having said this, however, we must acknowledge that this worldwide network represents a small minority (especially those who work at the peacemaking vocation intentionally) in a world that is in a rather desperate situation. We know of a number of major unresolved armed conflicts, people living in desperate situations of poverty and hunger, serious abuses of human rights, as well as a globe threatened by major environmental problems. These desperate needs of the world require that we extend and expand this global peacemaking network. One way that network can be expanded is for ethicists to seek to identify those norms that can provide a framework for increased cooperation and mission in the world by people of diverse cultural, national, and religious orientations.

Identifying ethical norms, however, will not be sufficient if we do not nurture moral communities that can form people of character. The analysis of North American society reflected in *Habits of the Heart* has shown how American society increasingly nurtures an individualism which erodes commitment to the common good.[3] Communities that nurture a commitment to a social vision are increasingly being eroded by an ethic of "self-interest" which acts on the premise that individual well-being is the ultimate value. Larry Rasmussen argues that we are living on "moral fragments" that are being destroyed more quickly than they are being replenished. He says increasingly our society is dominated by the instrumental value of "rational self-interest." In this view: "All society and its decisions can be fashioned and executed in the manner economic actors do—with the calculation of self- and group interest in relationships that are fundamentally instrumental in character. Stripped down, . . . rational self-interest is the one language everyone can understand and ought to apply to decisions and actions in every domain."[4]

We cannot take for granted the institutions of civil society (families, churches, synagogues, neighborhoods) that form people of character. Such communities can form people morally willing to commit their energies to just peacemaking because they believe it is right in and of itself. The conditions of our world require that we be willing to embrace the strangers, those with no voice, if we are really serious about just peacemaking. A calculating self-interest will not sustain us. A deep commitment to the intrinsic values of compassion and justice are essential for the costly and enduring commitment to just peacemaking required by the conditions in our world.

However, simply having a set of values is not enough to make someone an active peacemaker. In his book *Acts of Compassion: Caring for Others and Helping Ourselves*, sociologist Robert Wuthnow cites statistics to show that the likelihood for compassionate behavior requires a combination of belief in these values and regular participation in an organized religious community.

> Religious inclinations make very little difference unless one becomes involved in some kind of organized religious community. Once you are involved in such a community, then a higher level of piety may be associated with putting yourself out to help the needy. But if you are not involved in some kind of religious organization, then a higher level of piety seems unlikely to generate charitable efforts toward the poor or disadvantaged.[5]

As we stated in the introduction, religious communities keep alive the memory of their paradigmatic stories (such as the Exodus or the good Samaritan [Luke 18:18–30]). Such community memory is essential to the moral formation of people of character. Wuthnow notes that most Americans have a vague knowledge of the good Samaritan story as being about someone who helped a needy person.

But participation in a religious community nurtures the more profound meaning of the story: the "possibility of kindness existing among strangers."[6] Wuthnow believes that keeping alive such stories is important to the continued practice of a kind of compassion that reaches across barriers to generate reconciliation. Jesus' parable jars us to consider that it is the social outcast, the excluded one, who shows compassion. The story forces us to consider ways in which divisions between rich and poor, black and white, male and female, citizen and alien can be overcome.

The sacrificial, costly work of peacemaking, illustrated in the story of the good Samaritan, is vividly represented by women who organize in the struggle for peace and justice in repressive and violent societies in Central America. In her book *Voices of the Voiceless: Women, Justice and Human Rights in Guatemala,* Michelle Tooley documents the prominent role of women in human rights organizations in Guatemala in the last two decades. The violence of the 1980s especially served as a catalyst for women to become involved in collective action for social change. Rigoberta Menchu, winner of the 1992 Nobel Peace Prize, has been one of the primary leaders of her people in the struggle for justice amidst violence and repression.

One of the human-rights groups to survive longer than any other in Guatemala, despite the systematic repression by the police, army, and paramilitary death squads, has been Grupo de Apoyo Mutuo (GAM). Women formed the group to find their disappeared family and friends. Although GAM includes men, 90 percent of its constituency is female; 80 percent is indigenous. GAM seeks to be unified in all their activities, which have included a number of nonviolent interventions, including:

> public speeches, letters of opposition, public statements, declarations of indictment, and group petitions. They have written or supplied information for newspaper articles and have used banners and posters. They have sponsored vigils, marches, parades, funeral processions, and protest meetings. GAM has implemented sit-ins, nonviolent harassment, nonviolent occupation, and has created an alternative institution to investigate human rights abuses.

Tooley quotes an observer who says that GAM has been called "the moral conscience of Guatemala and the thorn in the flesh of the military and the right wing government ruling Guatemala."[7]

CONAVIGUA, the National Coordinator of Guatemalan Widows, formed in 1988, concludes its introductory statement of its purpose with the following words:

> In our villages only our great sacrifices have kept us alive together with our sons and daughters. Without men at home and without any help from the government, we have to take care of everything—work in the corn field, clean our house, go down to the coast for seasonal work. These and other things we have done in order that we and our children might live. So for this we have organized, to meet our needs, to defend ourselves from the abuses that we suffer, and so that we can forever live in peace.[8]

Since its beginning, CONAVIGUA has been the object of death threats and harassment from the military and right-wing groups closely associated with the military. Tooley concludes:

> Rigoberta Menchu and the women of GAM and CONAV-IGUA tell a story—a story of exclusion from economic participation, domination by powers and authorities, exploitation by the dominant culture, and violence from repressive regimes. But as they tell their story, they resist reacting with bitterness, cynicism, and hopelessness. Instead, they act as agents of transformation, turning the conspiracy of silence and the intimacy of pain into social protest. Mothers and wives and daughters, they enter the political arena as novices, novices who defiantly and openly question the state. No longer are they silently weeping women who privately bear their pain. Through collective action they are transformed into political actors helping to gain recognition for the 60 percent indigenous, for the 87 percent majority living in poverty, for widows and orphans, and all the people who lack access to the political system.[9]

Religious organizations in less-repressive and free societies are in a position to stand in solidarity with the people of Central America. Numerous examples could be cited. Among them are the following:

Witness for Peace, a North American ecumenical grassroots organization which challenged U.S. policy toward Nicaragua through the 1980s; the Roman Catholic Church, influenced by liberation theology, which served as a vehicle for lay leadership training and development through Catholic Action groups and Christian base communities; the Human Rights Resource Office for Latin America for the World Council of Churches; the American Baptist Churches, which challenged the injustice of U.S. refugee policy toward Central America by bringing a lawsuit against the Immigration and Naturalization Service;[10] and the role in the late 1980s of Moravian church leaders in Nicaragua and John Paul Lederach of the Mennonite Central Committee in North America to mediate the conflict between the Atlantic Coast Indians and the Sandinista government in Nicaragua.[11] According to Daniel Buttry, "the link in partnerships between the Nicaraguan Baptist Convention and the American Baptist Church had a definite impact upon the quest for peace."[12] The Nicaraguan bishops sent a series of pastoral letters to the churches in the United States. North American missionaries returned to the United States to provide a critique of U.S. policy toward Nicaragua, which lent support to the resistance against U.S. policy. American Baptists were also inspired to participate in Witness for Peace and the Pledge of Resistance.

Just peacemaking theory must empower ordinary people. The norms of a just peacemaking theory should not assume that the only or primary agents of action are heads of state or the leaders of revolutionary groups vying for power. Making peace is increasingly a function of a combination of many actors within the international system: people's movements, peacemaker groups in congregations and faith communities, nongovernmental organizations, leaders of nation-states, and international organizations.

Robert Putnam, international-relations scholar and political scientist, has shown the important interaction between achievements in international negotiations and the pressures of domestic politics.

The politics of many international negotiations can usefully be conceived as a two-level game. At the national level, domestic groups pursue their interests by pressuring the government to adopt favorable policies, and politicians seek power by constructing coalitions among those groups. At the international level, national governments seek to maximize their own ability to satisfy domestic pressures, while minimizing the adverse consequences of foreign developments. Neither of the two games can be ignored by central decision-makers, so long as their countries remain interdependent, yet sovereign.[13]

Putnam's thesis supports our argument that grassroots movements and voluntary organizations can have an important influence on the outcome of public policy on issues of peacemaking and justice.

In his book *Peace Works: The Citizen's Role in Ending the Cold War*, David Cortright argues that citizen peace activists from 1980 to 1987 played a significant role in ending the Cold War and that grassroots social movements have the power to shape history. Though the factors that influence policy were varied and complex (e.g., economic costs in both the United States and the Soviet Union, bureaucratic politics in the Soviet Union, the influence of U.S. allies), "if citizens groups had not campaigned constantly to prevent nuclear war, the military standoff between East and West might have become much more dangerous."[14] The Reagan administration's goal was to create a political climate that favored a "peace through strength" philosophy. But because of the creation of the nuclear-weapons freeze movement, the Physicians for Social Responsibility, the organization of religious leaders against the concept of nuclear superiority,[15] and media events like showing "The Day After" to a television audience of one hundred million people, the administration was forced to abandon the rhetoric and concept of nuclear superiority. Similarly, public resistance forced the administration to abandon large-scale civilian defense plans. Though the administration sought to delay arms negotiations until after a huge military build-up, pressure from the peace movements in the United States and Europe forced the administration to the bargaining table earlier and led to the moderation of U.S. positions. Massive peace mobilizations were unable to halt the deployment of intermediate-range nuclear forces in Europe, but the missiles were later abandoned in the INF Treaty.[16] There was partial success by the MX missile campaign to block mobile basing and reduce the number of missiles. The opposition to the Strategic Defense Initiative (Star Wars) by peace groups and scientists led Congress to cut funds and impose restraints, and though vast sums of money were still spent on development, no systems were deployed. Public opposition to the Reagan administration's Contra War against

Nicaragua was partially successful in blocking Contra aid and preventing direct U.S. intervention (though illegal funding of the war
continued until it was finally stopped by citizen pressure, Congressional vote, and eventual disclosure).

The larger structures of militarism, however, continued un-
abated. Unfortunately the peace movement was unable to halt the
overall strategy of military confrontation (which contributed to the
Persian Gulf War) and the massive increase in U.S. military spending,
which, combined with tax breaks for the wealthy, resulted in a huge
increase in the gross federal debt (from $1 trillion in 1981, after 205
years of U.S. history, to $4.02 trillion in 1992, after only 11 more years).

The nuclear-weapons freeze campaign phenomenon is evidence
that a set of shared norms that transcend national boundaries is shap-
ing large numbers of people. The development of a just peacemaking
theory, in fact, is largely possible because there exists, on an increasingly growing worldwide scale, a people's movement that shares an
implicit set of norms. In part, these shared values derive from common assumptions about the importance of the implementation (not
mere verbal assent) of human rights, reflected in the Universal
Declaration of Human Rights (1948), and the various expansions and
elaborations of those rights in the last several decades. Second, persons from both pacifist and just war traditions are increasingly
emphasizing that they need to implement the shared value of peacemaking implicit in their theories. Pacifists are stressing what the label
"pacifism" means: "pax" or peacemaking, not passivity or withdrawal from conflict. Just war theorists recognize that peace should
be the aim or intention of action and that war must be a last resort.
Both traditions, consequently, converge (even though disagreement
still exists about whether the use of violent force is ever justified) in
order to identify and practice the norms of just peacemaking.

A pacifist vision continues to shape my orientation and my sen-
sitivities, but I am less and less interested in defining the pacifist
position over against other positions. We must find ways to identify
common norms because of fundamental pragmatic (and ethical) reasons. Our task is to develop a "global civic culture," to use Elise
Boulding's phrase, if we are to have any chance of meeting the serious challenges of our globe.[17] Trends in the international system
(decline in the utility of war, economic trade and integration,
transnational networks of communication and cultural exchange, the

ascendancy of liberal democracy) that make just peacemaking more likely require individuals and groups to undertake kinds of action Paul Schroeder enumerated in chapter 9, "to sustain, criticize, goad, influence, reform, and wherever possible lead the many kinds of voluntary associations, governmental and private, which can contribute to transcending the contradictions and managing and overcoming the conflicts of an anarchic international society."[18]

Why is a "citizens' movement" of peacemakers and peacemaking groups so important? What do they do?[19]

1. A transnational network of people who are organized to learn from one another and act in concert can partially transcend the narrow self-interest and myopia that often characterize groups in conflict. A longer view of the root causes of a conflict can help overcome the failure to see the adversary's point of view.[20]

2. A citizens' movement, committed more to peacemaking processes than to defense of governmental or bureaucratic interest or to quick fixes (often with armed force) in a single conflict, can help maintain the long view, the kind of perseverance that is needed so that a just peace can emerge over generations. The ashram was central to the success of Gandhi's nonviolent struggle in India. Bishop Desmond Tutu and the South African Council of Churches were in the forefront in advocating nonviolence in the struggle in South Africa. As movements come and go and the popularity of a cause begins to wane, people's organizations and their leaders often provide key support and staying power. Rosa Parks had long been an active member of an ongoing organization, the NAACP, when she took her seat in the front of the bus in Montgomery, Alabama.

3. Citizens' groups often serve as advocates for the voiceless, especially those who are poor and powerless. Religious institutions, for example, can establish a space (a sanctuary), even in the most repressive societies, that is not easily controlled by the dominating political system. They can thus become a center for teaching and organizing. In 1981, a youth pastor and some young people started weekly Monday prayer services for peace at the St. Nicholai Church in Leipzig, East Germany, one of the small seeds planted early which contributed to the crumbling of the Berlin Wall. In 1988, these prayer services became the locus of increasingly larger groups of East German citizens who gathered to discuss social issues. By October, 1989, three hundred thousand persons gathered in Leipzig to demon-

strate despite police harassment and arrests.[21] In communist Czechoslovakia, the theater provided a space for social transformation. Vaclav Havel's courageous action is a profound demonstration of what it means "to live within the truth" rather than "living a lie."[22]

4. A transnational people's network has less investment in defending what has been. Persons in the movement can free our imaginations to think of alternatives to established patterns of behavior and the narrow range of options we often consider in resolving conflict. International nongovernmental institutions can model alternative ways of living that put the lie to so-called inevitable hatreds by bringing together persons of diverse religious, national, racial, ethnic, ideological, and economic background. Out of these interactions, people's imaginations are freed to consider ways of making peace where hatred and violence are assumed to be inevitable. An example is the effort in Bosnia and Croatia of David Steele and colleagues to work at local levels across lines of culture, religion, language, and class.[23]

5. People within citizens' movements can play a servant role, working behind the scenes in mediating conflict without needing to be in the limelight or to take credit. People without strong attachment to governments, or people who do not bring to a conflict a strong self-interest, can gain the trust of parties and serve in a mediating role. American Methodist leaders behind the scenes sought to help resolve the Iranian hostage crisis. This conflict might have led to a much more positive outcome if their advice had been heeded.[24]

6. Citizens' movements often help to initiate, foster, or support transforming initiatives,[25] where existing parties need support and courage to take risks to break out of the cycles which perpetuate violence and injustice. Charles Osgood's method of "independent initiatives" was widely adopted by church statements and peace movements in Europe and the United States. Eventually, they persuaded governments to adopt it, with striking success.[26] Stassen tells the fascinating story of the role of citizens' groups in encouraging the adoption of the "zero solution" in the late 1980s on intermediate-range missiles in Europe, referred to above in my report on David Cortright's book, *Peace Works.*

7. A citizens' network (particularly as that is institutionalized in voluntary associations) sustains concern and interest when the media and world opinion are unaware, forget, or flit about from one

thing to the next. One year it was Somalia; earlier it was Iraq. Where will our attention be next year? Sustainable development, one of the norms of just peacemaking theory, will require long-term advocacy and commitment by a host of citizens' groups.[27]

8. A citizens' network of NGOs and INGOs can often be a source of information and knowledge that persons in positions of governmental authority lack. One of the most important services performed by the Washington, D.C., office of the Mennonite Central Committee is to circulate returned workers from around the globe to the U.S. Congress. I have seen the power and significance of such testimony on a number of issues, as well as their impact in informing their home communities.[28]

9. Citizens' groups also sometimes resist governments when they behave unjustly, are short-sighted or arrogant, thinking they know more than they do or thinking they can control futures that are in fact not under their control. The revival of Islam nurtured in the mosques throughout Iran was critical in the overthrow of the Shah in 1978–1979. Islamic women played a vital role in the mass protests. While resistance to tyranny is sometimes called for, at other times religious groups and individual leaders can help to nurture a spirit of repentance and forgiveness in the political culture. Alan Geyer cites a number of cases where repentance and forgiveness, nurtured by church groups and church confessions, prepared the climate in which governmental leaders could then make repentance and forgiveness a public event, advancing international peacemaking and reconciliation.[29]

10. Churches and other religious groups can serve a special role in nurturing a spirituality that sustains courage when just peacemaking is unpopular, hope when despair or cynicism is tempting, and a sense of grace and the possibility of forgiveness when just peacemaking fails. In Vietnam, Thailand, and Burma, Buddhist monks have given leadership in protest of human-rights violations and movements for nonviolent social change. Aung San Suu Kyi, daughter of Burma's national hero, winner of the Nobel Peace Prize, and advocate of nonviolence and democracy, connects her struggle explicitly to the teachings and institutions of Buddhism.

Out of intense loyalty grounded in the authority of religious tradition, ordinary people act and shape social reality regardless of whether they are always conscious of how they impact the world.

Religious organizations are especially important in nurturing a spirituality that is essential to peacemaking: courage and the willingness to suffer; overcoming hatred of the enemy and the ability to endure abuse without retaliation; hope and patience during a long period of struggle; trust in the possibility of the miracle of transformation when the evidence for change appears bleak; joy even in the midst of suffering and pain; realism that guards people from disillusionment by making them aware of the depth of human evil and the persistence of systems of domination and injustice; and humility about one's own lack of knowledge and need for wisdom. Aware of our limits to predict and control the future, we can still embrace our common humanity through simple deeds of kindness and charity. In the context of hatred and violence, such deeds may disarm an opponent and provide the possibility for a transforming initiative for justice and peace. Any genuine religious act is potentially an act of peacemaking because it touches people with a transcendent spirit and power, which opens us to our common humanity and exposes the lie of human systems of injustice and violence.[30] In the words of Vaclav Havel:

> In today's multicultural world, the truly reliable path to coexistence, to peaceful coexistence and creative cooperation, must start from what is at the root of all cultures and what lies infinitely deeper in human hearts and minds than political opinion, convictions, antipathies or sympathies: it must be rooted in self-transcendence. Transcendence as a hand reached out to those close to us, to foreigners, to the human community, to all living creatures, to nature, to the universe; transcendence as a deeply and joyously experienced need to be in harmony even with what we ourselves are not, what we do not understand, what seems distant from us in time and space, but with which we are nevertheless mysteriously linked because, together with us, all this constitutes a single world. Transcendence as the only real alternative to extinction.
>
> The Declaration of Independence, adopted two hundred and eighteen years ago in this building, states that the Creator gave man the right to liberty. It seems man can realize that liberty only if he does not forget the One who endowed him with it.[31]

A just and peaceful society protects in law, and nourishes and encourages, and informs accurately rather than untruthfully, associations of citizens organized independently of governmental organizations that are linked together across the boundaries of nation, class, culture, and race. Governments that claim to seek peace are obligated to such protection, encouragement, and truthfulness. Even when this freedom of association is not protected by law and is threatened by hostile conditions, still the mystery of the human spirit is that independent associations of people emerge who seek the shalom of the city where they dwell, as did the Jews in ancient Babylon and as did people in our time in the churches of East Germany and the theaters of Czechoslovakia.

NOTES

1. Michelle Tooley, *Voices of the Voiceless: Women, Justice, and Human Rights in Guatemala* (Scottdale, Pa., and Waterloo, Ontario: Herald Press, 1997), 84.

2. *Kairos* is the Greek word for the kind of time when historical breakthrough occurs. It can be seen in Mark 1:15: "The *time* is fulfilled, the kingdom of God is near." This is different from clock time (*chronos,* in Greek). *Kairos* is the time of breakthrough or fulfillment. We believe a breakthrough is happening in our time and is too little noticed.

3. See page 141. Ironically, each of us who wrote parts of this introduction found that we had referred to one another's writings but never to our own. Out of mutual modesty, we considered deleting all such references but decided that would not be fair to our actual sources and intentions.

4. National Conference of Catholic Bishops, *The Challenge of Peace: God's Promise and Our Response* (Washington, D.C.: U.S. Catholic Conference, 1983), par. 23 and 24. Excerpts Copyright © 1983 United States Catholic Conference, Inc., Washington, D.C. Used by permission. All rights reserved.

5. For a fuller elaboration of the ethical-community concerns at the center of Pauline Christology, see Krister Stendahl, *Paul among the Jews and Gentiles* (Philadelphia: Fortress Press, 1976).

6. Larry L. Rasmussen, *Moral Fragments and Moral Community* (Minneapolis: Fortress Press, 1993), 142.

7. See, for example, John H. Yoder, *The Politics of Jesus* (Grand Rapids, Mich.: Eerdmans, 1972); Walter Wink, *Engaging the Powers* (Minneapolis: Fortress Press, 1992); and Glen H. Stassen, *Just Peacemaking: Transforming Initiatives for Justice and Peace* (Louisville, Ky.: Westminster/John Knox Press, 1992).

8. Stassen, *Just Peacemaking: Transforming Initiatives*, 46.

9. Donald Shriver, *An Ethic for Enemies: Forgiveness in Politics* (New York: Oxford University Press, 1995).

10. Wink, *Engaging the Powers*, 114.

11. David Hollenbach, S. J., *Justice, Peace, and Human Rights: American Catholic Social Ethics in a Pluralistic World* (New York: Crossroad, 1988), 16. He quotes the U.S. Bishops from Synod of Bishops, *Justitia in mundo*, no. 6.

12. This is taking place, however, not without defeats and subterfuges. See Tooley, *Voices of the Voiceless*, chap. 2.

13. John Langan, S. J., "Defining Human Rights: A Revision of the Liberal Tradition," in *Human Rights in the Americas: The Struggle for Consensus*, ed. Alfred Hennelly, S. J., and John Langan, S. J. (Washington, D.C.: Georgetown University Press, 1982), 70, 74, 82.

14. Ibid., 81, 85.

15. Ibid., 99.

16. Judy Gundry-Volf, "Spirit, Mercy, and the Other," *Theology Today* 51 (January 1995): 508.

17. Ibid., 510.

18. Ibid., 516.

19. Ibid., 518–22.

20. Duane Friesen, *Christian Peacemaking and International Conflict: A Realist Pacifist Perspective* (Scottdale, Pa.: Herald Press, 1986), 87, 89.

21. Lisa Sowle Cahill, *Love Your Enemies: Discipleship, Pacifism, and Just War Theory* (Minneapolis: Fortress Press, 1994), 244.

22. Yoder, *Politics of Jesus*, 40.

23. Ibid., 179–84.

24. Anthony Spaeth Davos, "@ the Web of Power," *Time* (February 17, 1997), 58.

25. Ibid., 59.

26. See also John H. Yoder, "To Serve Our God and to Rule the World," in Yoder, *The Royal Priesthood: Essays Ecclesiological and Ecumenical*, ed. Michael Cartwright (Grand Rapids: Eerdmans, 1994), 128–40.

27. Yoder, *Royal Priesthood*, 12ff., and 359ff.; John H. Yoder, *Body Politics* (Nashville, Tenn.: Discipleship Resources, 1993); Theophus Smith, *Conjuring Culture* (New York: Oxford University Press, 1994), 3, 172, 214–16, 253; Sharon Welch, *A Feminist Ethic of Risk*, 4, 25ff., 75f., 91, 154–58; Michael Walzer, *Obligations* (New York: Basic Books, 1970); Michael Walzer, *Just and Unjust Wars* (New York: Basic Books, 1977); Michael Walzer, *Spheres of Justice* (New York: Basic Books, 1983); Rasmussen, *Moral Fragments*; Stanley Hauerwas, *Against the Nations: War and Survival in Liberal Society* (Notre Dame, Ind.: University of Notre Dame Press, 1992), 169–208; Stanley Hauerwas, *In Good Company: The Church as Polis* (Notre Dame, Ind.: University of Notre Dame, 1995), 11, 14, 28, 73ff., 176–80; Stanley Hauerwas, *A Community of Character* (Notre Dame, Ind.: University of Notre Dame Press, 1981), 63; James William McClendon Jr., *Systematic Theology: Ethics* (Nashville, Tenn.: Abingdon Press, 1986), 165ff., 180ff., and chaps. 6 and 8; and transforming initiatives in Stassen, *Just Peacemaking:*

Transforming Initiatives, and Glen Stassen, Diane Yeager, and John Howard Yoder, *Authentic Transformation: A New Vision of Christ and Culture* (Nashville, Tenn.: Abingdon Press, 1996). See also the U.S. Catholic Bishops, "The Challenge of Peace," secs. 3, 4.

28. Desmond Tutu, "Stop Killing the Children," *The Washington Post*, November 24, 1996, C7.

29. Bread for the World, 1100 Wayne Avenue, Suite 1000, Silver Spring MD 20910; Peace Action, 1819 H Street NW, Suite 420, Washington DC 20006-3603; Amnesty International USA, 322 8th Avenue, New York NY 10001; Green Cross, 10 East Lancaster Avenue, Wynnewood PA 19096; World Peacemakers, 2025 Massachusetts Avenue NW, Washington DC 20036; Sierra Club, 730 Polk Street, San Francisco CA 94109; Greenpeace, 1436 U Street NW, Washington DC 20009.

30. Dietrich Bonhoeffer called prayer and action "the arcane discipline," with a sense of Christian devotion as well as irony, because so few churches were practicing the essential Christian discipline. See his *Letters and Papers from Prison*, ed. Eberhard Bethge (New York: Macmillan, 1972), 281, 286, 347ff.; and *Life Together* and *Prayerbook of the Bible* (Minneapolis: Fortress Press, 1996), 136, 139–40.

31. Tooley, *Voices of the Voiceless*, 21–25 and chaps. 3, 6. Some parts of this introduction were included in another form in Glen Stassen, "New Paradigms: Just Peacemaking Theory," *The Council of Societies for the Study of Religion Bulletin* 25, nos. 3 and 4 (Sept. and Nov. 1996): 27–32.

1. SUPPORT NONVIOLENT DIRECT ACTION

1. Daniel L. Buttry, *Christian Peacemaking: From Heritage to Hope* (Valley Forge, Pa.: Judson Press, 1994), 63ff.

2. Mark W. Charlton, *Do Economic Sanctions Work?* (Wynnewood, Pa.: Evangelicals for Social Action, forthcoming).

3. Mohandas Gandhi, *Nonviolence in Peace and War*, 2:363, as cited in *Gandhi on Nonviolence*, ed. Thomas Merton (New York: New Directions, 1965), 27.

4. Martin Luther King Jr., "Letter from Birmingham Jail," *Why We Can't Wait* (New York: Harper & Row, 1964), 88.

5. Henry David Thoreau, "On the Duty of Civil Disobedience," in *Social and Political Philosophy*, ed. John Somerville and Ronald Santoni (New York: Doubleday and Company, 1963), 283.

6. Margaret Miles, "The Female Body as Figure," in *Carnal Knowledge: The Female Nakedness and Religious Meaning in the Christian West* (Boston: Beacon Press, 1989), chap. 4.

7. Gandhi, *Nonviolence in Peace and War*, 1:282, as cited in *Gandhi on Nonviolence*, 27.

8. Dom Helder Camara, *The Spiral of Violence* (London: Sheed and Ward, 1975).

2. TAKE INDEPENDENT INITIATIVES TO REDUCE THREAT

1. Charles E. Osgood, *An Alternative to War or Surrender* (Urbana: University of Illinois Press, 1962).

2. See Stassen, *Just Peacemaking: Transforming Initiatives*, chap. 5, and David Cortright, *Peace Works: The Citizen's Role in Ending the Cold War* (Boulder, Colo.: Westview Press, 1993), chap. 8.

3. Harold Saunders, Address to the Middle East Institute of the World Affairs Council, Washington, D.C., Jan. 17, 1991 (manuscript), 6ff.

4. Susan Thistlethwaite, ed., *A Just Peace Church* (New York: United Church Press, 1986), 75, 136–37, 142–43; *In Defense of Creation* (Nashville, Tenn.: Graded Press, 1986), 77; National Council of Catholic Bishops, *The Challenge of Peace* (Washington, D.C.: United States Catholic Conference, 1983), par. 204–6.

5. Schritte zur Abrüstung, *Von der Abschreckung zur Sicherheitspartnerschaft* (Bonn: n.p., May 1985); *Ökumenische Versammlung für Gerechtigkeit und Bewarhung der Schöpfung* (Berlin: Aktion Sühnezeichen/Friedensdienste, 1990), 21, 92–93, 97–98, 196.

6. National Council of Catholic Bishops, *Challenge of Peace*, par. 204–6.

7. Thistlethwaite, *A Just Peace Church*, 136f., 142f.

8. Svenn Lindskold, "Trust Development, the GRIT Proposal and the Effects of Conflict and Cooperation," *Psychological Bulletin* 85 (1978): 770–93. See also Lindskold's research reports in *Journal of Conflict Resolution* (September 1983): 521–32; *Personality and Social Psychology Bulletin* 12 (June 1986): 179–86; in *Personality and Social Psychology Bulletin* 14 (June 1988): 335–45. See also E. H. Boyle and E. J. Lawler, *Social Forces* 69 (June 1991): 1183–1204.

9. Deborah Welch Larson, "Crisis Prevention and the Austrian State Treaty," *International Organization* 41 (Winter 1987): 27–60.

10. Robert Jervis, *Perception and Misperception in International Politics* (Princeton, N.J.: Princeton University Press, 1976).

3. USE COOPERATIVE CONFLICT RESOLUTION

1. Some practitioners refer to this practice as partnership conflict resolution, echoing the use of the term "partnership" by Olaf Palme and Helmut Schmidt (Dieter S. Lutz, *Lexikon: Rüstung, Frieden, Sicherheit* [Munich: C. H. Beck, 1987], 132–291). In the concept of security partnership Palme and Schmidt's recognition that each party's security depends on the degree of security felt by its adversary certainly states one important part of what we mean by conflict resolution. CCR, however, goes beyond security issues and reciprocal process. Other practitioners refer to this practice as collaborative conflict resolution, a phrase used widely in peer mediation programs in schools across the United States. The term "collaboration" is used to indicate the active nature of the engagement. It affirms that the goal is not only passive compliance or compromise. The problem with "collaboration" is the quisling connotation the term holds for many people who have suffered under fascism or communism. In contrast, CCR is never secretive or subversive.

2. According to Moltmann, unavoidable differences can be localized and relativized in a way that enables people to attend to common concerns (Jürgen Moltmann, *The Experiment Hope*, ed. and trans. with a foreword by M. Douglas Meeks [London: SCM Press Ltd., 1975], 175).

3. In the last two centuries, proponents of these teachings have included American Indians like Chief Joseph (*Chief Joseph's Own Story*, [Fairfield, Wash.: Ye Galleon Press, 1984]), Quakers opposing world wars, civil rights workers in the southern United States, Gandhian disciples in India, liberation theologians (like Jan Sobrino, José Míguez Bonino, and Gustavo Gutiérrez in South and Central America, religious and lay leaders in Eastern Europe during the fall of communism in 1989, the Catholic Church which opposed Marcos in the Philippines in 1986, and most recently, those following Desmond Tutu's and Nelson Mandela's paths in the anti-apartheid movement in South Africa.

One non-Christian example can be found in Islam, which stresses the inter-relationship between forgiveness and justice. Though the Koran states that justice must come first, it also emphasizes that a special reward will come to one who forgives:

> Those who avoid the greater crimes and shameful deeds and when they are angry even then forgive. . . . The recompense for an injury is an injury equal thereto (in degree): but if a person forgives and makes reconciliation his reward is due from Allah. . . . But indeed if any show patience and forgive that would truly be an exercise of courageous will and resolution in the conduct of affairs. (Surah Ash-Shura, sec. 4, ll. 37, 40, 43)

4. This vulnerability component resembles the risk-taking described by Glen | **193** Stassen in the previous chapter, on independent initiatives.

5. Richard Cohen, *Students Resolving Conflicts: Peer Mediation in Schools* (Glenview, Ill.: Scott Foresman, 1995), 42–43.

6. Brian Frost, *The Politics of Peace* (London: Darton, Longman and Todd, 1991), 85–100.

7. "Six Steps for Nonviolent Social Change," taken from the Martin Luther King Jr. Center for Nonviolent Social Change, Inc., (Atlanta, 1990), printed in *Nonviolence Anthology*, (n.p.: Golubka, 1991), 20.

8. Ivo Markovich, Franciscan priest from Guca Gora, Bosnia, as told during a roundtable, "The Role of Religion in the Conflict in Serbia, Croatia, and Bosnia and Herzegovina," sponsored by the Mennonite Central Committee and co-led by N. Gerald Shenk and David Steele, held in Vienna, Austria, May 16–18, 1993.

9. See Ulric Johnson and Patti DeRosa, *The 10 C's: A Model of Diversity Awareness and Social Change* (Boston: Cross Cultural Consultation, 1995); Manu Meyer and Albie Davis, "Talking Story: Mediation, Peacemaking and Culture," *Dispute Resolution Magazine*, (Fall 1994): 5–9; and Tunde Kovac-Cerovic and Steven Brion-Meisels, "Conflict Resolution in the Cultural-Historical Framework," working paper, 1994.

10. See John Paul Lederach, *Beyond Prescription: Perspectives on Conflict, Culture, and Transformation* (Syracuse, N.Y.: Syracuse University Press, 1995).

11. Joseph Montville, "The Healing Function in Political Conflict Resolution," in *Conflict Resolution Theory and Practice*, ed. D. Sandole and H. Van der Merwe (Manchester, Eng.: Manchester University Press, 1993), 115–23.

12. Cohen, *Students Resolving Conflict*, 42.

13. Wink informs us that in this seminal text from Jesus' teaching, *antistenai*, the Greek word translated "resist not" (also the term used in Rom. 13) actually means "do not rebel violently." So Romans 12 reports the teaching as: do not seek revenge or repay evil for evil. Jesus repeatedly resisted evil, but not by evil means. Wink interprets turning the other cheek, giving one's cloak, and walking the second mile as actions that rob the oppressor of the power to humiliate by taking the initiative oneself and publicly unmasking the oppression. He presents Jesus' teaching as a strategic measure for empowering the oppressed by pushing the unjust laws of the day to the point of absurdity in order to reveal them for what they are. At the same time, he portrays Jesus as preserving respect for the rule of law and lovingly challenging the Roman powers to change (Walter Wink, *Violence and Nonviolence in South Africa: Jesus' Third Way* [Philadelphia: New Society Publishers, in cooperation with the Fellowship of Reconciliation, 1987], 13–21 and 58–61).

14. In the slave/master conflict, Paul summons each man to responsible action. Onesimus was to return, and Philemon was to set him free. The mutual call to responsible hospitality was clearly intended to help each party to come to terms with its own misperceptions of both the ideal and the reality in the relationship. In addition, this demanded recognition of the "weaker party's" potential contribution. Philemon was confronted with Onesimus' value to Paul's mission and thereby to himself as well. Enhanced status as Paul's emissary and "son" must have been intended to empower Onesimus to view himself as a person of equal importance and value. Such esteem would have been critical as he came face to face with any latent dominance in the relationship with his master. Furthermore, Paul, as intermediary, exemplified the same commitment he demanded of others. He affirmed Onesimus' contribution and status within the Christian community and took on himself some of the responsibility and cost for initiating and enabling a just reconciliation. He risked jeopardizing his relationship with both men through this confrontation, yet he did it in a way that could truly be labeled as noncoercive (John Koenig, *New Testament Hospitality: Partnership with Strangers as Promise and Mission* [Philadelphia: Fortress Press, 1985], 78–80). (See also Koenig's treatment of seven additional biblical passages where he draws similar conclusions.) At the end of the conflict, all Paul's efforts seem to be rewarded, as intention appears to have become reality if the Onesimus mentioned in Colossians 4:7–9, a traveling missionary, is the same person as the one in the epistle, a contention supported by biblical scholarship (C. F. D. Moule, *The Epistle of Paul the Apostle to the Colossians and to Philemon* [Cambridge: Cambridge University Press, 1957], 16).

15. For further treatment of this subject, see David Steele, *Role of the Church as an Intermediary in International Conflict: A Theological Assessment of Prinicipled Negotiation,* Ph.D. dissertation (Edinburgh: University of Edinburgh, 1991), 300–330.

16. The origins of the realist paradigm reach back to Thucydides, Machiavelli, Hobbes, and Clausewitz. Modern proponents include George Kennan (see *American Diplomacy 1900–1950* [New York: Mentor, 1952]) and Hans J.

Morgenthau and Kenneth Thompson (see *Politics among Nations: The Struggle for Power and Peace,* 6th ed. [New York: Alfred A. Knopf, 1985]).

17. Michael Banks, "The International Relations Discipline: Asset or Liability for Conflict Resolution?" in *International Conflict Resolution: Theory and Practice,* ed. Edward E. Azar and John W. Burton (Brighton, Sussex: Wheatsheaf Books, 1986), 17–20, and John Burton, *World Society* (Lanham, Md.: University Press of America, 1987), 123–25, 140–49.

18. Helmut Thielicke, *Theological Ethics. Volume 2: Politics,* ed. William H. Lazareth (London: Adam and Charles Black, 1969), 167–70, 235–48, 635–36.

19. Robert Axelrod, *The Evolution of Cooperation* (New York: Basic Books, Inc., Publishers, 1984), 7–11.

20. Ibid., 19–23.

21. Martin Patchen, *Resolving Disputes between Nations: Coercion or Conciliation?* (Durham, N.C., and London: Duke University Press, 1988), 46–47; Anatol Rapoport, "Prisoner's Dilemma—Recollections and Observations," in *Game Theory as a Theory of Conflict Resolution,* ed. Anatol Rapoport (Dordrecht, Neth.: D. Reidel, 1974), 17–19.

22. Robert Jervis, "Realism, Game Theory, and Cooperation," *World Politics* (April 1988): 336–40.

23. Ibid., 131–32.

24. For example, see Roger Fisher and William Ury, *Getting To Yes* (Boston: Houghton Mifflin Company, 1981).

25. See Meyer and Davis, "Talking Story," 5–9.

26. Johnson and DeRosa, *The 10 C's.* Another good example can be found in the work of Cornel West, *Race Matters,* (New York: Random House, 1994).

27. Workshop evaluations from a range of sources including school-based evaluations of mediation programs and participant evaluations from three annual summer institutes conducted by the Center for Peaceable Schools at Lesley College, Cambridge, Mass.

28. Steele, *Role of the Church,* 365–67, 449–51.

29. Meyer and Davis, "Talking Story," 5–9.

30. Martin Luther King Jr., *The Words of Martin Luther King, Selected by Coretta Scott King* (New York: Newmarket Press, 1987), 90.

4. ACKNOWLEDGE RESPONSIBILITY FOR CONFLICT AND INJUSTICE AND SEEK REPENTANCE AND FORGIVENESS

1. Reinhold Niebuhr, *An Interpretation of Christian Ethics* (New York: Meridian Books, 1956), 45. Copyright © 1935 HarperCollins Publishers.

2. Ibid., 118.

3. Reinhold Niebuhr, *The Irony of American History* (New York: Charles Scribner's Sons, 1952), 42.

4. Andre Trocmé, *The Politics of Repentance* (New York: Fellowship Publications, 1953), 72, 74, 111.

5. Shriver, *An Ethic for Enemies,* 71.

6. Ibid., 108.

7. Ibid., 108, 110.

8. For one explication of this story in the context of Desmond Tutu's theology, see Michael J. Battle, *Reconciliation: The Ubuntu Theology of Desmond Tutu* (Cleveland: The Pilgrim Press, 1997).

9. Alan Geyer and Barbara G. Green, *Lines in the Sand: Justice and the Gulf War* (Louisville, Ky.: Westminster/John Knox Press, 1992), 170.

10. George F. Kennan, *At a Century's Ending* (New York: W. W. Norton, 1996), 186–87.

11. Gerald Ford, quoted in Shriver, *An Ethic for Enemies*, 165.

12. George Bush, quoted in ibid., 166.

13. George Bush, quoted in ibid., 143.

14. Arthur Moore, quoted in Michael McIntyre, "Efforts to Organize an 'Act of Repentance' in Washington," February 15, 1980; memo to Bishop James K. Mathews et al.

15. "A Call to repentance and Prayer for Iran and the United States," leaflet from Office of Bishop James K. Mathews, Washington, D.C., February, 1980.

16. Mansour Farhang, quoted in Walter Taylor, "Iranian Aide Suggests U.S. Apologize for Its Past Policy on Shah," *The Washington Star*, January 30, 1980, 1.

17. Alan Geyer, "A Proposal for a Presidential Statement on U.S.–Iranian Relations," Washington, D.C., draft memo, February 22, 1980, 1.

5. ADVANCE DEMOCRACY, HUMAN RIGHTS, AND RELIGIOUS LIBERTY

1. For comments on for this chapter, I am indebted to Glen Stassen, and I have incorporated some sentences on human rights and religious liberty from a draft paper for this just peacemaking project by John Langan, S.J. In part, the chapter summarizes research reported in detail in Bruce Russett, *Grasping the Democratic Peace: Principles for a Post–Cold War World* (Princeton, N.J.: Princeton University Press, 1993). See also James Lee Ray, *Democracy and International Conflict: An Evaluation of the Democratic Peace Proposition* (Columbia: University of South Carolina Press, 1995); Rudolph Rummel, *Power Kills: Democracy as a Method of Nonviolence* (New Brunswick, N.J.: Transaction, 1996); Spencer Weart, *Never at War: Why Democracies Will Never Fight Each Other* (New Haven, Conn.: Yale University Press, 1998). The larger project that I lay out here, including the effects of interdependence and international organizations, is discussed in Bruce Russett, "A Neo-Kantian Perspective: Democracy, Interdependence, and International Organizations in Building Security Communities," in *Security Communities in Comparative Perspective*, ed. Emmanuel Adler and Michael Barnett (Cambridge: Cambridge University Press, 1998).

2. My assertions have not gone uncontested, but the predominant evidence remains strongly in their favor. For a reply to some critiques, see Bruce Russett, "Counterfactuals about War and Its Absence," in *Counterfactual Thought Experiments in World Politics: Logical, Methodological, and Psychological Perspectives*, ed. Philip Tetlock and Aaron Belkin (Princeton, N.J.: Princeton University Press, 1996).

3. Russett, *Grasping*, chapter 4, reports much of this evidence, based on an analysis of the international behavior of nearly one thousand pairs of states in each of the years from 1950 to 1985. Similar results over a longer period are

reported independently by Stuart Bremer, "Dangerous Dyads: Conditions Affecting the Likelihood of Interstate War, 1815–1965," *Journal of Conflict Resolution* 36, no. 2 (June 1993): 309–41. A persuasive recent study is David Rousseau, Christopher Gelpi, Dan Reiter, and Paul Huth, "Assessing the Dyadic Nature of the Democratic Peace, 1918–1988," *American Political Science Review* 90, no. 3 (September 1996): 512–33.

4. Samuel Huntington, *The Third Wave: Democratization in the Late Twentieth Century* (Norman: University of Oklahoma Press, 1991).

5. Edward Mansfield and Jack Snyder, "Democratization and War," *International Security* 20, no. 1 (Summer 1995): 5–38 have suggested the dangers of democratization, but their systematic evidence does not indicate that democratizing states are more likely to fight either mature democracies or other democratizing states. For the important qualifications about neighbors and autocratization, see John Oneal and Bruce Russett, "The Classical Liberals Were Right: Democracy, Interdependence, and Conflict," 1950–1986," *International Studies Quarterly* 41, no. 2 (June 1997): 267–93, and William R. Thompson and Richard Tucker, "A Tale of Two Democratic Peace Critiques," *Journal of Conflict Resolution* 41, no. 2 (June 1997): 428–54 and subsequent responses in that issue.

6. Rummel, *Power Kills;* Matthew Krain, "State-Sponsored Mass Murder: The Onset and Severity of Genocides and Politicides," *Journal of Conflict Resolution* 41, no. 3 (June 1997): 331–60.

7. Harry Bliss and Bruce Russett, "Democratic Trading Partners: The Liberal Connection, 1962–1989," *Journal of Politics* 58 (forthcoming); Oneal and Russett, "The Classical Liberals Were Right."

8. Boutros Boutros-Ghali, *An Agenda for Peace* (New York: United Nations, 1993), par. 81; and Boutrous Boutros-Ghali, *An Agenda for Democratization* (New York: United Nations, 1996).

9. Bruce Russett, John Oneal, and David Davis, "The Third Leg of the Kantian Tripod for Peace: International Organizations and Militarized Disputes," *International Organization* 52 (forthcoming).

10. James Fearon, "Domestic Political Audiences and the Escalation of International Disputes," *American Political Science Review* 88, no. 3 (September 1994): 577–92; David Lake, "Powerful Pacifists: Democratic States and War," *American Political Science Review* 86, no. 1 (March 1992): 24–37; Daniel Reiter and Alan Stam, "Democracy, War Initiation, and Victory," *American Political Science Review* 92 (forthcoming); Bruce Bueno de Mesquita, Randolph Siverson, and Garry Woller, "War and the Fate of Regimes: A Comparative Survey," *American Political Science Review* 86, no. 3 (June 1992): 639–46; Bruce Bueno de Mesquita and Randolph Siverson, "War and the Survival of Political Leaders; A Comparative Study of Regime Types and Political Accountability," *American Political Science Review* 89, no. 4 (December 1995): 840–55; Michelle Garfinkel, "Domestic Politics and International Conflict," *American Economic Review* 84, no. 5 (December 1984): 1294–1309; Zeev Maoz, *Domestic Sources of Global Change* (Ann Arbor: University of Michigan Press, 1997).

11. Michael J. Smith, *Realist Thought from Weber to Kissinger* (Baton Rouge: Louisiana State University Press, 1986), 48.

6. FOSTER JUST AND SUSTAINABLE ECONOMIC DEVELOPMENT

1. See Gustavo Esteva, "Regenerating People's Spaces," *Alternatives* 12, no. 1 (1987): 125–52, and Gustavo Esteva, "Development," in *The Development Dictionary: A Guide to Knowledge as Power*, ed. Wolfgang Sachs (London: Zed Books, 1992). There is a vast recent literature on development, looking at the ways that words embody values and an exercise of power of which people are only dimly aware. Generally, these authors are writing about the set of techniques, attitudes, and prescriptions found in large, "official" development agencies like the World Bank, UNDP, AID and other Northern governmental aid organizations, and not as much about nongovernmental organizations (NGOs). This literature is insightful and useful but rarely includes the perspective of the poor on development. See Geof Wood, "Labels: A Shadow across Reality: An Introductory Note," *Development and Change* 16, no. 3 (July 1985): 343–45, and Geof Wood, "The Politics of Development Policy Labelling," *Development and Change* 16, no. 3 (July 1985): 347–74; James Ferguson, *"The Anti-Politics Machine: "Development," Depoliticization, and Bureaucratic Power in Lesotho* (Cambridge: Cambridge University Press, 1990); Tim Mitchell, "America's Egypt: Discourse of the Development Industry," *Middle East Report* (March–April, 1991): 1834; Stacy Leigh Pigg, "Constructing Social Categories through Place: Social Representation and Development in Nepal," *Comparative Studies in Society and History* 34 no. 3 (1992): 491–513; Arturo Escobar, *Encountering Development: The Making and Unmaking of the Third World* (Princeton, N.J.: Princeton University Press, 1995).

2. The problems of defining "the poor" are outside of the scope of this paper. We refer the reader to any number of definitions available in the literature on development.

3. This includes changes in attitudes, in values, in morals, concerning others and oneself. In addition, it also includes changes in relationships among nation-states. It can also be seen as including changes in relationships with one's God. This last one is trickier to define, requires a whole theology, and is beyond the scope of this essay. Development as consisting of changes in relationships is not a new idea. See Patrick Breslin, *Development and Dignity: Grassroots Development and the Inter-American Foundation* (Rosslyn, Va.: Inter-American Foundation, 1987), for how one agency, the IAF, defined it this way already in the 1970s.
The stark human need of poor people in poor countries is an obvious rationale for development aid. Further, the suggestion that development may not be a good or ought to be subordinated to ecological or spiritual concerns is often offensive to people from those countries, because richer or "more-developed" countries evidently seek further wealth for themselves. This has been an issue of contention at least since the 1928 International Missionary Conference, and it has surfaced in international events such as conferences on the environment.

4. Of course, many times the two parties attach different meanings to the word "development." Nevertheless, material (or economic) progress is always one of the most important meanings attached by both sides. Depending on the context and people involved, other meanings include political, social, cultural, spiritual, and personal changes. As indicated below, we adopt the more holistic definition.

The "South" is used to refer to those countries considered "poor. " Previous designations such as "underdeveloped," "developing," "less developed," "Third World," have dropped by the wayside in an attempt to avoid pejorative connotations. Another alternative use that has found favor in the literature, especially in the missiology literature, is "Two-Thirds World. " (See Vinay Samuel and Chris Sugden, eds., *Sharing Jesus in the Two Thirds World: Evangelical Christologies from the Contexts of Poverty Powerlessness and Religious Pluralism*, The Papers of the First Conference of Evangelical Mission Theologians from the Two Thirds World, Bangkok, Thailand, March 22–25, 1982 [Grand Rapids, Mich.: Eerdmans, 1983]).

5. See Norman Uphoff, "Assisted Self-Reliance: Working with, Rather than for, the Poor" in *Strengthening the Poor: What Have We Learned?*, ed. John P. Lewis, U.S.–Third World Policy Perspectives, No. 10, Overseas Development Council (New Brunswick, N.J.: Transaction Books, 1988); Norman Uphoff, "Fitting Project to People," in *Putting People First*, ed. Michael M. Cernea, 2nd ed. (New York: Oxford University Press, 1991), 467–511; Thomas F. Carroll, *Intermediary NGOs: The Supporting Link in Development* (Hartford, Conn.: Kumarian Press, 1992); and John Farrington and Anthony Bebbington, with Kate Wellard and David J. Lewis, *Reluctant Partners? Non-governmental Organizations, the State, and Sustainable Agricultural Development*, Non-Governmental Organizations Series, Coordinated by the Overseas Development Institute (London and New York: Routledge, 1993). This "capacity-building" literature has roots in the work done by Norman Uphoff and Milton Esman, *Local Organization for Rural Development: Analysis of Asian Experience*, Special Series on Rural Local Government (Ithaca, N.Y.: Rural Development Committee, Cornell University, 1974), and Norman Uphoff et al., *Local Institutional Development: An Analytical Sourcebook with Cases* (Hartford, Conn.: Kumarian Press, 1986). The concepts on which it is based have much in common with those employed in the community development efforts of the 1960s and with those advanced by Paulo Freire's work on education, *Pedagogy of the Oppressed*, trans. Myra Bergman Ramos (New York: Seabury Press, 1970). These commonalities are seldom mentioned in the literature cited above, which focuses on detailed comparative development case-study research designed to identify the crucial variables in development-project success.

6. John W. Sewell, "Foreword" in Lewis, ed., *Strengthening the Poor.*

7. See Ted Gurr, *Why Men Rebel* (Princeton: Princeton University Press, 1970).

8. The so-called "Earth Summit" was held in Rio de Janeiro, Brazil, in June 1992.

9. Roger C. Riddell and Mark Robinson, with John de Coninck, Ann Muir, and Sarah White, *Non-Governmental Organizations and Rural Poverty Alleviation* (Oxford: Clarendon Press; London: ODI, 1995) have an excellent summary of the literature comparing NGOs to "official" agencies, and the meteoric trend toward funding NGOs.

10. This refers not just to the "physical" aspects of their environment but also to the political ones.

11. See Uphoff et al., *Local Institutional Development.*

12. "Political consequences" is an easy way to refer to changing relationships of power. As people acquire increased access to resources, they can become less

199

dependent on others, who may resent it for a variety of reasons. As examples, the wealthy may lose the labor, market, and deference of those who had depended on them, and men may lose leverage and control over the women as the latter engage in their own productive activities.

13. See Farrington and Bebbington, *Reluctant Partners,* for a good summary of the rise and decline of state-driven development. For additional material on the state and development and development ideas and theories in general, see H. W. Arndt, *Economic Development: The History of an Idea* (Chicago and London: University of Chicago Press, 1987) and A. F. Robertson, *People and the State: An Anthropology of Planned Development* (Cambridge: Cambridge University Press, 1984).

14. Among others, see Stephan Haggard, *Pathways from the Periphery* (Ithaca and London: Cornell University Press, 1990), and Duncan Green, *Silent Revolution: The Rise of Market Economics in Latin America* (London: Cassell, 1995). Singapore and Hong Kong are essentially city-states lacking rural peasants.

15. Bruce Rich, *Mortgaging the Earth: The World Bank, Environmental Impoverishment, and the Crisis of Development* (Boston: Beacon Press, 1994).

16. Green, *Silent Revolution.*

17. Ibid., 202.

18. Thomas F. Homer-Dixon, "On the Threshold, Environmental Changes as Causes of Acute Conflict," *International Security* 16 (Fall 1991): 76–116, and Thomas F. Homer-Dixon, "Environmental Scarcities and Violent Conflict, Evidence from Cases," *International Security* 19 (Summer 1994): 5–40.

19. The Arab League and Syria in the early and mid-1960s attempted to divert Jordan River headwaters away from Israel. Israel responded with air strikes, creating tensions that contributed to the 1967 war. For details of the Middle East conflicts over water, see Peter H. Gleick, "Water and Conflict, Fresh Water Resources and International Security," *International Security* 18 (Summer 1993): 79–112, and Peter H. Gleick, Peter Yolles, and Haleh Hatami, "Water, War and Peace in the Middle East: Conflict over Water Rights," *Environment* 36 (April 1994): 6–15, 35–42.

20. Thomas F. Homer-Dixon, *Environmental Scarcity and Global Security,* Headline Series, no. 300 (New York: Foreign Policy Association, 1993), 52, and Ashok Swain, *The Environmental Trap: The Ganges River Diversion, Bangladeshi Migration and Conflicts in India,* Report No. 41 (Uppsala, Sweden: Department of Peace and Conflict Research, Uppsala University, 1996). See also by Homer-Dixon, "On the Threshold" and "Environmental Scarcities and Violent Conflict."

21. Boutros-Ghali is quoted in Anthony Shadid, "Cairo May See Waters of Nile Diminish," *Los Angeles Times,* December 17, 1995, A38. Sadat is quoted in Gleick, "Water and Conflict"; Engelman is quoted in Shadid.

22. Information in this section comes mostly from Miriam R. Lowi, "Bridging the Divide, Transboundary Resource Disputes and the Case of West Bank Water," *International Security* 18 (Summer 1993): 113–38.

23. Joe Remenyi and Bill Taylor, "Credit-Based Income Generation for the Poor," in *Christianity and Economics in the Post–Cold War Era: The Oxford Declaration and Beyond,* ed. Herbert Schlossberg, Vinay Samuel, and Ronald J. Sider (Grand Rapids, Mich.: Eerdmans, 1994); Farrington and Bebbington, *Reluctant Partners.*

24. See for example, Herbert Schlossberg, "Destroying Poverty without Destroying Poor People," in *Christianity and Economics*, ed. Schlossberg, Samuel, and Sider, 116, 117. The "cultural" characteristics listed by Schlossberg and those he quotes come from a stream of analysis introduced in the 1960s by Oscar Lewis in "The Culture of Poverty," *Scientific American* 214, no. 4 (1966): 19–25. At its worst, the legacy of this literature sees the "cultural" characteristics of the poor as the main barriers to their own success and implies that the poor have different values than the middle classes. At its best, this literature shows that many of the poor share middle- and upper-class values, and pays close attention to the complexity of the interaction of structural and cultural constraints that perpetuate poverty and lead to differences in the behavior of some of the poor.

25. See, for example, Gavin Smith, *Livelihood and Resistance: Peasants and Politics of Land in Peru* (Berkeley: University of California Press, 1989).

26. See Farrington and Bebbington, *Reluctant Partners*, and Remenyi and Taylor, "Credit-based Income Generation."

27. The literature on linking the state with efforts at the micro level for maximum impact is important here. See Farrington and Bebbington *Reluctant Partners*; Lewis, ed., *Strengthening the Poor*; John Friedmann, *Empowerment: The Politics of Alternative Development.* (Cambridge, Mass.: Blackwell, 1992). However, these sources do not address how these efforts are linked up with the structure of the international economic system.

28. For references to development education, how it came about, and the difficulties agencies have with it, see material throughout Maggie Black, *A Cause for Our Times: Oxfam the First 50 Years.* (Oxford: Oxfam, 1992); Ian Smillie, *The Alms Bazaar: Altruism under Fire: Nonprofit Organizations and International Development* (Ottawa, Can.: International Development Research Centre, 1995); Anne Gordon Drabek, ed., "Development Alternatives: The Challenge for NGOs," *World Development* 15, Supplement (1987).

29. Robert Moffitt, "The Local Church and Development," in *The Church in Response to Human Need*, ed. Vinay Samuel and Christopher Sugden (Grand Rapids, Mich.: Eerdmans, 1987), advocates church-community links and details some experience in this area. The "Sister City" projects are another example.

30. The Global Environment Facility, a new multilateral agency that targets assistance to make ongoing development projects sustainable, is required to consult extensively with NGOs, and is therefore a step in the right direction. See Rodger A. Payne, "The Limits and Promise of Environmental Conflict Prevention; The Case of the GEF," *Journal of Peace Research* (forthcoming in 1998).

31. Toby Ash, "Jordan: Water Authority Forges Links with Israel," *MEED Middle East Economic Digest* 39 (March 10, 1995): 14.

32. As argued above, this is not meant to deny that there are cultural traits that prevent some poor from making a transition to a new style of social, economic, and political relationships inside and outside of their community. However, a significant body of anthropological literature on development shows that cultural traits are not the major impediment to development and that many times what appears to be a cultural barrier is really a way in which the poor resist and rework changes that are detrimental to their welfare. See James Scott, *Weapons of*

the Weak: Everyday Forms of Peasant Resistance (New Haven, Conn.: Yale University Press, 1985); Thayer Scudder, "The Institute for Development Anthropology: The Case for Anthropological Participation in the Development Process," in Production and Autonomy: Anthropological Studies and Critiques of Development, ed. John W. Bennett and John R. Bowen (Lanham, Md.: University Press of America, 1988); Anne Fleuret, "Some Consequences of Tenure and Agrarian Reform in Taita, Kenya," in Land and Society in Contemporary Africa, ed. R. E. Downs and S. P. Reyna (Hanover, N.H., and London: University Presses of New England, 1988), 136–58, among many others.

33. Rodger Payne wishes to thank Joshua Easton and Jason Renzelman for research assistance.

7. WORK WITH EMERGING COOPERATIVE FORCES IN THE INTERNATIONAL SYSTEM

1. Hedley Bull, The Anarchical Society. A Study of Order in World Politics (London and New York: Columbia University Press, 1977).

2. I am borrowing this scheme (acronym OWL) from a colleague in political science, Edward A. Kolodziej, "Order, Welfare, and Legitimacy: A Systemic Explanation for the Soviet Collapse and the End of the Cold War," International Politics 34 (June 1997): 111–51.

3. Richard Rosecrance, The Rise of the Trading State: Commerce and Conquest in the Modern World (New York: Basic Books, 1986).

4. I develop this historical perspective more fully in the following works: "Historical Reality vs. Neo-Realist Theory," International Security 19, no. 2 (Summer 1994): 108–48; "The Nineteenth Century Balance of Power: Balance of Power or Political Equilibrium?" Review of International Studies 15 (April 1989): 135–53; "Did the Vienna Settlement Rest on a Balance of Power?" American Historical Review 97, no. 2 (June 1992): 683–706, 733–35; and The Transformation of European Politics, 1763–1848 (Oxford: Clarendon Press, 1994).

5. Aaron L. Friedberg, "Ripe for Rivalry," International Security 18 (Winter 1993–1994): 10–13, 19ff.

6. William L. Kissick, Medicine's Dilemmas (New Haven, Conn.: Yale University Press, 1994), 150.

8. STRENGTHEN THE UNITED NATIONS AND INTERNATIONAL EFFORTS FOR COOPERATION AND HUMAN RIGHTS

This essay draws substantially on a joint work in progress with Professor Stanley Hoffmann of Harvard University.

1. On this distinction, see Stanley Hoffmann, Primacy or World Order (New York: McGraw-Hill, 1978). Of course, the distinction in reality is far from perfect. In the realm of economic interdependence, states try to combine the logic of competition (the quest for relative gains) with that of a world economy that has rules and a dynamism of its own. Chaos or crises caused, in that realm, either by aggressive state competitiveness or by economic recessions and dislocations, can spill over into the traditional arena.

2. Susan Strange, "The Name of the Game," in *Sea Changes,* ed. Nicholas X. Rizopoulos (New York: Council on Foreign Relations, 1990), 238–73.

3. The image comes from Hoffmann, *Primacy or World Order.*

4. Henry Shue, *Basic Rights,* (Princeton, N.J.: Princeton University Press, 1980).

5. See Carl Kaysen, "Is War Obsolete? A Review Essay," *International Security* 14, no. 4 (1990): 42–64.

6. Cf. Thomas M. Franck, "The Emerging Right to Democratic Governance," *American Journal of International Law* 86, no. 1 (January 1992): 46–91.

7. Cf. Stanley Hoffmann, "The Delusions of World Order," *New York Review of Books* 39, no. 7 (April 9, 1992): 37–42.

8. See Jessica Matthews, "The UN and the Congress," *Washington Post,* March 5, 1995.

9. Charles F. Kegley, "International Peacemaking and Peacekeeping," *Ethics and International Affairs* 10 (1996): 26; other data are taken from this article.

10. Carl Kaysen and George Rathjens, *Peace Operations by the United Nations: The Case for a Volunteer U.N. Military Force,* 1996, 51, 52; available from the American Academy of Arts and Sciences, Cambridge, Mass.

11. Quoted in Kegley, "International Peacemaking," 40.

12. Quoted in Alison Mitchell, "Clinton Lays Out His Case for Troops in Balkans: 'We Have to Do What We Can,' " *New York Times,* November 28, 1995, A1.

13. Cf. Walzer, *Just and Unjust Wars,* 102–10.

| 203

9. REDUCE OFFENSIVE WEAPONS AND WEAPONS TRADE

1. Most of the cases of war we cite to illustrate our theme also illustrate additional factors described in other papers: isolation from international forces of cooperation, including the United Nations; authoritarian rather than democratic leaders; historical guilt and resentment unforgiven and unhealed; negative economic development; lack of respect for human rights; lack of willingness to engage in cooperative conflict resolution, nonviolent direct action, or independent initiatives; lack of a civil society with strong grassroots peace groups.

For research assistance we thank Fran Teplitz of Peace Action Education Fund and Lora Lumpe, senior researcher at the Federation of American Scientists.

2. National Academy of Sciences, *The Future of the U.S.–Soviet Nuclear Relationship* (Washington D.C.: National Academy Press, 1991), vii.

3. Jonathan Dean and Kurt Gottfried, *A Program for World Nuclear Security* (Cambridge, Mass.: Union of Concerned Scientists, February, 1992), 8.

4. Ibid., 18.

5. Ibid., 12–13.

6. Ibid., 18.

7. Ibid., 13.

8. National Academy of Sciences, *Future of U.S.–Soviet Nuclear Relationship,* 37.

9. Lisbeth Gronlund and David Wright, *Beyond Safeguards: A Program for More Comprehensive Control of Weapon-Usable Fissile Material* (n.p.: Union of Concerned Scientists, 1994), 11.

10. Thomas Graham Jr., Acting Deputy Director, USACDA, "The Nuclear NPT: A Twenty-five-year Success Story," Rome, Italy, July 2–3, 1994, 3.

11. Ibid., 1–2.

12. Steven Greenhouse, "US Cuts Nuclear Arsenal, Hoping Russia Will Follow," *New York Times,* Sept. 23, 1994, A3.

13. William D. Hartung, quoted in Jim Bridgman, ed., "September 1996 Weapons Trafficking Campaign Update," *Peace Action Grassroots Organizer,* September 1996.

14. "A U.S. Conventional Arms Transfer Policy," *The Defense Monitor* 23, no. 7 (1994): 6.

15. Peace Action Education Fund, "Factsheet: Timeline of U.S. Landmine Policy," Washington, D.C.

16. "A U.S. Conventional Arms Transfer Policy," 5.

10. ENCOURAGE GRASSROOTS PEACEMAKING GROUPS AND VOLUNTARY ASSOCIATIONS

1. Susan Thistlethwaite, ed., *A Just Peace Church* (New York: United Church Press, 1986), 60.

2. See chap. 1, "Support Nonviolent Direct Action," by John Cartwright and Susan Thistlethwaite.

3. Robert Bellah et al., *Habits of the Heart: Individualism and Commitment in American Life* (Berkeley: University of California Press, 1985).

4. Rasmussen, *Moral Fragments,* 48.

5. Robert Wuthnow, *Acts of Compassion: Caring for Others and Helping Ourselves* (Princeton: Princeton University Press, 1991), 156.

6. Ibid., 179–84.

7. Tooley, *Voices of the Voiceless,* 81. See particularly chapter 3, entitled "Voices of the Voiceless: The Response of Women in Guatemalan Human Rights Groups."

8. Ibid., 86.

9. Ibid., 96.

10. Tooley describes the American Baptist case, ibid., 177.

11. See the documentation of this case in Buttry, *Christian Peacemaking,* 132f.

12. Ibid., 182f.

13. Robert D. Putnam, "Diplomacy and Domestic Politics: The Logic of Two-Level Games," in *Double-Edged Diplomacy: International Bargaining and Domestic Politics,* ed. Peter B. Evans, Harold K. Jacobson, and Robert D. Putnam (Berkeley: University of California Press, 1993), 436. Copyright © 1993 The Regents of the University of California.

14. Cortright, *Peace Works,* 248. The summary of the impact of the peace movement on policy is taken from a chart on page 247.

15. For example, in the early 1980s, major statements were made by the U.S. Roman Catholic Bishops, the General Assembly of the United Presbyterian Church, the United Methodist Council of Bishops, as well as other denominations. Riverside Church in New York City, through the leadership of William Sloan Coffin, played a very significant role through its convocations and publications.

16. Richard C. Eichenberg corroborates Cortwright's argument. An initial hard-line U.S. position against negotiation with the Soviet Union was changed

by the pressures of domestic politics. "This flexibility on the part of the American administration represented a shift from its initial preference, and it was the result of domestic pressure within the United States as well as West Germany. " Richard C. Eichenberg, "Dual Track and Double Trouble: The Two-Level Politics of INF," in *Double-Edged Diplomacy*, ed. Evans et al., 54.

17. Elise Boulding, *Building a Global Civic Culture: Education for an Interdependent World* (New York: Teachers College, Columbia University, 1988).

18. See chap. 7, "Work with Emerging Cooperative Forces in the International System," by Paul Schroeder.

19. Parts of the concluding section of this chapter have been published by Duane K. Friesen in the essay "Religion and Nonviolent Action," in *Protest, Power, and Change: An Encyclopedia of Nonviolent Action from ACT-UP to Women's Suffrage* (New York: Garland, 1997).

20. See chap. 4, "Acknowledge Responsibility for Conflict and Injustice and Seek Repentance and Forgiveness," by Alan Geyer, which cites the recent conflicts in Somalia and the Persian Gulf War as case studies of this myopic view.

21. For an account of the role of the churches in East Germany, see Jörg Swoboda, *The Revolution of the Candles: Christians in the Revolution of the German Democratic Republic* (Macon, Ga.: Mercer University Press, 1996). For an eye-witness account of the events, see Mark Jantzen, *The Wrong Side of the Wall: An American in East Berlin during the Peaceful Revolution* (Beatrice, Nebr.: Author), 1993. Jantzen was a student studying in East Germany under the auspices of the Mennonite Central Committee. The book is available through Henry and Gretl Jantzen, 1415 Summit St., Beatrice, NE.

22. See chap. 1, "Support Nonviolent Direct Action," by John Cartwright and Susan Thistlethwaite, who cite numerous examples of practices by citizens' groups which advocate for the voiceless.

23. See chap. 3, "Use Cooperative Conflict Resolution," by David Steele, Steven Brion-Meisels, Gary Gunderson, and Edward LeRoy Long Jr.

24. See chap. 4, "Acknowledge Responsibility for Conflict and Injustice and Seek Repentance and Forgiveness," by Alan Geyer.

25. Stassen, *Just Peacemaking: Transforming Initiatives*, chaps. 3, 4, and 5.

26. See chap. 2, "Take Independent Initiatives to Reduce Threat," by Glen Stassen.

27. See chap. 6, "Foster Just and Sustainable Economic Development," by David Bronkema, David Lumsdaine, and Rodger A. Payne.

28. See the documentation of this impact in Keith Graber Miller, *American Mennonites Engage Washington: Wise as Serpents, Innocent as Doves?* (Knoxville: University of Tennessee Press, 1996).

29. See chap. 4, "Acknowledge Responsibility for Conflict and Injustice and Seek Repentance and Forgiveness," by Alan Geyer.

30. Several paragraphs of this paper are included in Friesen, "Religion and Nonviolent Action."

31. "Post-Modernism: The Search for Universal Laws," by Vaclav Havel, president of the Czech Republic, delivered on the occasion of the Liberty Medal Ceremony, Philadelphia, Pa., July 4, 1994.

INDEX

206

Saunders, Harold, 49
self-transcendence, 77, 85–86
Sermon on the Mount, 8, 61
Shaefer, Edward, 172
Sharp, Gene, 33
Shriver, Donald, 9, 79
Shue, Henry, 149
Silkwood, Karen, 42
Smith, Theophus, 23
spirituality, 22, 186–187
"Star Wars" program. *See* Strategic
    Defense Initiative (SDI)
state sovereignty, 136, 153–55
Strange, Susan, 148
Strategic Arms Reduction Treaties
    (START) I & II, 159, 165
Strategic Defense Initiative (SDI), 49,
    182
strikes, 35–37; hunger, 36, 37
sustainability. *See* development, sus-
    tainable

Taylor, Bill, 121
terrorism, 1, 32, 160; state, 153
Thatcher, Margaret, 94
Thielicke, Helmut, 62
Thoreau, Henry David, 39
Tooley, Michelle, 1, 13, 28, 179, 180, 189
transnational corporations, 111, 117
transnational network. *See* interna-
    tional system
Trocmé, Andre, 79, 80
Tutu, Bishop Desmond, 75, 82

United Church of Christ, 50, 176
United Nations (U.N.), 13, 19, 93,
    104–41, 144, 146, 148, 168; General
    Assembly, 150–53, 155, 163, 166,
    170, 175
United States Catholic Bishops, 4, 50,
    189

violence, 1, 17, 22, 31, 31, 36, 41, 43,
    45, 64, 71, 76, 112, 119, 124, 187
Voices of the Voiceless (Tooley), 1, 179
voluntary associations, 2, 139,
    140–41, 142, 176, 185
Von Weizsacker, Richard, 81

Waldheim, Kurt, 87, 88
war, 2, 4, 13, 20, 24, 25, 26, 27, 32, 35,
    44, 47, 58, 70, 73, 80, 83, 102, 112,
    133, 135, 137–38, 150, 154–59, 161,
    174, 182, 183; Cold War, 3, 48, 64,
    84–88, 94, 98, 143, 146–48, 161,
    165; Gulf War, 49, 83, 157–58;
    nuclear, 1, 137, 138, 142–49,
    160–61; post–Cold War, 147–48;
    World War II, 3, 80, 82, 93, 104,
    106, 115, 150–52
weapons: biological, 157, 168; build-
    ups, 158; chemical, 49, 157, 168;
    conventional, 157; nuclear, 3, 46,
    48, 50, 154, 157–65, 168, 182; offen-
    sive, 156, 158; trade, 156, 163, 165,
    168. *See also* arms
Welch, Sharon, 23
Wilson, Woodrow, 95
Wink, Walter, 8, 11, 61
World Bank, 93, 105, 116
World Commission on Environment
    and Development (Brundtland
    Commission), 111, 119
Wuthnow, Robert, 17, 178

Yoder, John H., 8, 19, 23

zero solution. *See* INF Treaty; Nuclear
    Weapons Freeze Campaign

209